I Hear My People Singing

I Hear
My People
Singing

VOICES OF
AFRICAN AMERICAN
PRINCETON

Kathryn Watterson

PRINCETON UNIVERSITY PRESS
Princeton & Oxford

Requests for permission to reproduce material from this work should be sent to Permissions, Princeton University Press

Published by Princeton University Press, 41 William Street, Princeton, New Jersey 08540
In the United Kingdom: Princeton University Press, 6 Oxford Street, Woodstock, Oxfordshire OX20 1TR

press.princeton.edu

Jacket art: Photograph from the early 1900s, "Family of Five on Front Porch"; courtesy of the Collections of the Historical Society of Princeton

ISBN 978-0-691-17645-1

I hear my people singing

Library of Congress Cataloging in Publication Number: 2016048694
British Library Cataloging-in-Publication Data is available

This publication has had the support and cooperation of the Historical Society of Princeton and the Princeton Public Library.

Photographs are courtesy of the Historical Society of Princeton; the Rose Family Photographic Studio, Collections of the Historical Society of Princeton; the Seeley G. Mudd Manuscript Library and Archives of Princeton University; with photographs by Romus Broadway, Eileen Holmuth, Iming Lin, Henry F. Pannell, and Katrina Robinson.

This book has been composed in Garamond 3 LT Std and Ex Ponto

Printed on acid-free paper. ∞

Printed in the United States of America

10 9 8 7 6 5 4 3 2 1

Dedication

We dedicate this book to all of our children—our greatest hope for the future. Specifically, we pay tribute to the "jewel" of the neighborhood—Princeton Nursery School—the oldest continuous nursery school in Mercer County, New Jersey. Since 1925, children from the Witherspoon neighborhood have played and discovered songs, words, numbers, languages, and life lessons in the nurturing environment of Seventy-Eight Leigh Avenue.

Many of the residents you'll meet in the following pages still talk about their beloved Princeton Nursery School teachers and its staff of nurses and cooks, who often were one and the same person, particularly Mary Moss, for whom a park on John Street is named, and Jean Riley, who devoted fifty years to the children and families of the nursery school—first as head teacher and then as director.

Numbers of these elders have watched their own children, grandchildren, great-grandchildren, and even great-great-grandchildren thrive at the Princeton Nursery School.

We also dedicate this book to Hank Pannell, whose lifelong mission has been supporting Princeton's children and their families. Without him this book would not exist, and Princeton certainly wouldn't be the same.

For Larry

Hard-working people, and poor, most of them, in worldly goods—but how rich in compassion! How filled with the goodness of humanity and the spiritual steel forged by centuries of oppression! There was the honest joy of laughter in these homes, folk-wit and story, hearty appetites for life as for the nourishing greens and black-eyed peas and cornmeal bread they shared with me. Here in this little hemmed-in world where home must be theatre and concert hall and social center, there was a warmth of song. Songs of love and longing, songs of trials and triumphs, deep-flowing rivers and rollicking brooks, hymn-song and ragtime ballad, gospels and blues, and the healing comfort to be found in the illimitable sorrow of the spirituals.

Yes, I heard my people singing!—in the glow of parlor coal stove and on summer porches sweet with lilac air, from choir loft and Sunday morning pews—and my soul was filled with their harmonies.

—"I HEARD MY PEOPLE SINGING,"
PAUL ROBESON (1898–1976)

Contents

Foreword

A Fascinating World

Cornel West

Princeton, New Jersey, is a special place. This historic town looms large in the founding and sustaining of the American Republic, and it houses one of the world's great institutions of higher learning—Princeton University. Yet in my thirty-four years of association with this town and university, I have always identified with and been fascinated by the vital and vibrant black community in Princeton. I have been informed and inspired by the dignity and grace of my black brothers and sisters "down Witherspoon Street." Their struggles in the midst of this Northern outpost of the Confederacy, attended by many Southern gentlemen, buoyed up my soul and spirit. And though I have been blessed to experience the best of Princeton University, my memories of the great Paul Robeson and the courageous Bruce Wright keep me in touch with the worst of Princeton's often overlooked recent past.

This historic book now allows all of us to enter the fascinating world of black Princeton—to learn of its gallant efforts to forge meaning, preserve families and communities, sustain love, endure sorrows, and contribute to the making of modern-day Princeton. Kathryn Watterson—a highly acclaimed writer, Princeton University and University of Pennsylvania professor, and community activist—has performed a monumental service in laying bare the rich humanity of black Princetonians in this magnificent and marvelous book. With the wisdom and guidance of towering black community leaders such as Henry F. Pannell, Clyde Thomas, and Penney Edwards-Carter, and the work of many dedicated Princeton students, whose hearts and minds were opened by the people they met and interviewed, Watterson has made available for the first time the powerful voices, piercing viewpoints, and poignant stories of twentieth-century black Princetonians. We all owe her an enormous debt for her vision, courage, and love.

As a black Princetonian, I now walk the streets of Nassau, Prospect, Witherspoon, Harrison, and John with more dignity and grace owing to this talking book of the blues people of Princeton—with their voices as wind at my back. We all stand tall because of them.

I Hear
My People
Singing

First Baptist Church of Princeton in 1925
(founded as Bright Hope Baptist Church, 1885)

Introduction

"THE NORTH'S MOST SOUTHERN TOWN"

I

The time is the twentieth century and the place is the center of the borough of Princeton, New Jersey, where white church spires and flowering, tree-lined streets reflect the aura of the world-renowned Princeton University, well known for a steady stream of Nobel Prizes and accolades for its illustrious professors, graduates, and alumni. Every year, thousands of visitors from around the world walk the hallowed grounds where famous predecessors have tread, not only at Princeton University but also at the nearby Institute for Advanced Study, Princeton Theological Seminary, and Westminster Choir College.

Unknown to most of those visitors, as well as to most university students and local white residents, is the existence of an active, yet historic African American community in the very heart of Princeton, only a few minutes' walk from the university. This book, *I Hear My People Singing: Voices of African American Princeton*, gives testimony to the firsthand experiences of individuals who built a close-knit and vibrant community within a segregated Northern Jim Crow town, where "the doctrine of white supremacy was held almost as tenaciously above the Mason-Dixon Line as below it."[1]

This neighborhood took shape in the 1700s across the road from what would become Nassau Street and Princeton University's Nassau Hall. Originally established by the Presbyterian Church as the "College of New Jersey" in 1746 in Elizabeth, New Jersey, and permanently situated in Princeton in

1756, the school, like the town, prospered from slavery—so much so that local black residents dubbed Princeton "The North's Most Southern Town," as well as "The South's Most Northern Town."

Only one dirt road, formerly an Indian trail, led from Nassau Street into the neighborhood. That thoroughfare, then named Hill Street, was referred to by generations of white Princetonians as "African Lane" or "African Alley." Today that thoroughfare, called Witherspoon Street, still takes us from Nassau Street into the African American neighborhood. In the 1800s and 1900s, the vicinity covered eighteen blocks, which included what is now Palmer Square. The neighborhood had active black businesses mixed in with a stables and a fire station. Today, it's an eleven-block area, still proximate to the university and yet still a world apart. Its narrow streets, shaded by overhanging trees, continue their turn-of-the-century appeal. From Paul Robeson Place (formerly Jackson Street) to Birch Avenue, Witherspoon to John Streets, you will find neat two- to three-story single houses, as well as wooden and brick row houses with front porches and small, well-tended yards planted with flowers, bushes, and trees.

The area is also home to four long-standing churches: the First Baptist Church of Princeton on John Street, founded as Bright Hope Baptist Church of Princeton in 1885; Witherspoon Street Presbyterian Church, founded in 1838; Mount Pisgah African Methodist Episcopal Church (AME), founded in 1832 on Witherspoon Street, and Morning Star Church of God in Christ, founded in 1941 on Birch Avenue. Members of social clubs and fraternal organizations meet in the American Legion building, the Elks Lodge, and the Masonic Temple. A large multi-unit residential building called The Waxwood sits at the former site of the Witherspoon School for Colored Children and, central to the neighborhood, is a community learning center and businesses that include an urban planning center, a beauty parlor, a convenience store, and restaurants.

The presence of African Americans in this predominately white town may not be well known, but their existence here is older than the town itself, which became known as "Prince Town" in the early 1700s. The first black people in the Princeton area are thought to have been free blacks dating back to the 1680s.[2] Seven enslaved Africans arrived in 1696 with white colonialist Richard Stockton, who had bought and brought them,

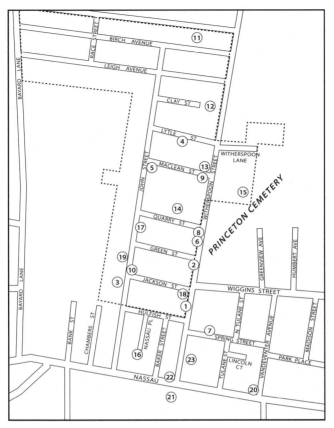

The Borough of Princeton in 1917, based on a map created by William L. Ulyat.

1. Griggs' Imperial Restaurant
2. The Colored YW/YMCA
3. Dorothea House
4. Charles Robinson American Legion Post 218
5. Masonic Temple, Aaron Lodge #9, Inc.
6. Paul Robeson's birthplace
7. "Sport" Moore's family property
8. Witherspoon Street Presbyterian Church
9. Mt. Pisgah A.M.E. Church
10. First Baptist Church of Princeton
11. Morning Star Church of God in Christ
12. Barclay's Ice, Coal, and Wood Plant
13. Witherspoon Street School for Colored Children
14. Witherspoon ("Quarry Street") School
15. Negro Cemetery (inset for Princeton Cemetery)
16. Palmer Square (after 1937); previous site of Baker's Alley
17. Ball's Confectionary
18. Thomas Sullivan's grocery store
19. Princeton Rug Washing and Carpet Cleaning Works
20. Public Library (later the Historical Society)
21. Nassau Hall and FitzRandolph Gate
22. Cesar Trent's property (1795)
23. Office of the *Citizen*

In April 2016 the area inside the dashed line was designated a historic district on the recommendation from the Historic Preservation Committee of Princeton.

along with his wife, Susanna, and their children, to a 400-acre tract he pur-chased that year—land that includes what is now the campus of Princeton University and the grounds of the Theological Seminary. In 1701, Stock-ton purchased from William Penn an additional 6,000 acres that are ap-proximately the center of the present town of Princeton, for the sum of 900 pounds.[3] The enslaved Stocktons not only worked the land but also cleared and built the Stocktons' stately home, as well as their own slave quarters in the back. The Stocktons' mansion, "Morven," later became the official residence of New Jersey's governors.[4] Today it is known as the Morven Mu-seum and Garden.

It's most likely that Richard Stockton, and perhaps his father before him, was among the beneficiaries of land in exchange for the purchase of slaves. When the English seized New Netherland from the Dutch in 1664 and New Jersey became a royal colony, the Crown, which profited from the slave trade, encouraged slavery by offering white settlers 150 acres each "for every full-grown, able-bodied male slave he owned and 75 acres each for those not fully grown."[5] Elsewhere in New Jersey, Africans arrived with settlers from England, Sweden, and Holland, possibly as early as the 1630s.[6] By 1726, there were some 2,600 enslaved Africans living within the state—roughly 8 percent of the colony's population.[7] Their origins varied, but ships brought them directly from West Africa and the Caribbean to New Jersey's ports in Perth Amboy and Camden, where they were advertised and sold to slave traders and the highest bidders from New York, New Jersey, and Pennsylvania. New Jersey imported Africans in larger numbers than any other Northern colony.[8]

Throughout the 1700s and into the early 1800s, slavery was woven into the financial and social fabric of Princeton, as it was into the college towns of Cambridge, New Haven, Providence, New Brunswick, and elsewhere in the North. The sale and purchase of African men, women, and children was business as usual. Across generations, "For Sale" advertisements were printed on flyers or run in local newspapers, not just for newly arrived Africans, but also for those previously owned. After the fifth president of the College of New Jersey died in 1766, for instance, a sale was held on campus right in front of the president's house, now known as the Maclean House. On July 31, 1766, the *Pennsylvania Journal* ran this notice:

TO BE SOLD,

At public venue, on the 19ᵗʰ of August next, at the presidents house in Princeton, all the personal estate of the late Revd. Dr. SAMUEL FINLEY, consisting of:

Two Negro women, a negro man, and three Negro children, household furniture, horses, and neat cattle, a light wagon, a new chaise, a sleigh, some hay and grain, together with a variety of farming utensils. Also a choice collection of books, religious, moral and historical, containing the complete library of the deceased. The Negroes will be disposed of at private sale previous to the day appointed for the venue, should a suitable price be offered for them. The Negro woman understands all kinds of house work, and the Negro man is well suited for the business of farming in all its branches. The conditions of the venue will be made known on the day of sale. All those that are indebted to the said estate by bond, note, or book debts, are desired to make immediate payment to the subscribers, and such as have any demands against the estate are desired to lend in their accounts properly attested to.

> JONATHAN SEARGEANT, jun,
> in Princeton, or
> SAMUEL BREESE, Executor,
> in New York.[9]

As the town of Princeton grew, so did the number of Africans sold to local residents, businessmen, and estate owners for work in private homes, brickyards, quarries, farms, stables, and lavish properties.[10] According to Robert Ketchum, in his book *The Winter Soldier*, "Lush agricultural land around Princeton resembled the plantations of Virginia, both in its gentleman farmers and the number of Negro slaves who toiled in their fields."[11]

Just as most white families in Princeton had a team of horses, they also had slaves. "Most white families in Princeton owned at least one black human being," writes historian and professor of American History at Massachusetts Institute of Technology, Steven Craig Wilder, author of *Ebony & Ivy: Race, Slavery, and the Troubled History of America's Universities.* By the 1780s, one of every six residents of Princeton was an enslaved person. Similarly at that time, enslaved people were one fifth of the population of New Brunswick, where Rutgers University had been chartered as Queens College in 1766.[12]

It's clear that colonial institutions of learning greatly relied on the use of slave labor and profits from the slave trade to build and maintain their facilities. Princeton was no exception. Its seven founders, named as trustees who in the king's name established the College of New Jersey in 1746, each owned African people who were bound to them for life. In addition, the first eight presidents of the College, at the school's helm from 1746 to 1822, are all known to have been slave owners.[13] As Wilder recounts, "The first five colleges in the British American colonies—Harvard (est. 1636), William & Mary (1693), Yale (1701), Codrington (1745) in Barbados, and [Princeton in] New Jersey (1746)—were instruments of Christian expansionism, weapons for the conquest of indigenous peoples, and major beneficiaries of the American slave trade and slavery."[14] Among these college towns, however, Princeton created a unique niche for itself as the most welcoming intellectual environment for children of the Southern elite. Its sixth president (1768–94), Rev. John Witherspoon, a Presbyterian minister, who began buying slaves shortly after his arrival in America from Scotland, actively recruited students from slaveholding families in the South and the West Indies, so as to acquire funding for his initiatives to restructure the college and enhance the curriculum. By doing this, Witherspoon reached beyond the intense competition for students from New England and the Mid-Atlantic states to welcome the sons of Southern families hostile to Harvard's and Yale's abolitionist sentiments.[15]

In important ways, Witherspoon—whose name came to identify the African American neighborhood—embodied Princeton's relationship with slavery. The contradictions in white behavior were always apparent to the Witherspoon residents. They understood Witherspoon's slave-owning and proslavery status yet appreciated his preaching that blacks and Indians should be educated—something forbidden in many other slaveholding states. Witherspoon also privately acted upon this belief by tutoring two free black students from Rhode Island, a free black man from North Carolina and several Delaware Indians, in the hope they would preach the Gospel.[16]

Later in his life, President Witherspoon spoke in favor of abolishing slavery, but an inventory at his death still included "two slaves . . . valued at a hundred dollars each."[17]

And so it was that Princeton's African American neighborhood was born within the framework of slavery—an institution that stripped people of their own names, languages, families, homes, and tribes, and also, by law, denied them all rights and liberties. As the DC Slave Code of 1860 mandated, "A slave is a human being who is by law deprived of his or her liberty, for life, and is the property of another. A slave has no political rights and generally has no civil rights."[18] Despite this legacy, Princeton's African American residents found personal freedom through their steadfast faith and deep understanding of the essential equality of all people.

When the College of New Jersey's Nassau Hall hosted the first New Jersey state legislative body in 1776 and housed sessions of the Continental Congress in 1783—when, for several months, the town of Princeton was the capital of the United States—Princeton's free and enslaved African Americans did the heavy lifting. They stoked fires, cooked meals, served, cleaned, washed dishes, laundered clothes, shaved white men's cheeks, powdered them, polished shoes, floors and silver, emptied chamber pots, built lecture platforms, readied furniture, and did other service jobs. When one of the first public readings of the Declaration of Independence took place on the lawn in front of Nassau Hall in early July 1776,[19] several signers of the Declaration—John Witherspoon, Richard Stockton II, and Benjamin Rush, class of 1760, all slave owners—were part of the crowd gathered for the occasion in defense of American freedom. As Craig Steven Wilder observes, "[Witherspoon] and his contemporaries had established their own intellectual freedom upon human bondage. They had also bound the nation's intellectual culture to the future of American slavery and the slave trade."[20] We don't know how many of Princeton's free or enslaved black residents were standing on the outskirts of the crowds in front of Nassau Hall, but it is certain that the Declaration's message of "freedom, equality, and liberty for all" reached their ears and stirred their aspirations.

When it came to the American Revolution, African Americans were eager to fight for freedom—a concept they wholeheartedly embraced. Both free and enslaved black men seized the opportunity to prove themselves.

Some slave owners throughout the colonies promised freedom to enslaved black men willing to fight in their places, and their places were quickly filled. Two Princeton men were known to have served for their owners during this time. And when the British realized their manpower shortage and offered freedom to slaves in exchange for their service to the Crown, thousands of black men enlisted in the British army and navy.

Thousands of black men signed up to fight for the army of the colonies as well. Eventually, the Continental army, pressed for manpower, also offered to liberate enslaved men at the end of the war.[21] Some two dozen black men from Princeton—enslaved and free—joined nearby state militias and fought against the Crown. Several others signed on as seamen and marine pilots. At the end of the war, most of the formerly enslaved men who had fought for the Crown—approximately 14,000—departed on British ships. Some settled in Nova Scotia while others were taken to Canada as freemen, making many Americans, particularly slaveholding Americans, furious at the British for confiscating their "property."[22]

Formerly enslaved men who had fought for the colonies also earned their freedom, which was sometimes accompanied by a reward of land.[23] Another victory was the fact that the nature of a war waged in the name of "liberty" inspired more Americans to reflect upon the wrongness of slavery. "During the war, anti-slavery sentiment became a moving force, highlighted by the law of March 1780 gradually abolishing slavery in Pennsylvania."[24]

In 1804, the New Jersey legislature passed a Gradual Abolition Act mandating that "all slave children born in New Jersey" after July 4, 1804, be set free upon a woman's twenty-first birthday and a man's twenty-fifth birthday. This arrangement actually extended slavery until 1825 and gave slave owners two decades more of free labor. Throughout the first half of the nineteenth century, many free blacks began settling in Princeton because of the South's pressure on them to leave: "In the South the free Negro was unwanted, branded both a nuisance and a menace. . . . He was viewed as a threat to the institution of slavery, not only by arousing the slaves' dissatisfaction by his very presence, but by actively encouraging them to steal, to escape, and to plot against their masters. All whites agreed that the Free Negro must be kept in check."[25]

New Jersey, like other Northern states, replaced outright slavery with strict controls of free blacks. An 1807 law disenfranchised free Negroes and women from the voting rights they'd been granted by the state constitution in 1776. In Princeton, as elsewhere in New Jersey, free blacks were required to carry "free papers," which included a certificate of freedom that stated his or her name, a physical description, and the manner in which freedom had been obtained. Throughout the state, free Negroes could not walk on the streets after dark, travel between towns without a pass, vote, purchase property, enlist to fight in a militia, serve on a jury, testify against a white man, or enter public or private white establishments.[26] By 1850, when the town's total population was just over three thousand, the Witherspoon neighborhood had become home to between five and six hundred free blacks.[27]

During the Civil War—one-sixth of Princeton's black male population volunteered to fight for Union forces. Since the black regimental army units known as United States Colored Troops (USCT) were still not permitted to form in New Jersey, Princeton's black men enlisted mainly in Pennsylvania and New York. Some eighty black Princeton men volunteered and fought in the Union army, many serving in the Sixth or Eighth Pennsylvania Regiment, USCT.[28] At least twenty-two joined the US Navy.[29] Princeton's men joined some 200,000 other black soldiers to help turn the tide of victory for the Union forces.

African American men from Princeton also served in large numbers in World War I, World War II, the Korean War, the Vietnam War, and, more recently, the Gulf War. Three of the men interviewed in this book won Purple Hearts and higher honors for their bravery during World War II, but their presence abroad earned them no special gratitude from their government in America, which still treated them as second-class citizens. "When we got out of the service, [and we went to a restaurant,] they stopped all of us black guys and said, 'You can't eat here,'" recalls Floyd Campbell, who earned a Bronze Star in the Battle of Iwo Jima during World War II. "We said, 'But, we're soldiers.' They said, 'We don't serve colored.' So they brought food out to us—plain white bread with mayonnaise and onions. That was the first incident of hurt. You mean to tell me I went to war for my country, and I can't eat with fellow soldiers? It brought tears to my eyes."

Witherspoon residents resisted the injustices in large ways and small. In the neighborhood, the churches served as hubs of mutual support and community action. In the 1800s, they formed their own independent congregations, apart from the white churches where they had to sit in balconies or "colored" pews. These churches were not only sanctuaries for worship, but they also served as social centers, meeting places, and avenues for mutual aid and social justice; they provided hiding places for escaped slaves and schools for uplifting and empowering black people, as well as sites for Bible study and activities for young people. Churches in Princeton also worked cooperatively with churches of their denominations in nearby Trenton, Camden, and Newark. A preacher from the African Methodist Episcopal Church (AME) in Trenton, Samson Peters, helped establish the first black church in Princeton, Mount Pisgah AME Church, in 1832.[30]

Witherspoon residents also traveled to colored church conventions, which began in 1830 at Bethel Church in Philadelphia and were designed to galvanize Negro leaders.[31] Princeton's congregants joined other delegates from New Jersey, New York, and Pennsylvania at annual meetings that addressed public issues affecting Negroes. Church pastors played key roles in the lives of their congregations, not only by preaching against the laws and public policies of slavery and segregation but also in providing needed counsel, food, goods, jobs, and housing in times of hardship for families and individuals.

Princeton's black community, particularly members of the Mount Pisgah AME Church, became active participants in the Underground Railroad, work that connected them to a large network of both black and white abolitionists. Beginning in the late 1830s, Princeton was "one of the switching points in a circuit for runaways that stretched from Morristown to New Brunswick."[32] This system of transporting their black brethren out of slavery depended on secrecy. It was dangerous work. But the Witherspoon neighbors and their white cohorts were passionately committed to the holy imperatives: "Remember them that are in bonds, as bound with them," and "Do unto others as ye would they should do unto you."[33]

To combat discrimination in housing and employment and strive for racial betterment, residents established mutual aid and self-help groups, along with secret fraternal organizations such as the Witherspoon Elks Lodge, founded in 1913, and a chapter of Prince Hall Freemasonry, Aaron Lodge No. 9F & AM, which was descended from the country's first African Masonic Lodge chartered in Boston in 1787. In 1922, World War I veterans organized the Charles W. Robinson Post 218, American Legion. Witherspoon residents established an active and influential chapter of the National Association for the Advancement of Colored People. (NAACP), in Princeton in 1917. The author and intellectual giant W.E.B. Du Bois, who founded the NAACP, often visited the Princeton chapter, which actively advocated for integration, housing, civil rights, and an end to police abuse.

Neighborhood men organized, staffed, and maintained numerous social and civic organizations, including the community's YMCA, which became a local branch of the National YMCA in 1917. Neighborhood women were equally active in forming the YWCA, which met in private homes before joining the YMCA in their central location at the corner of Witherspoon and Jackson Streets in 1938. The YM-YWCA was a lively center of activity that hosted national speakers, as well as sports, recreation programs, field trips, father-son banquets, mother-daughter teas, and social activities for boys, girls, adults, and families. It was the vital heart of the community up until the 1950s, when both black and white branches of the YM-YWCA in Princeton were racially integrated and established in a new building on Avalon Place. In 1932, Witherspoon women formed a "Friendship Club" to advance the cause of racial justice, provide local students with college scholarships, and offer support to families in need. They sponsored concerts and fund-raisers and made contributions to the NAACP and the New Jersey State Federation of Colored Women's Clubs. Families also actively worked through their churches to create a caring environment.

In the years that followed, Witherspoon neighbors founded the Elizabeth Taylor Byrd Scholarship Fund, in honor of Elizabeth Byrd's lifetime effort to develop leadership among the African American youth through education and cultural exposure. They organized events and invited guests, including Daisy Bates, the president of the NAACP in Little Rock, Arkansas, to talk about her efforts to integrate the school system there. Bates commented that in her visit to Princeton, she did not find even one Negro working as a salesperson or in any capacity on Nassau Street—the retail center of Princeton then and now. She told the crowd, "I'll take care of Little Rock. See to it that you take care of Princeton."[34] In 1963, Witherspoon residents created the Princeton Association for Human Rights. Including residents of the greater Princeton area, together with faculty and students at educational institutions, it worked with the Interfaith Council to organize civil rights work in Princeton. Two hundred and fifty people from Princeton traveled together to the March on Washington in 1963.

———

A good number of the speakers in this book were among the six million African Americans who fled the violence of the South and came north during what is now called the Great Migration, which occurred from 1910 to 1970. Many Witherspoon residents recall their surprise upon finding Princeton as segregated as the Southern Jim Crow towns they had left behind. Racial divisions in Princeton, they discovered, were vigorously enforced in the schools, in housing, and on other fronts. Despite the vagaries of "race" and multiracial mixtures, persons were defined as "Negro" if their appearance conveyed any suggestion that their rainbow of ethnicities contained a drop of Negro blood. Internationally renowned actor, singer, and human rights advocate Paul Robeson, born in Princeton in 1898, later wrote, "Rich Princeton was white: the Negroes were there to do the work. An aristocracy must have its retainers, and so the people of our small Negro community were, for the most part, a servant class. . . . Princeton was for all the world like any small town in the deep south. Less than 50 miles from New York, and even closer to Philadelphia, Princeton was spiritually located in Dixie."[35]

———

Most of the contributions of Princeton's African Americans have not been recorded or accounted for in white newspapers or history books, yet their labor fueled the growth, maintenance, and economic success of the town and the university. As did blacks in similarly segregated communities all over this country, generations of Witherspoon residents, no matter how bright or how educated, worked to exhaustion for paltry wages. Within the neighborhood, adults traded goods and services to sustain life for themselves and their children. Together in communion, they created an island of ingenuity in an ocean of pervasive, invasive, and persistent racial discrimination.

This is the world, neighborhood, and community in which the elders of this book lived from 1900 to 2000. They were an exceedingly motivated group of individuals committed to education and intellectual advancement for their children. Upon arriving, some may have been inspired by the institutions of higher learning they found around them, but they soon understood they were not welcome or considered worthy of the privileges and the opportunities reserved for whites. A potent symbol of the racial division between the all-white, all-male university and its black neighbors was the tall iron FitzRandolph Gate in front of Princeton University. This gate, locked year-round, opened only on graduation day and then was closed and locked again. Ironically, the gate opens onto Nassau Street in front of Nassau Hall, at its intersection with Witherspoon Street.

"Probably one of the most ominous things I can remember about growing up in the shadow of the university is the gate," recalls educator Leonard Rivers. "You go [up] Witherspoon Street [to the] University, and that gate was always locked shut. . . . We had the John Witherspoon area that was our community. We knew that when you crossed Nassau Street and you went to the university, that was not us."

II

I Hear My People Singing: Voices of African American Princeton took root one summer day in 1999 when I met with two men from the Witherspoon neighborhood for advice about a writing seminar I was planning for students at Princeton University, where I was a lecturer. The course required my students to volunteer weekly in soup kitchens, crisis centers, rescue missions, homeless shelters, after-school sessions, or other programs, and to write about what they learned. Both Henry (Hank) Pannell and Clyde (Buster) Thomas were actively engaged in mentoring children and teenagers, driving older folks to church and to doctors' appointments, and working to keep housing affordable for black residents. They suggested several programs they knew of in the area that could use volunteers.

We had been talking a while when Hank sat forward. "Your poverty course sounds just wonderful." His voice grew louder. "But what *we really want* is an oral history of our community. *Before it's too late.*"

I was startled. "Are you saying there's never been an oral history of this community?"

"It's never been done. And people are dying. If it doesn't happen now, if we don't get their stories now, it's going to be too late."

Sitting there, I felt a jolt of lightning pass through me. During the summer of 1964, crossing through Mississippi on my way to Florida as a young bride, blinders had been ripped off my eyes. It was the "Whites," capital W, and the "coloreds," small c, signs over water fountains, plus the headline, "Mixers Missing" about the disappearance, and ultimately the deaths, of three civil rights workers, that first shocked me. Like most white people, I'd grown up in a sea of whiteness, oblivious to the depth of racist assaults against black people in America. When I got to Florida, I joined the NAACP, and began tutoring teenagers from the segregated black high school even before I got my first job as a newspaper reporter. At that time, it was *illegal* for my students and their taxpaying parents to cross the train tracks that segregated them after 9:00 p.m. It was *illegal* for them to use public beaches or swim in the ocean. The police arrested the father of one of my students for driving across the tracks at 9:30 p.m. to pick up his daughter. They beat him up and threw him in jail. What I learned in those tense, volatile years changed me forever.

Later on, I went as a Peace Corps volunteer to Malaysia, where I lived in a Chinese neighborhood and taught English as a second language in a teachers' training college. I came back in 1969 to Philadelphia, where I lived in the inner city, worked as a daily newspaper reporter, and became even more deeply cognizant of the viciousness of institutionalized racism—particularly as it pertained to police abuses and the courts. I taught a writing workshop at Holmesburg Prison, which led me to investigate Pennsylvania's state prison system and interview hundreds of prisoners, as well as guards and administrators. My first book looks at prisons and the criminal justice system from the perspectives of women prisoners, who know it from first-hand experience. In a later book. I examine a leader in America's white supremacist hate movement, a Grand Dragon of Nebraska's Klu Klux Klan, who was transformed by the love of a Jewish cantor and his family, whose synagogue he had planned to bomb. I'd been drawn to this true story because it epitomizes Rev. Martin Luther King Jr.'s message: "Let us not seek to satisfy our thirst for freedom by drinking from the cup of bitterness and hatred. . . . We must not allow our creative protest to degenerate into physical violence. Again and again, we must rise to the majestic heights of meeting physical force with soul force."[36]

Of course, on that spring day in 1999, Hank Pannell didn't know my history, my love of stories, or the wild symphony stirring inside me at the very idea, even the impossible idea, of my managing to conduct this oral history. But Hank is a fisherman, and I've come to know his patience, his powers of observation, and his joy in making a catch. That day he had light in his eyes, and in that light I felt the intensity of his love for the remarkable community that I would later learn had sheltered and nurtured him after his mother's and grandmother's deaths, when he was a young teenager in charge of his younger sister and two brothers.

Hank sat there quietly for a while. Then he leaned back and let out his lure. "We have one member of the community, Mr. Albert Hinds, who is ninety-eight years old right now. That man has a wealth of stories."

"I don't know. I don't think there's any possible way I could do this."

Hank began to smile. "But you're gonna try, aren't you? You're going to try."

———

Two weeks later, on a Sunday afternoon, I walked by the bank at the corner of Witherspoon and Nassau Streets, which I would later learn had been the first property in Princeton owned by a black man, Cesar Trent, who bought it in 1795, during a lull in enforcement of laws prohibiting such a purchase. I continued down Witherspoon Street. I passed what in the early 1900s had been the office of a black-owned newspaper called the *Citizen,* and past the Princeton Arts Council, former home of the black YM-YWCA, where many hundreds of black kids in segregated Princeton had played, performed, and been coached in a variety of programs that had grounded them in their young lives with a powerful sense of inclusion and belonging.

At the corner of Witherspoon and Clay, I walked into the air-conditioned Clay Street Learning Center, a community gathering place with a big after-school program, and yoga, exercise, business, and computer classes.[37] Hank called me up to a large, airy room on the second floor, where I was surprised to see him setting up video equipment. Buster (Clyde Thomas) and I arranged two chairs and a small table in front of Hank's curtain-draped backdrop. I wasn't used to being filmed while I interviewed someone, and I silently was worrying about whether this setting, the camera, and my tape recorder would inhibit Mr. Hinds. About then, I heard someone slowly climbing the stairs. His hat appeared first, then his brown suit jacket, and then all of him—Mr. Albert Hinds, a small, trim man with the stature of a former athlete.

"My knees make it slow," he said as he took off his hat. "Concrete and steel wear out over time, so I guess knees do, too. But I'm not getting them replaced." He smiled. "I'm going out with everything I came in with, except my teeth."

That day, nearly two decades ago, I treasured hearing Albert Hinds talk about his life. He'd watered horses, walked horses, driven a hack, and shined shoes as a young kid, and at ninety-eight, he was still living in his own home, driving his own car, teaching yoga to seniors three times a week, and playing bridge every afternoon. His deep, bright eyes filled at different times with laughter and sadness as he spoke about his childhood and years as an athlete-scholar at Princeton High School, which gave blacks certificates instead of diplomas. Stories flowed about his work, dreams, and life experiences, most of which, except for a few years in Louisiana, he'd lived within a three-block radius of his house on John Street, where he was born in 1902. He told of his first wife's dying during childbirth in the 1940s, when she was not admitted to Princeton's hospital because she was black.

He spoke freely, with no trace of self-consciousness—not a bit bothered by the video camera, lights, or tape recorder. At the end of three hours, he said he was happy to have recalled so much, but it made him regret he'd never interviewed his own relatives. "My grandfather [a former slave] never talked about slavery much. My family wasn't a very talkative family. Now I realize how important it is to talk to your children."

After meeting Albert Hinds, I had a brainstorm. That fall, I was teaching a writing seminar titled "Finding Voice: Perspectives on Race and Class" at Princeton. I realized I could change one of my assignments: instead of interviewing a grandparent, each student could interview an elder resident. This could be a great learning opportunity for the students—and at the same time, it could provide at least a dozen more interviews.

Hank, Buster, and I started meeting in Hank's workshop on John Street or over sausage sandwiches at Conti's Restaurant, across from Community Park Elementary School, to figure out how to accomplish our task. Soon, Penelope S. Edwards-Carter joined us. Penney had also grown up in the neighborhood, where everybody knew everybody. The three of them began compiling a list of people sixty years old or older—the oldest first—who had lived or grown up in the Witherspoon neighborhood. We sent out close to one hundred letters, and Hank, Buster, and Penney made calls to talk about the project and ask for suggestions of anyone who might have been forgotten or overlooked. We wanted everyone included. The only criterion was that they currently or formerly had lived in the neighborhood. Every person had stories to tell, and we wanted to hear them all.

These efforts led to an afternoon in late September 1999 when I walked with fourteen Princeton undergraduates from campus into this neighborhood so intimately linked to their university but unknown to them. At the Clay Street Learning Center, we sat in a circle with about twenty older neighborhood residents, whose parents, aunts, uncles, grandparents, great-grandparents, and even great-great-grandparents had served Princeton University, its faculty, its students, and its grounds and facilities for more than two hundred years.

Buster, who was a retired labor negotiator, began the conversation. My students looked uncomfortable. In our class, they were reading Frederick Douglass, examining white privilege and patterns of discrimination, but the majority of them had very little experience in conversing about race or unconscious assumptions they might carry. Certainly, most of the students had never been in the same room with this many black people or old people. Seeing everyone sitting a little too stiffly, avoiding one another's eyes, eating too few cookies, reminded me of how racially segregated we still are in America. Traditionally, one group had advantages associated not only with whiteness but also with an elite university, and the other group, given secondhand books since they were small, and denied freedoms, opportunities, prospects, and power, had known far more humble circumstances.

One lifelong resident, Lois Craig, cut through the reticence and began to tell stories about the way it used to be in the neighborhood. "When we were kids, we were poor, but we never knew it. We always had enough food on our table from the leftovers Dad brought home from his work on Prospect Avenue [at the Cap and Gown eating club]."

"The university don't let them take food home anymore," said another woman. "It's really too bad for the families."

That meeting, for all its discomfort, was a beginning. We were together. Some of the residents said they were willing to be interviewed. Others weren't. Several expressed skepticism about the university's involvement. They said that for years they'd been approached as "subjects" by Princeton students doing research for politics or sociology classes. For them to believe that this project would celebrate their lives—rather than just use them—required a leap of faith that was aided by the fact that Hank, Buster, and Penney, beloved and respected community activists, had initiated this project with me.

One woman in her late seventies said that she wouldn't be comfortable telling her personal stories to a white student; she would participate only if the student were black. This posed a challenge, but we agreed with her wishes. We wanted to hear her story.

Hank, Penney, and Buster handled the logistics of scheduling, and at least one of the three accompanied each student to the initial interviews, which the students tape-recorded and Hank videotaped. By the end of the semester, we had fourteen completed interviews that my students transcribed and shaped into first-person narratives. The students said they felt their eyes had been opened to a whole new world.

———

With our semester complete, it became clear that we needed a larger and more focused effort to put together a collection of interviews, which now seemed a logical goal. In September 2000, I launched a seminar, AAS 204,

"Life Stories: Writing Oral History"—the first academic course at Princeton University focused entirely on Princeton's African American community—under the aegis of what was then the African American Studies Program and the Princeton Writing Program. The students in this class embarked on a journey with me that took on a life of its own. They started learning about the Witherspoon neighborhood and black history through literature, film, guest speakers, scattered newspaper accounts, and research from the First Exhibition on the African-American Community in Princeton, by the Historical Society of Princeton in 1996.

The students said their *real education* began, however, when they walked out of "the Princeton bubble," down Witherspoon Street, and past the swanky shopping area across Nassau Street that is Palmer Square, which bore little resemblance to the black neighborhood that occupied it in previous centuries. When the students crossed Paul Robeson Place, the complexion of people they passed took on a darker hue, and the atmosphere changed. People greeted them warmly as they passed, and students said they felt a welcoming friendliness they previously had not experienced in Princeton. Lauren Miller, a junior at the time, wrote, "It's a wonder how much of a difference it makes to step several blocks off campus and to interview the amazing people of the community and learn the rich history of the area. . . . Every day when I step into that neighborhood, I feel my spirit has been uplifted."

Walking in the neighborhood, the students saw the house where Paul Robeson, the neighborhood's great champion of human rights, had been born. Throughout the 1930s and 1940s, the internationally known singer, actor, athlete, scholar, and orator Paul Robeson was "arguably the most popular and influential black public figure in the United States and the world."[38] Students saw the Witherspoon Street Presbyterian Church with its tall spire, where Paul's extraordinary father, the Reverend William Robeson himself, an escaped slave who earned a bachelor's and two doctoral degrees from Lincoln University, had preached the Gospel in the late 1800s and early 1900s. They also saw the stained-glass window Rev. Robeson had installed in honor of his mother, Sabra, who had been born into slavery in 1825 in North Carolina. On Quarry Street, they saw the former Witherspoon School for Colored Children, which had been formally established in 1858 at 184 Witherspoon Street. As the population grew, the school, still called the Witherspoon

School for Colored Children, was relocated in 1908 to Thirty-Five Quarry Street, where it was reconstructed in 1939 to include more classrooms, a gymnasium, and an auditorium.[39] Now it is used as a nursing home.

The students soon learned that they were treading the same streets where the world's most famous scientist, Albert Einstein, had regularly walked. As a Jew who had "felt a definite coldness" when he first arrived in Princeton in 1933, Einstein had been acutely aware of racism, which he called "America's worst disease."[40] Throughout his life in Princeton, Einstein attended NAACP meetings and sat on neighborhood porches, conversing with his Witherspoon friends and kindred spirits.

Several students visited the neighborhood churches that residents had attended for worship and Bible studies, community dinners, social events, plays, political discussions, and spiritual solace since they were children. Students also visited organizations established by neighborhood residents, such as the Elks, Masons, and Veterans Association, and saw the site of the former Charcoal Inn and Tavern. They learned about black businesses in the neighborhood and the entrepreneurial spirit that created them.

Two or three of the students visited James ("Jimmy") Mack's barbershop on John Street, a go-to place for black men to get haircuts. Up until the 1970s, black men were turned away from barbershops on Nassau Street. Students learned that for many years, the one black physician in Princeton had a general practice and also made house calls. However, the Princeton Medical Center and Hospital refused to give him hospital privileges, so he could not admit any of his patients there. If black people needed hospitalization, they had to go to a hospital in Trenton or elsewhere for treatment.

During our weekly three-hour seminar, students responded to readings, discussed racism, practiced interviewing skills, and researched different aspects of the community. As they began their interviews, they started to learn more specific details about the discrimination African Americans had experienced in Princeton. At Lahiere's Restaurant on Witherspoon Street, for instance, blacks who appeared to be African in full African garb were served, but American blacks dressed in suits and ties were refused service there well into the late 1960s. Many Witherspoon residents continued to boycott Lahiere's until the day it closed in 2010. Similarly, even though black Princetonians broke through the hiring barrier in the 1950s to cook and wait tables at the Nassau Tavern (now the Nassau Inn) and the Nassau Club, they themselves were not allowed entry or served there until well into the 1970s.

To see a movie at the Playhouse theater, located on Hulfish Street and demolished during the urban renewal of the 1980s, blacks had to sit on the back right side of the theater. "I used to wonder why we always sat in the back on the right-hand side," resident Shirley Satterfield recalls. "I thought it was just where we always sat, but actually that's where we *had* to sit." The only black person who sat in the front of the theater was Donald Moore's Aunt Kissey (1899–1972), who played the piano there during silent films in the early 1920s. At the Garden Theatre on Nassau Street, blacks had to climb the staircase to the balcony—the only place they were allowed to sit. Albert Hinds recalled how it hurt him as a young man when his father could no longer climb those stairs. The last time they went, he carried his father up to his seat. After that, they stopped going to the movies.

Until the 1970s, African Americans could not sit at the counter in Woolworth's (located on Nassau Street until it closed in the late 1990s), or shop in the fancy stores that sold everything from jewelry to dishes, let alone be hired as clerks in those stores. Certain clothing stores along Nassau Street "permitted" black women to purchase clothes, but they were not allowed to try on any clothing in the store. If they were black, once they had purchased the clothing, they could not return or exchange the item for any reason.

Alice Satterfield remembers going with her mother into a store, where they had once felt welcomed. The ownership had changed, however, and the clerk, saying nothing, closely followed them around the room until they left. "We didn't need to go there anyway," Satterfield said. "We could get what we needed in our own neighborhood."

At Princeton restaurants, such as "the Balt" (the Baltimore Daily Lunch) on Nassau Street, black people could not sit down, be served food, or pay for takeout food well into the 1960s. One of the greatest authors of the twentieth century, novelist and essayist James Baldwin, worked at a defense plant near Princeton in the 1940s. In *Notes of a Native Son*, Baldwin writes about waiting to be served at Renwick's, a restaurant on Nassau Street.

I knew about jim-crow but I had never experienced it. I went to the same self-service restaurant three times and stood with all the

Princeton boys before the counter, waiting for a hamburger and coffee; it was always an extraordinarily long time before anything was set before me; but it was not until the fourth visit that I learned that, in fact, nothing had ever been set before me: I had simply picked something up. Negroes were not served there, I was told, and they had been waiting for me to realize that I was always the only Negro present. Once I was told this, I determined to go there all the time. But now they were ready for me and, though some dreadful scenes were subsequently enacted in that restaurant, I never ate there again.

It was the same story all over New Jersey, in bars, bowling alleys, diners, places to live. I was always being forced to leave, silently, or with mutual imprecations.[41]

No local hotels welcomed black Americans—no matter how famous they were. The Nassau Inn and other local inns were reserved for whites only.[42] In 1902, when Woodrow Wilson, Princeton class of 1878, was about to be inaugurated as Princeton's thirteenth president, Booker T. Washington was invited to attend as an honored guest. Washington, founder of the Tuskegee Institute and one of the most prominent black educators, orators, and authors of the late nineteenth century, joined the procession of dignitaries walking behind Woodrow Wilson, and also attended the luncheon that followed, where President Wilson gave a speech. Washington was the only black person and the only black visiting dignitary present. He was also the only celebrity who was not housed with a Princeton faculty member's family during the inaugural events. Instead, Washington stayed at a black boardinghouse in the Witherspoon neighborhood. He was further snubbed by the Wilsons, who did not invite him to either of the dinners they gave during the inaugural festivities.[43]

In 1937, when opera contralto Marian Anderson, one of the most celebrated singers of the twentieth century, gave a concert to a standing-room only audience at Princeton's McCarter Theatre, Princeton's Nassau Inn refused her a room. When Albert Einstein heard about the insult, he invited Anderson to stay with his daughter and him in their house on Mercer Street. Anderson accepted the invitation, and she and Einstein formed a friendship that lasted for the rest of his life.[44]

Throughout the neighborhood's history, black boardinghouses were, for the most part, bedrooms hired out by neighborhood residents to black folks who were not welcome "uptown." When Carmen McRae and other musicians, including Count Basie, Cab Calloway, Lionel Hampton, Ella Fitzgerald, and Duke Ellington, came to perform at the McCarter Theatre or at university events, they found lodging in various neighborhood homes. A number of the people we interviewed recalled how as youngsters they helped their parents clean bedrooms and change sheets, move chairs, and set up tables on their family's front porch or in the living-dining room, to transform those spaces into guest rooms or dining rooms for paying customers. The visiting musicians often put on mini-concerts for the community—sometimes at the old Charcoal Inn on John Street, the YMCA, the Masonic Temple, or in a boardinghouse where they were staying. Often, neighborhood musicians, including jazz stride pianist Donald "the Lamb" Lambert (1904–62), well known in Harlem nightclubs in the 1920s and '30s, joined in with them. When Harriett Calloway, born in Princeton in 1906, recalled the life of her musician father, she said, "He didn't have a band like Count Basie or any of those, but he entertained a lot, and did a lot of work around Princeton. He had a little jazz band, and he went to Florida every year to play—that was [starting] back in 1910."

Music—from gospel to jazz, classical music to opera, bop to rhythm and blues—filled the Witherspoon neighborhood. The Harlem Renaissance in the 1920s and the flourishing of African American voices being heard throughout the world—poets, writers, artists, musicians, intellectuals, and performers—lifted spirits and reminded Witherspoon residents of the joy of being alive and connecting to others in this long walk toward freedom.

———

While we were learning from residents about national events that had sparked unity in the community and what local initiatives they'd created to right the wrongs against them in employment, housing, urban development, and police-community relations, my students were scouring old issues of newspapers and magazines and looking for relevant files at the Historical Society of Princeton, the Archives of Seeley G. Mudd Library at Princeton University, and the Princeton Public Library. In the process, they discovered firsthand how ignored and underrepresented African Americans were in the written history of this town, state, and nation by a white press that rarely covered black life on any level. No full copies of the black-owned paper the *Citizen*, "A Weekly Newspaper Dedicated to the Moral, Intellectual, and Industrial Improvement of the Negro Race," are known to exist.[45] Only one front page of the *Citizen* ("Volume 1, no. 16, March 12, 1909. Price Five Cents") has survived. "This document alone provides ample testimony to the struggles and successes of Princeton's African Americans in forging their own ideals, institutions, and community," says Professor and writer Kevin Gaines. At a time the mainstream press expressed indifference to black aspirations, the black press articulated them and promoted black advancement and combatted antiblack prejudice."[46]

The students were galvanized when they realized this neighborhood had a history that, on paper, did not exist. They began to unearth significant documents and fill in missing gaps. Lou Arrindell, a junior researching civil rights and local politics for our class, wrote:

Up until this point, the library was simply a quiet place to do homework or check out a book. A few weeks ago, the idea of doing research in newspapers and microfilm was more than an unnerving task; it was absolutely terrifying. The idea of scrolling through a year's worth of microfiche seemed impossible. I thought the needle-in-a-haystack type research we were doing was reserved for junior papers and senior theses.

After all the research we've done in this class, I have not only gained confidence, but also learned how to research topics efficiently. Despite the fact that the actual process became tedious at times, whenever I found a gem of information, I was overcome with a feeling of satisfaction that sustained me for quite a while. The greatest moment research-wise for me was when I found a copy of the *Black Word*.[47] Several of the founding members of the newspaper had expressed regret over not having any of the old issues, and did not know where any existing copies were. When I found a copy of the *Black Word* in the public library, I thought it typified the research of the class, as we were not only finding tangible objects with a real connection in history, but also emotional connections with people.

The students found great motivation when they realized that their scholarship might help enlighten others and deepen their perspective on African American experience. Jenny Hildebrand, then a sophomore, wrote:

> I am amazed at the interesting and shocking events that have occurred in Princeton. Finding historical information has not been easy, but along the way, I have learned a lot. Sitting in Mudd Library the other day, I spent about three hours sifting through ancient documents. I found myself reading articles that didn't pertain to my topic just because they were interesting. At the end of the three hours, I stood up and there were little pieces of browned paper all over my lap. It was then I realized how fragile those old documents were and that future generations would not be able to handle them. In the same light, people's stories would be dying along with them, burying valuable history.

I felt exhilarated as I watched my students discover for themselves the humanity I'd been experiencing from my black friends and mentors since the 1960s and '70s. I loved seeing the students tearing off the blinders, and moment by moment being given unexpected insight into the false notions of race and racial superiority. I loved seeing the Witherspoon old-timers decimate stereotypes of blacks as less intelligent, less diligent, less ethical, less capable, and more dangerous and volatile than whites.

Many of the students *saw and felt* racism in whole new ways. I heard amazement in their voices when they talked about how many of the residents *looked* white but were classified as black. The variety of skin shades made illogic the myth of "race" and highlighted the inconsistencies of how we define it.

All of the students were captivated by the keen sensibilities of the people they interviewed. They were also startled by some of the elders' abrupt observations about them. Kappy (Kathleen Montgomery Edwards) chided a black student for her privileged background and challenged her to become more active in social and political justice issues. Another, one-hundred-year-old Johnnie Dennis, kept interrupting her own story to tell the white student interviewing her, "Get your hat and go home."

Again and again, students said they were "blown away" by hearing about living life on a daily basis under oppressive white assumptions and the daily terrorism of Jim Crow racism. At the same time, they felt humbled and inspired by the genuine openness of people who had transcended the tremendous wrongs done against them to live with such humor, imagination, and intellect. Student Celia Riechel wrote:

With Mr. Phox and Ms. Twyman, I forgot almost immediately what information I was looking for. I just wanted to sit and listen, and follow their thoughts. I wanted to sit at their feet in wonder and awe. So this is real. This is raw. . . . Nothing could adequately convey how I feel. . . . Were I to sum up my experience this semester, I should like to have the luxury of time, to serve as an intermediary. Will it weave itself into some spiraling arabesque throughout the rest of my life? I do not know. I am in the midst of this, still waking each morning with something new because of it. Still glowing/flushed/tingling from the listening. . . .

To really know (and I will never really know, but maybe that is what is so wonderful about it), I need the focalization that time can only give—not time as defined by seconds, minutes, years, but time defined by distance traveled, things done and not done, happiness and pain felt and shared. . . . I do not know how my time will go, but ask me in a year or ask me in fifty, and maybe then I'll know.

The more interviews we did, the more it became clear how much more we had to do. We couldn't possibly complete all the interviews or research in the few weeks that remained in the semester.

When the course had ended, we couldn't let it go. Lauren Miller, a sophomore, suggested we call the oral history "a work in progress." Our core group was committed, and more volunteers joined us. With funding from Princeton University's president, the Program in African American Studies, Community-Based Learning Initiative, and vice president for Campus Life, we were able to subsidize students' work and pay for professional transcriptions of the taped interviews. With this backing, our endeavor turned into a much larger project. We began to gather one evening a week to share stories, check facts, eat pizza, read the narratives aloud, and make notes about following up on various interviews to fill in missing details.

We held events at the Princeton Public Library, Princeton University, and the Clay Street Learning Center, and students read dynamic excerpts from the interviews that moved and sometimes shocked our audiences. Many Witherspoon residents attended these sessions and afterward often confirmed, elaborated upon, or corrected information they heard. The most significant intervention was one night at the library when a student read from his interview with a former Tuskegee Airman, who had described in phenomenal detail his experiences in World War II as one of the first African American military pilots.

After our presentation, three women from the neighborhood took me aside to say this man's story was absolutely untrue. He never was a Tuskegee Airman. He claimed to have been with the 302nd Fighter Squadron in Italy in 1944, but at the time, he was still in high school. They showed me a photograph of him and themselves at their graduation under a "Class of 1944" banner. He was not in the records of Tuskegee Airmen. Memory may be unreliable, but this was fiction, so we deleted that story from this collection.

In May 2001, we celebrated our progress at the Henry F. Pannell Learning Center, formerly known as the Clay Street Learning Center. By then we had been working for more than two years. We had thirty-four taped interviews, with written transcripts of most of them—some as long as thirty pages. From the transcripts, we'd shaped short biographies, as well as first-person narratives of varying lengths that related stories of important or pivotal moments of the residents' lives.

The oral history was under way. Neighborhood retirees and university students—black, white, Asian, Caribbean, Native American, and Middle Eastern—had been mobilized by this extraordinary community. People who normally didn't cross paths had worked together, often in a state of elation, over the rich first-person histories we were collecting. To witness the strength of individuals who saw so clearly beyond the corrosive effects of racial prejudice was awe-inspiring. Coming together to preserve these irreplaceable stories gave all of us the gift of seeing and being seen.

At our celebration in May 2001, we ate soul food prepared by George Cumberbatch, owner and chef of the Downtown Deluxe on John Street. The large room was filled with the loud noise of people talking and laughing together. A hush fell, however, when Buster Thomas spoke and students began to read excerpts from their interviews with the residents. As we listened, a feeling of reverence seemed to settle over the room. At one point, Saloni Doshi, a junior then, read from her interview with Romus Broadway about a time he went to explore the slave records of his ancestors and ran into a cousin of his who was white. Broadway sat rapt as he heard his own words spoken back to him. Later, he said, "When I was listening, it was all I could do to stop the tears. I felt I was walking in the footsteps of all of my forefathers."

Now, nearly two decades after it began, with *really* the last interview completed, we are seeing Hank Pannell's dream, now our collective dream, come true. Altogether, we now have gathered more than fifty-five oral histories. These incorporate interviews with Sophie Hinds, Burnett Griggs, Emma Epps, Estelle Johnson, and Eva Redding, which we unearthed at the Historical Society of Princeton. We've regretted that some people died before we had a chance to record their stories. But it wasn't too late for these.

———

This book's organization was inspired by presentations we gave based on the interviews. Each chapter presents a particular focus, followed by speakers talking about their own experiences. The residents' birth dates are given after their names, before they are quoted, to allow readers a sense of time and perspective from the late 1800s up to 2000. In chapter 10, residents discuss more modern times and look to the future of the neighborhood. In the back of the book, short biographies of each speaker are listed in alphabetical order by surnames.

Given the history of Jim Crow and all the barriers erected against black success, the Witherspoon residents have always been well aware that their value as individuals is not equated with the status of their jobs. Whether people wash pots or pans, open doors, or shine shoes for pay does not measure their intellect, dignity, courage, or generous spirit. Residents show loyalty and respect for one another based on character, unrelated to spurious measurements. As Emma Epps told her mother's employer, "Miss Wright, the fact that my mother was a laundress in your house was not the fact that she didn't have a brain but that she didn't have a chance."

A large number of the speakers in this book did service work and jobs below their aspirations. For many, their life experience has been their schooling. Holding a job for twenty or thirty years and moving to the top of it may show a steadiness of purpose and a pragmatism that has supported their families, but looked at more closely, it can also be an index of their intellect and their character. For instance, Jay Craig, superintendent of maintenance for the Jewish Center of Princeton for thirty years, used to go to the Carousel, a breakfast spot, to drink coffee and solve the problems of the world with former Princeton president Harold Shapiro. A voracious reader, Craig, who lives on-site at the Jewish Center, traveled around the world on the funds he saved on rent. I imagine that if, as a young man, he'd had a chance at college, he would have been, at the least, a US senator by now. Similarly, Hank Pannell did such outstanding work as a maintenance mechanic for the Housing Authority that he ended up as chief of maintenance for the Housing Authority of the Borough of Princeton for thirty years. Yet he would have much preferred to follow his dreams at Princeton's Jet Propulsion Lab, where he worked as a young man—the first and only African American at that time.

———

Our intention for this book was to bring the historic Witherspoon neighborhood into view and to share the sweep of its rich history. An unplanned result of the process is that the wealth of individuals' life stories has provided a fresh lens for illuminating the persistence of racism's harsh realities and the legacies of slavery as they have been and still are experienced in our country today—particularly in law enforcement's disproportionate focus on young black men and women. This stereotypical focus has created a discriminatory cycle of arrests, prosecutions, prison sentences, and an industry of mass incarceration and felony disenfranchisement that has taken the vote away from millions of black men and women and split up families in ways reminiscent of slavery.

Close up, this book has allowed us to witness the personal ways in which discrimination and institutional inequalities work in our society and the lengths to which entrenched power will go to suppress black advancement, black leadership, and independence. It also has allowed us to see how African Americans have fought for self-determination in the face of continuing prejudice. In these pages, we hear how a tight-knit community faced these adversities and formed strategies to protect their children from them. As individuals, neighbors, children, and parents, they have gone through all life's passages—growing up, working, forming friendships and partnerships, marrying, divorcing, raising children, celebrating, burying loved ones—with an awe-inspiring ability to challenge yet put aside, step over, leave behind, and transcend the demeaning, destructive stereotypes others keep imposing on them.

In the pages that follow, you'll meet black Princetonians who have risen to challenges every day and have worked to live just lives despite the injustices. Although the speakers certainly have cause for bitterness, they rarely dwell on it. This was true for Emanuel Rhodes, a World War II veteran awarded the Bronze Star Medal for valor and heroic service in a combat zone. Rhodes returned after the war to a segregated Princeton and a nation where black soldiers were being shot, and lynched by white mobs that were never held accountable. He shook his head. "I still don't have hate in my heart," he said. "I'm seventy-eight years old and I don't hate nobody."

The words from this little-known neighborhood, in this well-known town can teach us lessons for living, for finding freedom by standing up against wrongs and working together for justice. We hope that this book will inspire readers to create a world of caring where every one of our children can thrive.

1

Our Grandmother
Came from Africa
as a Little Girl

Thomas Sullivan Grocery Store at 74 Witherspoon Street,
on the corner of Jackson Street, 1887

IN PRINCETON, PEOPLE OFTEN repeat the myth that claims Princeton's black population began when Southern students brought their slaves with them to the college. This simply is not so. As stated previously, free and enslaved Africans lived in this area long before the town was founded or the university was established.

When the College of New Jersey moved from Elizabeth to Princeton in 1756, its first buildings were Nassau Hall, a house for the college president, and a separate kitchen building that had slave quarters above. The charter president, Jonathan Dickenson, a slave owner and minister, had died in 1647, four and a half months after being appointed to lead the infant college in Elizabeth.[1] His successor, Aaron Burr, Sr., the first to move into the president's house, came to campus with his wife, daughter, and baby son.[2] He also brought with him a man named Caesar, whom he had purchased in 1755. The bill of sale, still in Princeton University's archives, specifies that for eighty pounds, the former owner sold Mr. Aaron Burr "a certain Negro Man named Caesar"—"To HAVE and to HOLD the said Negro Man Caesar unto the said Mr. Aaron Burr his Executors, Administrators and Assigns for ever."[3]

Certainly, many college students came from slave-owning Southern gentry, but Southern students did not "bring their slaves" to the tiny but growing campus.[4] The white male students lived and studied in one large stone building—Nassau Hall—which, at the time, was the largest building in all of the American colonies. This building would house the entire college—library, chapel, classrooms, and residential space—for the next fifty years.[5]

The enslaved people living on campus belonged to the college's presidents. Following Aaron Burr, six more slave owners presided over the college and lived in the same presidential home (Maclean House) that sits on Princeton University's campus today. They legally owned people who, because of the bodies into which they'd been born, were sentenced to a lifetime of bondage. In 1766, the six people held by the fifth president, Samuel Finley, most likely lived above the kitchen, as had Cesar. That may have been home to them for five years before both Finley and his wife died during a stay in Philadelphia, and they were put up for sale. On August 19, 1766, it was those two women, one man, and three children who stood on the lawn in

Nancy Greene and Emma Greene (Epps) (1904)

front of Maclean House, where buyers looked them over and bid on them, as they did on horses, cattle, and other household possessions.

Enslaved blacks were not the only new arrivals to Princeton in those days. Freed Negro men and women also settled here as paid servants, domestics, carpenters, laborers, and entrepreneurs. At the end of the Revolutionary War, men who had earned manumission from slavery by fighting for the Continental army also found employment at the college.

Quite a number of formerly enslaved people arrived in Princeton in the 1700s and 1800s by terrifying means of escape. Some traveled north on the Underground Railroad—the secret interstate network that took shape by the 1830s to help Southern slaves flee to freedom in Northern states and Canada—decided they liked Princeton. One legendary resident, who changed his name to James C. Johnson after he escaped from his owner in Baltimore in 1839, was penniless by the time he got to Princeton, which was why he chose to stay. Within a few days, he was earning wages as a servant at the college. Like others, he kept students' rooms swept and clean, started fires on cold mornings, and blackened the students' boots. Because of emptying their chamber pots, he got the nickname "Stinky" from some of the students.

Another brave soul who escaped slavery was Albert Hinds's maternal grandfather, Robert Hall, who traveled north with the aid of the Underground Railroad in the 1850s. He stopped in New York and got work helping to build the Brooklyn Bridge. Then he chose to settle down as a farmer in New Jersey, right outside Princeton, where he and his wife had nine children.

Another former slave, Rev. William Robeson, escaped from North Carolina and worked for the Union army during the Civil War. He made his way north to Lincoln University, outside Philadelphia, where he worked as a farmhand while he learned Greek, Latin, and Hebrew, and earned a bachelor's degree and two additional degrees in theology. He married and came with his bride from Philadelphia, Maria Louisa Bustill Robeson, to Princeton, where they moved into the parsonage of the Witherspoon Street Presbyterian Church (founded in 1837 as the First Presbyterian Church of Color) and had seven children. Rev. Robeson served as the Presbyterian Church's beloved pastor for twenty-one years.

For each person who settled in the Princeton neighborhood, siblings, cousins, or friends often followed. Two of Rev. Robeson's brothers, for instance, trailed him to Princeton from North Carolina, and each married, had children, and built families that became part of the Witherspoon community. By the mid-1800s, historical records mention the presence of paid servants—both Irish and African American—who'd found low-income housing in the Witherspoon neighborhood.

The College of New Jersey was a major draw for African Americans looking for work, as was the Princeton Theological Seminary, which had been founded in 1812. Unlike the college, the seminary welcomed black students and played a strong role in educating black clergy and supporting black churches. It, too, became a source not only of employment, but also its welcome drew many free blacks to the area and substantially increased the African American population in Princeton.

Following the Civil War, during a short period known as Reconstruction, when the federal government attempted to rebuild the South, African American men exercised their first-time voting rights to overwhelmingly elect black representatives to state and national offices. During this time,

> newly freed men were able to exercise rights previously denied them. They could vote, marry, or go to school if there were one nearby, and the more ambitious among them could enroll in black colleges set up by northern philanthropists, open businesses, and run for office. . . . In short order, some managed to become physicians, legislators, undertakers, insurance men. . . . But by the mid-1870s, when the North withdrew its oversight in the face of southern hostility, whites in the South began to resurrect the caste system founded under slavery. Nursing the wounds of defeat and seeking a scapegoat, much like Germany in the years leading up to Nazism, they began to undo the opportunities accorded free slaves during Reconstruction and to refine the language of white supremacy. They would create a caste system based not on pedigree and title . . . but solely on race, and which, by law, disallowed any movement of the lowest caste into the mainstream.[6]

The South denied African Americans any right to due process and unleashed ruthless violence against them. "The status of former slaves in the first two generations following emancipation is a dramatic example of the attempt to make the color line a distinctive and permanent feature of American life," the imminent historian John Hope Franklin writes. "After participating in the political process for less than a decade in the 1860s and 1870s, they were stripped of every vestige of citizenship by one of the most merciless, terror-driven assaults in the annals of modern history. Black men who dared to vote were lynched, and schools that black children dared to attend were burned to the ground."[7] Politicians justified this behavior on

Stereographic portrait of a Princeton man (about 1800)

high moral grounds: "In spectacles that often went on for hours, black men and women were routinely tortured and mutilated, then hanged or burned alive, all before festive crowds of as many as several thousand white citizens, children in tow, hoisted on their fathers' shoulders to get a better view."[8]

Many families who decided to flee the terrorism of the South were drawn to Princeton by relatives and friends who lived there, work opportunities, and the town's relative peacefulness. The small black community of Princeton was enticing for its manageable size and social fabric. In 1900, one in every five residents in the town of 4,000 was African American. Census figures show a spike in the black population from 585 in 1890 to 1,148 in 1910, which was 22 percent of the borough population. Many of these newcomers to Princeton had migrated from Georgia, North Carolina, South Carolina, and Virginia.[9] Princeton's churches, schools, wealthy businessmen, building projects, and entrepreneurial opportunities within the Witherspoon community continued to attract African Americans eager to put down new roots.

At the turn of the century, when the College of New Jersey was turning into Princeton University, when new job opportunities opened up for

African Americans, they also opened up for others. Specifically, the college brought in Italian stone masons, artisans, and carpenters to construct new, ornate, Gothic-style buildings on campus. The college helped the Italian workers find affordable rental housing for their families in and around the Witherspoon neighborhood. By then, most of the Irish had moved on, into white neighborhoods, so the Italians, despite the language differences, settled in. "Our connection with Italians was that we were all poor," said one black resident. "We got along fine."

Travelers who came north after World Wars I and II as part of the Great Migration were motivated not only by the Southern violence against blacks but also by the deteriorating economic realities of the South. They were searching for stable jobs and the chance to create and maintain a safe environment for their children. Most of the migrants traveling north moved into cities, such as Atlantic City, Newark, and New York. But those who stopped in Princeton found a lively community with strong ethical values and an active resistance to the Jim Crow laws that limited their freedoms.

Yesterday and today's Witherspoon residents speak about their own roots in the following pages—starting with Sophie Hinds, born in 1875, whose voice we found in the Historical Society's records. She and others descend in large part from those early neighborhood settlers, and they've continued to build on the courage and tenacity of those who came before them.

Hey, wait a minute here. That slavery business wasn't that long ago.
—LAMONT FLETCHER

Sophie Hall Hinds (1875–1974)

They were Northern people, my mother's folks. My father's were Southern people. My father was born a slave. The master that kept him had plenty of people. So none of my father's people were ever sold. They were given away, but never sold. This man that came down from Africa who was related to my father was head of the tribe or something like that. I don't know much about him, but he came down and he asked that none of his people be auctioned. He said, "Don't ever sell any of my people." And none of them were ever sold. I guess my father was a runaway slave. He got up here in the North and helped build the Brooklyn Bridge. When I was a grown-up girl, I used to hear from [my father's] one sister who was still living and was given away to Mississippi. . . . [My father] never heard much from [his family] until after a number of years . . . he somehow got in touch with one or two of his sisters who lived in Mississippi. And that's how I knew both of them, so I used to be the one to do the writing backward and forward to them. But the only one I ever saw was one of his sisters.

Jacqui Swain (1944–)

My great-grandmother and grandfather came from Lawrence, South Carolina. They were Maddens. Our family tree goes as far as a white slave owner by the name of Alex Madden. The Ku Klux Klan was tearing up South Carolina about that time, 1920ish. My grandmother on my mother's side used to always tell a story about how my great-grandfather sent his boys to find a place where they could live in relative comfort. She remembers being awakened in the middle of the night, at two a.m., by her parents because they had to get out of Lawrence, South Carolina, under the cover of the dark.

So they all came to Princeton and found a house on old Clay Street and had various jobs here. I don't know a lot about my father's family. His people were the Princeton Prior family, and I think a lot of them are still in New York.

My grandmother is Mary Madden Sullivan. She worked in a private family for a while. She worked at Princeton Hospital doing laundry. She must have had seven or eight brothers and sisters that I knew. Some of her sisters were professionals and her brother Gally worked for the Borough Garage. My Uncle Clarence was an entrepreneur, he did his own thing. Many of [my grandmother's] brothers and sisters could pass for white and did. When one of her sisters died, there was some question as to whether a child that that sister had could actually be her child because the child was obviously black. My grandmother had to go to court to prove that she was the sister and aunt.

Nana, my father's mother, was Elnora Prior Johnston. She was widowed and raised her two boys alone. Both my mother and father went to segregated schools here in Princeton. They didn't always give black students diplomas; they got these certificates of proficiency indicating that they knew

Women in the Witherspoon neighborhood (about 1800)

how to mop floors and scrub dishes. But my father graduated from the high school and he received a diploma. He and his brother went into the navy right out of high school during World War II.

Johnnie Dennis (1903–2007)

I'll be ninety-eight years old in September. I was born in South Carolina. I went to school in South Carolina, and they started a school made from a church. I had brothers and sisters. They lived to a certain age and then they died. Our grandmother came from Africa as a little girl. Our father is American Indian. My parents did what they could do. Born way back there in slave time. My father was a barber and he worked cutting hair. So they had jobs then, but nobody went out and created jobs like now. I told you, you got to read your history. They had to make the jobs. We had to work—any kind of work you could find. We built this country! We built it! Black folks from Africa. It just wasn't built by white men. It was built up by everybody.

Bruce Wright (1917–2005)

My father came to Princeton from Montserrat. He came to Princeton because of an older brother who ended up there, running one of those eating clubs that they had for students. His brother was a bit on the snobbish side, and, to me, a very strange guy. In fact, we had invented all kinds of nicknames for him. His name was Oscar, and he had a big nose, so we called him Oscola Schnozola, behind his back, of course. But he was a decent guy. And my track coach told me that if you don't have a nickname, you're not a regular guy, so I thought my uncle was a regular guy, Schnozola. He may not have thought so.

So my father worked at a restaurant on Nassau Street called the Balt. They let you work there but not eat there. He was a cook. And then he got rescued and he worked for one of the deans at the university. He was the cook, chief bottle washer, and servant for Dean Robert Russell Wickes—a sort of a divinity guy, if I'm not mistaken. And he was full of shit.

I worked in the kitchen with my father, especially when the Wickes family had guests for dinner. My father suffered from rheumatism all his life. He was only five foot four. And I used to weep sometimes, knowing the hard work that he did. He suffered from asthma, which made breathing even worse. So I used to help him when I got big enough. The dean entertained all the time, especially students. So there was a lot of work to be done. And in those days, I don't know what they do about people with asthma today, but my father had to pause now and then. There was some terrible-looking powder that he would put on a little piece of tin, and he would light it and inhale the fumes. He worked there until he died in his sixties.

My mother worked for a professor also, but she didn't cook, she took care of the house. My mother was a lousy cook. I mean, she would have told you that, too. She was not a good cook. My dad did a lot of cooking. But then, when I got drafted and my brother was drafted and my sister was married, she worked in a defense factory, I guess in New Brunswick. She liked motors and things. She was a good driver.

Fortunately for me, I had Aunt Katherine, my mother's sister, who lived mostly in New York, and she liberated me from Princeton when I was thirteen. Aunt Katherine became friendly with me and wanted me to have something better than Princeton. So I went to high school in New York City at Townsend Harris, an elite public high school for boys. There were probably three black kids in it, but it was integrated. The New York City public school system was, to my knowledge, never segregated.

Aunt Katherine was a typical poor Irish housekeeper. Of course, the Irish were known as the white niggers. They had almost as difficult a time as blacks, especially in the early days of the century. But they were smart. They knew how to manage the political system. My grandparents came here as kids from Ireland and they became cops and firemen. My mother's parents were typical white people in that they couldn't understand my mother's marriage. I think there was a lot of Indian blood in those people. But they were very white. My mother's twin brother was a cop, so I used to see him now and then. He remained friendly with my mother, even though she married a black guy.

But he'd come by to see her and ignore my father completely. I detested him, and I have all my life, since then, been suspicious of policemen, especially white policemen. I had incidents with police officers almost every day when I was a judge in the criminal court in New York. It was my mother's twin brother, too. Marion Thigpen. A big Irish brute of a man. Unfortunately, I was named for him. And, of course, I became a runner, because

I got used to being chased through the streets, "Marion! Little girl!" So I changed my name to my father's first name in fourth grade, Bruce, which is much more masculine. But it was good practice, because I became a runner, and the state champion of New York in the mile run in high school in 1935.

Floyd Campbell (1924–2005)

I have lived in Princeton nearly all my life. I was born February 27, 1924, in Memphis, Tennessee. I lived there five years, then I came here June 30, 1929. My grandfather came to Princeton first and built the house at Eleven Race Street, and my mother and I joined him. I can't begin to tell you about the changes in town. At the time our house was the only house on Race Street. We used to play all our games in the middle of the streets, since we didn't have to worry about the cars. The neighborhoods were segregated. This was predominately an Italian neighborhood.

As a child I didn't notice racism much. There were class differences. . . . But the nasty things you hear that go on today—like that case in Texas recently where a black man was tied up and dragged from the back of a truck because he was black—didn't seem to be happening. The children all played together, white and black. There was a park at the bottom of this hill and we used to play softball, baseball, and football there together. We had our fights and problems, but we had them as children would be [when] confronted with problems. They were not about race. Those problems were between our parents.

Of course, the park where we played was part of the township school that was reserved for the white kids in the town. I had to walk to Quarry Street School. But I wasn't much aware of the differences in education between the two. As a child you didn't ask too many questions. That was just the way things were.

Helen Ball Hoagland (1920–2009)

My mother first came to Princeton with a white family. She was a little maid girl in a family in Virginia, and when they moved to Princeton, they brought my mother. She was just a young child, twelve years old, and her job was to be the maid to the woman she came here with, and this meant

Kane children on the front steps of their Jackson Street home (1898)

fanning the woman at mealtime, fanning her at night. And Mom said the fan was a large fan, but it was something that she had to do to keep her cool. That was the main source of her job—keeping her (the white lady) comfortable. My father lived in Annapolis, Maryland. He was born down there. He came from a large family. He had very little money, because his father was in the marines and would go out on long journeys at sea. My father would play hooky from school to help feed his family, and when his father would come in from the sea, he would stack up barrels of food. They would purchase food in large amounts that would last until he returned to Annapolis. Well, this went on and on, but there's always something that makes you laugh. My Pop skipped school all the time to help feed his family, and I said to him at one time, "How could you get away with that?" and he said, "Well, Mom, Ma"—that's how he talked—"Ma was glad to see what I brought in." I said, "Well, what did you bring in?" He said (he called us dear), "Dear, I'd go down to that bay and sit all day and catch catfish in the sewer and when I went home Ma didn't even spank me, 'cause she was so glad to get the food." And so this is the funny part to me, though after he'd tell me the story about catching catfish in the sewer, I could never, never even look at a catfish. The last three years I've learned to eat catfish.

Albert Hinds (1902–2006)

Now my grandfather, of course, he was a slave, and I guess he was pretty young when he came up. But he helped build the Brooklyn Bridge. And then I guess he migrated to this area, somehow, and was working mostly as a farmer, I believe, and that's why, I presume, he was up in Harlington. In fact, he lived just the house up the street here, after he left working on the farms in Harlington. He lived in the various areas of Princeton. He never talked about [slavery] much. My family wasn't a very talkative family. Now I realize how important it is to talk to your children and so forth, so you can have something to present.

The only story that my grandfather told—as a slave he had very fast feet. Runner, they used to call him. And I don't see how he survived—as a runner for the hound dogs—the dogs that they used to hunt down slaves. So they used to use him, and he had to run and jump over a fence while the dogs were chasin' him.

Fannie Floyd (1924–2008)

My father was from Greensborough, North Carolina, and he had been up working in New England when he was just a teenager. He had met some young black fellas up there who told him about Princeton and helped him to come here. It worked that way. That was about 1906 when he came and got a job over at the clubhouses. He was a steward at Tower Club for all his lifetime,

I guess; he worked there for about forty-five years. He also was the cook at the Blairstown camp. He loved Blairstown! Come spring, he was always happy that he'd be going to Blairstown. He cooked there from 1910 until his death in 1951. After his death, they were building that new building up there and they dedicated part of the dining area to his memory. So we went up to the dedication. And the Tower Club, when he died, they recognized him for his work.

When my son went to Princeton—he graduated in '69—he became a member of the Tower Club and an officer of the club. And after he graduated, he became a member of the board of trustees of the club, so it was quite a change between the way it was back in '47 to now.

Jim Carson (1909–2001)

I was born and raised in a little town called Old Fort, North Carolina. . . . My father and mother didn't have much schooling. My father went to maybe the third or fourth grade. [They] had five children—three boys and two girls. When I was about six or somewhere along there, I went to live with my grandmother, because we lived close together . . . and she was old and living by herself. I went to stay with her so she'd have some company.

She lived to be 104 years old, as far as we can figure out. She said she was about eleven years old when the slaves were freed. And she used to tell us about having to go get the cows, bring them in, milk them—sometimes in the snow barefooted—because they only gave her one pair of shoes, and that had to last. And she didn't even know who her mother and father were. At the time, I didn't get as much history out of her as I should have gotten until it was too late. But, as far as what she was telling us, she raised ten children practically by herself . . . and in the end, she ended up raising me. 'Course, we didn't have no record of births and deaths way back then, only with the slave owners wherever she was. . . . She lived a long life, didn't know what a hospital was.

Thomas Phox (1920–2008)

I was born in a little town called Pals, Virginia. My father and mother worked there on what's now a historical plantation. It didn't pay real well, and there were a lot of people there, so they started looking for other work, looking up North. They came to Princeton in 1927. My sisters and brother and I—at that time there were five of us—we stayed with my grandmother in Virginia until the fall of 1929, when we came to Princeton. We lived on Witherspoon Street, right across from the hospital, in a house we shared with the Buggs family. That was when I was in second grade, and I went to the Quarry Street School through eighth grade and then to Princeton High School. It was a mixed neighborhood; there were a lot of Italians and Irish, and everybody knew everybody. We grew up, we played sports, we had fights like you normally do when you're boys. We were all pals, we'd come over every day. Even in our seventies and eighties, we cherish some things and we see each other just like [when] we were kids—it's that kind of feeling.

Lamont Fletcher (1942–)

My father was born in Princeton, so I'm a bit of an oddity in that I'm second generation Princeton. So that's kind of odd—not only second generation but black. Very few Afro-Americans who are second generation are still living in Princeton.

My grandfather came up from Virginia, and he was raised on a horse farm in Virginia. When he came up, he and his brothers worked on a farm on Cherry Valley Road. And from there, he got a job as a jockey for the Stocktons—the Stocktons of the Declaration of Independence. I don't know how many years he was a jockey for them, but he got a job at one of the clubs as a cook. I don't remember my grandfather, because I was still young when he passed away. But he lived with us for a little while.

I tried to do some genealogy work on my grandfather, and it's interesting, in that being black we talk about slavery and the events of slavery—we study the history of slavery and things of that sort, but you really don't realize—I didn't realize how close I was to slavery. I found out that my grandfather—looking at his death certificate—was born in approximately 1865, which was about the time of the Emancipation Proclamation.

So I went to the Records Office, and, lo and behold, I got the year 1865, and went down to Fletcher, so and so—like that. The surprising thing to me was that the only first names that were listed were whites. If there was

Three generations of Moore-May-Satterfield women (1944)

a slave who had taken on the name Fletcher, the record said, "Fletcher, Slave," or "Fletcher, Boy Slave," or "Fletcher, Girl Slave," but never a first name with it. So I couldn't find out really, precisely where my grandfather was born because the records just said, "Fletcher, Boy Slave." How can you find that particular person if you don't know which Fletcher family you belong to?

Not only that, but back in that period of time, the census taker had to go around to each farm, with the books, and say, "Okay, any new births to register?" If the county—if the census taker never got around to that farm, it may not have been registered on the census for that particular county. . . . So maybe there's something out there that's a little more accurate. . . .

But it's just—it's fascinating to me that I'm not that far removed from possible slavery. If my grandfather was born in 1865, he may have been born into slavery, so my great-grandfather may have been a slave. So if my grandfather was a slave, I'm just two generations away from slavery, which kind of says, "Hey, wait a minute here. That slavery business wasn't that long ago. I'm not that far removed from it." And it makes it that much more real to me. And imagine someone whose parents or grandparents were in the Holocaust. They may get the same revelation that, "Wait a minute. This Holocaust business is not that far away. . . ."

My mother was born in Georgia. And they lived on a farm. And my mother's sister came up to Trenton. I don't know how she got up or what brought her up—probably knowing someone in the Trenton area—she worked and eventually brought all of her sisters and brothers up.

Leonard Rivers (1934–)

As near as I can tell, my father came to Princeton in 1916, just before World War I. He was an orphan. He was orphaned when he was two or three years old. He sort of migrated this way with my aunts and uncle. They found there was work in the Princeton area, so my Aunts Bessie and Mabel and Uncle Tom and my father came together. My aunts and uncle took a job working at the university infirmary. [Bessie, Mabel Hillian, and Tom Hillian worked at the university infirmary for more than forty years.] And my father took a job as a dishwasher in Commons up on Nassau Street. My mother was from this area. Her parents were Dave and Mary Evelyn Lewis. My grandfather worked at Princeton Nursery, and my mother was born and raised in the Kingston area.

My father worked in Tiger Inn, oh thirty-five, forty years. My brother and I, when we were kids, used to go over with him in the summertime and cut the grass and do all the rest of that stuff. During house party weekends, we'd go over there early Sunday morning to help him wash glasses and clean up the bar. When he retired there was no pension, nothing.

Romus Broadway (1939–)

My father was born in Wadesboro, North Carolina, in 1891, and my mother was born there in 1904. My father's grandfather—my great-great-grandfather—was brought to North Carolina from England when he was thirteen years old and sold into slavery there. He hadn't been a slave in England. His father was white, and his mother was African. They say down in North Carolina that he was brought here by his father and put into slavery. He was moved from plantation to plantation, the way they were, but he taught all of his children to read and write. So there's been a writing gene in our family that's been there since Day One.

My other great-grandfather, Benjamin Gaddy, was half African and half Cherokee. In North Carolina in those days, they were trying to breed the perfect slave, and so they bred Africans and Cherokees, and he was a result of that. His wife, Vina, was half white and half African. Everyone down there knew that her father was the plantation owner. His family was into banking and industry. She knew her cousins. She and my great-grandfather had eight children—five born during slavery and three after, and they never were separated. My mother's father was one of the ones born into slavery. They say he never had trouble getting a loan when he needed it. My mother's grandfather, the plantation owner, died during the Civil War. And all my mother's and my aunt's grandchildren, 99.9 percent of them are college graduates—the University of Wisconsin, the University of Chicago, Hampton, the University of Massachusetts, Georgia State.

Once when I was working down at Duke University on a documentary project, I went into the town offices to get information on my grandfather, William David Gaddy, and when I said his name, the [white] clerk looked up, all startled. Later, when I told my aunt about it, she said, "He should look startled. He's your cousin."

Eric Craig (1934–)

Our father, Peyton Craig. There's a fellow that was asked many times what he was doing in the Jim Crow car. Clarence Craig, his father, was white. Never fully recognized him. He had like seven children with our grandmother and she brought them north for a better life. She left out of Lawrenceville, Georgia. She was very strong. Her name was Rebecca Cleveland but they called her Anna. But we had the name Craig, after our grandfather. Anna worked at the McLean House. She worked there, and she went to the Presbyterian Church. She lived on Jackson Street.

Anna's parents were Indians. That's what she always said. Our father's brother, Maron, looked exactly like an American Indian. He could've passed for an Indian chief. And, not that it really makes a difference to us, Daddy wasn't black. He was a half-breed. When Maron and our dad used to go south, they would just automatically go into the Jim Crow car. And there was more than once when the conductor said, "Well, what are you all doing back here?" They said, "Well, this is where we belong." They could've sat anywhere they chose to sit. Every last of them could've passed, eyes the color of the sky. They all came, though, and married black.

It used to be that our family was all very close. But it's drifting now. . . .

If you ever rode down the Great Road, there was always a fellow on the bridge waving. That was our first cousin, Charles. He walked with a cane, a stick, or a staff. He lived at the senior citizen housing there—everyone up and down the road knew him. Walter and Blanche's son. Walter had twelve kids.

Gaylord was another one of Walter's kids. He married a German girl. Married [her] in Germany. All the years she was married to him, she never told her parents that he was black. Gaylord was very fair. We don't know where their kids are, two boys. We'll never see them. We have cousins that are out there, and for all intents and purposes, are probably gone in time. They're passing, you know.

I'd like to know a lot more about the family. But when we were coming up, we just didn't have the where-with-all like some people to ask the questions. So, therefore, we're sort of in the dark. *The World Book*, they have a book this coat of arms, your family genealogy. I picked up, out of *The World Book*, between Atlanta, Lawrenceville, and Stone Mountain, about seventy some names of Craig. So I'm going to send out letters, tell them that if you are in fact related to these people, then you have some cousins in the North. I want them to know. It's something I think needs to be done. And with times changing, I may even get a response.

I think of the original sadness, I think of our grandmother having to leave Lawrenceville, Georgia, with her family for a better life. And then [our grandfather] letting her go, because he probably, at that time, felt he had no choice. He didn't want to be blackballed or blacklisted. So, he'd rather let his family go. And it probably happened many times.

2

I Grew Up Hugged

to the Hearts

of My People

YMCA Father-Son Banquet at the First Baptist Church of Princeton (1934)

AT THE HEART OF childhood in the Witherspoon community was a feeling of comfort, safety, and belonging. Many of today's elders, who were growing up during the 1900s to the 1950s, recall experiencing the essence of the African proverb that "it takes a village to raise a child." Person after person remembers how when they were small and dinner bells rang at five o'clock in the afternoon, they ran home as fast as their small legs could carry them. "It was a beautiful place to grow up," says Alice Satterfield, a small, slender woman born and raised in Princeton, who raised her own daughter Shirley here during World War II. "Everybody was family. We all took care of each other."

The feeling that the community was family was literally true for a large number of residents surrounded by their relatives—brothers, sisters, cousins, grandparents, aunts, and uncles, who also had settled in Princeton. As Paul Robeson recalls, "My early youth was spent hugged to the hearts and bosoms of my hard-working relatives. Mother died when I was six, but just across the street were my cousins the Caraways, with many children—Sam, Martha, Cecelia. And I remember the cornmeal, greens, yams, and the peanuts and other goodies sent up in bags from down in North Carolina."[1]

Harriett Calloway explains the curfews the adults had established to get the children off the street by nine o'clock. "I was living with Uncle John and Aunt Lizzy up on Humbert Street and, of course, then we had little yards all fenced in," she said. "Well, if I was up a couple of doors up to the neighbors and I heard the Nassau bell ring, I would fly home. Everybody started running to where they belonged. So that was the time. It was that kind of community, you know? And everybody knew everybody, and you didn't lock the doors."

One of the greatest concerns was protecting the children from danger. "On Birch Avenue, everybody's mother was your mother," recalls Hattie Smith Black, the second African American woman to be hired as a secretary by Princeton University in the 1950s. "So you didn't do anything wrong, because somebody was always watching out for you."

The neighborhood had a vitality that grew out of the common situations the inhabitants shared. This was a place where black adults could feel free despite the white bans and assaults from the outside that limited their options. Adults could see each other, and be seen, as individuals, with their own quirks, flaws, talents, and dreams—not just for the roles they played in serving others or for the color of their skin. Here, in this island, they could share stories of injustice, speak frankly, show anger, and be sarcastic and funny. They could laugh without being misunderstood, joke, make music, listen to music, relax, and be themselves.

"My grandmother was a beautiful woman," says Donald Moore. "She was a very, very sweet lady. They called her Mother Moore. On Christmas and the Fourth of July, she used to fire her .38 pistol out the back window. This was to celebrate. Fortunately, those bullets must have landed someplace else. She was the only one who ever beat me as a child. I guess she decided, 'Let me straighten him out before he goes too far.' But she taught me about honesty, integrity, and all good things. There used to be a trolley that came up to the corner of Spring and Witherspoon Streets called the Johnstown Trolley. I remember one day getting on this trolley with her, and she said, 'A whole fare and half fare.' And the conductor said, 'How old is he?' She said, 'Four.' I said, 'I'm five.' She said, 'Shut up.' You often wonder how you walk that fine line between honesty and all of the good things."[2]

Hank Pannell, who grew up in the house his grandfather bought on Jackson Street, recalls his friendships with Italian kids and black kids in the neighborhood. "I wouldn't trade one second of my childhood," he says. "We'd go to the Italian bakery right across the street on Witherspoon and buy sticks of pepperoni and hot loaves of Italian bread, and steal butter out of the house, and go make a campfire and go camping. One of our favorite spots was on the university grounds across from the train station. There used to be a stream that ran down along there, and we could go down to Carnegie Lake. That and Stony Brook are where I learned to fish."[3]

Many of the speakers in this book reminisced about going to church. As children, they attended First Baptist Church of Princeton, Witherspoon Street Presbyterian Church, or Mount Pisgah African Methodist Episcopal Church. These churches were sanctuaries and sacred places that were vital to their lives. Through sermons and stirring songs, they heard lessons that shaped them, and when they let their voices soar with the music, they felt connected to one another and to something greater that lifted their spirits.

Most of the speakers, as children, attended church not only on Sundays, but also on Wednesday nights. At other times throughout the week, they were there for meetings, classes, celebrations, and choir practice. Church also

Fred and Carrie Hoagland family (1907)

provided a place where men and women could discuss news and events of the day and make plans and take action to right certain wrongs, while their children played and thrived. Alice Satterfield's bright eyes lit up as she recalled her mother's door-to-door visits to collect food for the church's "Harvest Home" feast—"one of the best events of the year!" The whole community—not just the Presbyterians—celebrated Harvest Home in the parish hall of Witherspoon Presbyterian Church every autumn.

Prior to the building of Witherspoon Street Presbyterian Church in 1840, Satterfield says, "the coloreds in the area, we didn't have a church, and so we used to go to Nassau Presbyterian Church. But in those years, the coloreds weren't allowed to sit in the regular pews; they had to sit up in the balcony and they weren't allowed to take communion. You know, they were really discriminated against and the prejudice was kinda rough in those years, but we managed because we stuck together, worked together and overcame a lot of those things. . . . The Nassau church burned down after a July 4th celebration; it seems some fire got down in the church and destroyed it, burned it down. So then our people had no place to worship, and so we used to worship in various homes each week—go from one home to the other and worship. Then the parishioners and all decided that we would build our own church, and that's how Witherspoon Street Presbyterian Church began, through the work and the perseverance of a lot of old-time parishioners and members."[4]

For generations, Witherspoon neighbors not only focused on children but also on those who were sick and distressed. Men and women formed clubs to help young people and those in need. In the 1930s, Emma Epps, Carrie Pannell, and other neighborhood women who had organized "The Friendship Club" put twenty-five cents into the club's coffers every week. With their funds from dues and money from fund-raisers, they contributed to the NAACP, fed the elderly, and awarded scholarship funds to help neighborhood youngsters go to school or college.

Romus Broadway, now a photographer, historian, and storyteller, still lives in the house he grew up in on Birch Avenue. "It was idyllic growing up here—even with the racism from outside," he says. "I remember my father telling us, 'Just try to understand people. If you like them, fine. If not, then don't bother.'"[5]

As children, the speakers in this book felt protected by the adults, who rarely spoke in front of them about the assaults of racism they'd experienced or witnessed. Buster Thomas had heard adults talking about lynchings, but none of them ever mentioned or explained them to him or the other children, and he was afraid to ask. The pain of what they knew of racism was lifted by the magical moments of childhood, when being alive—being surprised by a bird, or a butterfly, a new idea, a sense of fun, or a kindness—mattered most.

Their neighborhood had that kind of magic. It was unique, if for no other reason than it was the only black neighborhood in America where two of the world's greatest icons—Paul Robeson and Albert Einstein—were a presence in their midst. When they were children, they saw Albert Einstein, a Nobel Prize–winner who developed the Theory of Relativity, even more regularly than they saw their own Paul Robeson, who was hailed internationally as the most gifted black man in America for his accomplishments as a singer, actor, athlete, and orator. Einstein, an exile from Nazi Germany who had a lifetime appointment at the Institute for Advanced Study, lived on Mercer Street, not very far away from Witherspoon residents. Every few days, he walked or rode his bicycle through the neighborhood, often on his way to the ice-cream store or to pick up an armful of wood at Barclay's Ice, Coal, and Wood Plant. He knew the neighbors quite well and frequently spent time visiting with them. The children were always happy to see him because he gave them candies and small coins. Hank Pannell's grandmother Carrie, who made all the baked goods for the Nassau Club, was a treasured friend of Einstein. Often, Einstein would stop to visit with her on her front porch, where she held forth from her rocking chair. They'd drink iced tea and converse about what was unfolding in the world.

Alice Satterfield was also friends with the scientist. Einstein and she had met when she worked in the kitchen of the Institute for Advanced Study. Her daughter, Shirley Satterfield, laughs with delight when she recalls being a small child taking long walks with Einstein at the Institute, where she first met him. "I loved his uncombed shock of white hair, his baggy sweaters, sneakers, or slippers—with no socks!" she says. "That's how he looked! He never wore socks!"[6]

Fannie Floyd met Einstein at an NAACP meeting when she was a teenager and forever after felt that he was a deep and meaningful part of their community. It seemed only fitting that the humanitarian scientist would became close friends with the great artist who was working to "[tear] down the walls of oppression imposed by the inequities of race and class anywhere he encountered them in the world."[7] In Berlin in 1920, Einstein had missed Paul Robeson's performance of "The Emperor Jones"; but in 1935, in Princeton, Einstein was in a packed audience at McCarter Theatre to hear Robeson sing spirituals. Afterward, Einstein went backstage and energetically shook Robeson's hand. Robeson, "taller, broader, nineteen years younger . . . was awed. 'I am honored,' he began in his deep, gentle voice, but Einstein interrupted: 'No, it is I who feel honored.'"[8]

Lloyd Brown, Paul Robeson's friend and biographer, says Robeson's eyes always brightened when he recalled that first meeting. Einstein and Robeson both spoke about their alarm at the Nazi regime in Germany canceling citizenship for Jews, and Mussolini's fascist troops invading Ethiopia. "[They] discovered that they shared not only a passion for music, but a hatred of fascism."[9]

In the eyes of the neighborhood children, not only Einstein and Robeson, but all the hardworking men and women in their community were great people. "Back in those days, people really were neighbors," recalls Rev. Judson Carter, who was born in Princeton in 1938. "You didn't need to lock your doors. In the event my mother needed something for cooking, she could always go into somebody's house and right into the refrigerator and grab whatever she needed—an egg, a cup of sugar, or some milk. When the neighbor came home, my mother would say, 'I owe you one.' We all watched out for each other. One thing that brought a lot of unity was a garden down on the Y field. Everybody in the neighborhood could go down and grow whatever kind of crop you wanted."[10]

Rev. Carter remembers several men and women concerned about young-sters, particularly a man named Raymond Holmes, who helped set up struc-tured activities: "He would always try to take them under his wing and form different clubs and organizations. We would go to different places playing basketball and baseball. We also had a YMCA where we could go after school. We even had a fathers and sons' banquet at the Y, and the director would invite maybe a celebrity or have a speaker. There was always some-thing to do. You didn't have to hang out on the corner or anything like that. I always had two or three jobs. I worked down to my grandfather's on Satur-day, and during the week, I would work up to the bowling alley setting up pins or at the golf course caddying. There also was the Playhouse, a movie theater. It was a hangout spot for most of us. We would wait for the doors to open up and slide in, and that was our little mischievous fun. We didn't drink or smoke or do any of the rough stuff. We just did little things. But, children, don't you start doing that, okay?"[11]

> Like it says, it takes a village to raise a family, well, we were all a vil-lage. And we raised and looked after each other.
> —JOAN HILL (1942–)

Sophie Hall Hinds (1875–1974)

When I was a child I had one rag doll. I don't know if my mamma made the rag doll or not. And I had one boughten doll, as we called 'em in those days and times. And that's all I ever had in my life. The boughten one, I

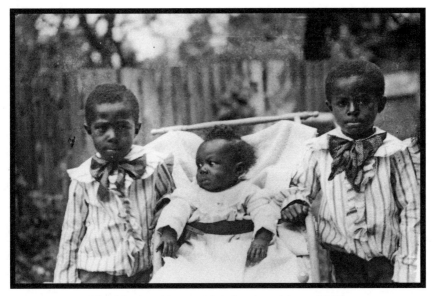

Neighborhood boys with baby sister (about 1840)

got maybe between eight and nine, ten years old maybe. I thought it was something when I got that doll.

We didn't have too many games in those days and times to play. Maybe we would know something about hide 'n' seek, and that was one game we thought was wonderful. I guess children in them days didn't know much about games like they do nowadays. Kids know everything nowadays—more than their parents, more than the teacher for that matter. To sled on we had an old piece of board with a hole cut into it. And we'd tie a rope past it. And if you got a hill you'd sit down on that flat board and that's all the sleddin' you got. Children nowadays would say that stuff was nothin' but we enjoyed it because I guess we didn't know any better.

You wouldn't have any inside heat and water in those days, so that also meant bringing in water and wood. We had to bring in corncobs. We had to get off all the corn and greens then let 'em get dry. And they'd burn like nobody's business. You had to fill the lamps every night, and wash them lamp chimneys every day so they were clean at nighttime so you could see. If I had anything to peel, I could help out with that. I could go and get apples and something my mother was going to make. Didn't can applesauce in those days, but you'd dry apples in them days and times. You had to peel 'em and slice 'em and put them out in the air. And when the weather was good, we'd cover them up with spy netting to keep the flies off of them. And every night we had those things to bring in and then wrap 'em and put them out the next day.

The way we used to do our strawberries, we used to cook 'em, just a little. 'Cause by the time you're pickin' strawberries, they're ready, like they was cooked almost. They're so moist. And you add sugar and water and such stuff as that, and then you put them in a can. For strawberries in canning, they have to be packed in cans and sealed tight right away, 'cause if you didn't, they wouldn't last very good. But jellies and preserves—they'll keep. They'll do all right if you don't tighten them up right away.

Harriett Calloway (1906–2005)

Our community was beautiful, more so than it is now. That's all I can say. Beautiful. Everybody looked after everybody. We had curfews here. The children had to be off the street by nine o'clock. My sister was six years older than me, and my brother was three years older. When my brother and I were small . . . we used to go out and lay our heads down on the track to hear the trolley coming up, and we didn't get too close, but then we'd get up and run into the house. . . . [My] mother didn't know anything about that until the motorman, he just went up and knocked on the door and said, "Would you please keep your little boys off the trolley track?" So I don't know whether we got a spanking or not, but anyway, that was one of the little things we used to do.

The older people [while I was growing up], they would have dances in the basement of the Branches building and we would go over and lay on the grate and look through the window. And we would look on and watch and hear the music, you know. And only once a year we children could go, and that was Memorial Day. We'd put on our Sunday best, I guess you would call it, and then that's when the men would dance with us. I loved to waltz. And we did the line dancing they're doing now; that was the same thing we were doing way back then. Yeah, the same thing.

Ping Pong at the YMCA (about 1940)

Albert Hinds (1902–2006)

See, I always loved horses. I'd jump in order to go up to the livery stable, to be around horses. The horses really could have prevented me from finishing even elementary school! I'd sometimes do something, the teacher would keep me out of class, I'd jump the fence and go to that livery stable! Because all these horses were there.

I was just sitting there, up at the stable. So I don't know anybody. There were three brothers who owned this livery stable. And people would come back for the horse—it was ten cents to put the horse under the shed. So, the owner, I was sitting there, and he said, "Boy, go up there and let that horse out!" So I go up and back the horse out the shed, and he give me the dime. So I bring it down, and gave it to Mr. Brown, and he put it in his pocket. So I [was] still sitting there. "Go get that horse out. Put it in your pocket." Now, so you see, this is happening so much, that they even gave me a job! I was driving a hack, before high school, like a taxi.

So I was the richest boy in school, but I smelled like a horse, all the time! I used to go over to Princeton Junction at 12:01 a.m. to meet the train—it was called the "L" train. I'd pick up passengers coming in from New York, Philadelphia, with a horse, like a taxi.

So then my sister caught up to me, in school, in about seventh grade. She started one or two grades behind me, maybe, but we went to high school, graduated together. So that changed me. I say to myself, "My sister caught me, but she'll never pass me," and that's when I stopped foolin' around with horses. I decided, I guess, I just said, "My word, she caught me, but I ain't going to let her pass me."

But unfortunately that stable burned. I don't know how many horses [were] there, but all the horses burned up. They had two very beautiful black horses that they used for funerals, and they also used to pull the fire engines, because fire engines were pulled by horses, back there in those days. Now, there was no way to save the horses, because the horses that pull the fire engines were in the fire!

Hazel Lewis Rivers (1910–2007)

I remember my grandmother, Margaret Ann Martin. She was a hard worker. And she walked; she didn't have a horse. She walked from Little Rocky Hill to Princeton to do housework. She worked for a farm, the Howe's, somewhere back there by Riverside School was the Howe's farm.

She was very, very sweet. My grandfather [Henry Salter] died—I barely remember him, and she went to work. All of her children were grown. And there wasn't all this welfare. And you had to eat. . . . But my grandmother was able to work.

Her home burned down, and then my uncle Raymond lived with her. They moved up the road to another house, and that's where she got sick. My mother would go up to see her, but that was a big deal. So she brought her down to our house. Her bed was in the dining room. We made the dining room into a bedroom; we improvised. And it was there that she passed—at our house.

I can remember when my uncle married—my mother's brother—we all walked to his wedding over in Big Rocky Hill. We went all the way down by the Old Mill Bridge and turned up that road. When you're used to walking, you don't mind it. Boy, it would kill these kids today. They can't walk two blocks. I remember little kids walking that much when I went to high school. There weren't many cars on the road—not like now. Little kids, they can't do it now. There's too many cars in the road.

I rode in a wagon sometimes. One time I got thrown out of a wagon. Well, I was standing up; I had no business standing up. And they went around the corner and out I went. I was not that little, but I wasn't big. Automobiles came in fashion and wagons went out of fashion. But I'll never forget that. I don't know where we were going. I got all dusty and dirty.

Emma Epps (1902–1989)

This area where this house is was the city dump. Up at the end where the trolley turned was the coal yard, Anderson's coal yard. And Pierson's Milk Farm. That was where the [Princeton] Hospital is. I went up there with my little pail every day. It cost ten cents a pail for your milk. I don't know how much is in a pail, I wish I did. All I know is he just filled up our little white pails with lovely milk. My mother used to sit it in what we had, the ice box. She'd let the cream come to the top and then she'd skim it off. Then she made cheese, it's called cottage cheese now, but she used to make pot cheese. You let the milk sour, and then scald it, all those things they used to do to it, you see, which was the only way they could live, really.

There was a candy store on Quarry Street, by an Italian named Tony. That drive there by Yancy's house on Quarry Street didn't used to be. There used to be a little Italian store there right across from Reeves'. We used to always try to get a penny to get candy and I know they used to sell dill pickles for a penny. I think that's the reason I don't like dill pickles to this day. I had too many of them. There used to be an ice-cream man that pushed a cart, and we called that the hokey-pokey wagon. He had the ice-cream cones— instead of shaped the way they are now they were shaped like little boats and boxes, kind of dirty ice cream, but we seem to have thrived off it. Now that I think of it, it must have been really dirty.

And I remember, oh, we used to trim our Christmas trees with popcorn and cranberries, and my mother used to make cookies and things to hang up 'cause we just couldn't afford to buy things. We made various things for each other. Like little handkerchief bags. Just something silly that kids now wouldn't even think about, you know. But we got a lot of fun out of it. Pincushions, little aprons, various things. We always had a big family Christmas dinner that went from—this year it would be at this aunt's and next year at my mother's and go on all of the family. It was a really great day. Christmas isn't really Christmas now. Kids don't work now, but we did. You see, because first thing, we had coal and we were poor, so we had to pick the cinders. That was our Saturday chore.

On Saturday, I remember, they had a class at the Presbyterian parish house on Quarry Street, and they had what they called Kitchen Guard, and it was run by Miss Paxton, Mrs. Hibber's daughter, and one of the Delafields. So I remember Miss Paxton. I didn't like her. I remember her very well. I think I didn't like her because they always wanted to teach us cooking, and I already knew how to cook, 'cause my mother knew how to cook so I knew how to cook. And they would do things and I would say, "I don't want to know how to cook. I want to do something else." And so, of course, they resented me.

Shirley Satterfield (1940–)

Everybody knew everybody. I grew up on Clay Street, and everybody took care of everybody's children. It used to be a time when nobody would lock any doors, and if I walked down the street, everyone would know where I was, and they'd call my grandmother or my mother to say that I went up the street. It was a close-knit neighborhood. We used to call going to Nassau Street "going uptown." It was a big thing to go uptown, but, as I said, there were certain places we couldn't go in. Like there's a restaurant called Lahiere's up on Witherspoon, well, we couldn't go in Lahiere's. Where Victor's pizza shop is, and Burger King. Well, that used to be a big store when I was growing up called the Balt, short for Baltimore I guess, and at one time, we couldn't go in that restaurant, and when they did open it up to blacks—we were called Negroes then—we used to go there after we went skating at Baker Rink, and we used to go there for cherry Coke and French fries, and that was a big thing. There were also two theaters, one where the

Garden is, and one on Hulfish Street, where Mediterra restaurant is, there was a big, beautiful theater called the Playhouse. We used to go and sit there all Saturday, and watch newsreels and comics and movies over and over, and I used to wonder why we always sat in the back, up on the right-hand side. I thought that was just where we wanted to sit, but actually, that was where we had to sit. I didn't know what segregation was, until the Princeton Plan in 1948 when two schools in Princeton Borough—Witherspoon School for Colored Children and Nassau Street Elementary School—were integrated. That's when I knew I was different, because I was treated differently.

Estelle Johnson (1919–2011)

I grew up in a mixed neighborhood, mostly Italians and blacks. It was evident that our parents did not want us really to play, but children will play if you give them half a chance. We would play over the side of the porch and talk out the windows at night, but we never went from porch to porch. And the only time we entered their homes was if it was for a christening, and then they would call us in, and they might give us a sip of wine and some candy. Other than that, there were no interactions between the Italians and my family because we didn't go to the same school, so we really didn't have too much in common, except that we lived side by side. So, we got to know who each other were but if you went down the street a little farther, there was a family there, they would smile at you but if they thought you were coming too close, every once in a while their dog would come out and nip at you to keep you at bay.

Alice Satterfield (1922–2010)

In those times we were mostly all colored in this area. We could walk to church, we could walk to Nassau Street, we could walk to the hospital, we could walk to the stores. We had everything we needed right in our neighborhood—so we had no need to go out of the area for a lot of things. We had the candy store on Leigh Avenue, and Matty's grocery store. A Polish man who repaired shoes, and Bill the Greek had a little restaurant. Mr. Ball owned the confectioner on this side of John Street. We had a little worldly community with all kinds of people.

Years back we used to have what they called the Harvest Home every year. It was usually in the fall, the end of October or beginning of November—after harvest time, you know, after the vegetables are just about finished at the end of the summer season. My mother would walk to Lawrenceville, Cranbury, and Plainsboro, and go to the farmers' houses and beg for food for Harvest Home. So they'd give her 'tatoes, sweet potatoes, beans, corn, and all that. And she'd walk back home, and then get someone with a car and go back and get all these vegetables. For many years she carried on this tradition, so that they got to know her. We'd gather up all of the vegetables, potatoes and string beans and lima beans, and sweet potatoes, corn and all that. We'd make fresh succotash from the corn and the lima beans, fresh string beans, fresh candied yams, and mashed potatoes— she got bags of potatoes. And then the meats; the turkey and ham. We'd just set it all up family style on our tables, which we then held in the parish hall of our church. People would look forward to Harvest Home every fall of the year.

James A. Carter (1928–2000)

My grandmother raised us, and ah, she was the sergeant of the house. She was something else, and we all loved her. I had seven aunts and six uncles. You know, when you have thirteen people at one supper table, it's going to be crowded. No food that you dropped off your fork would ever hit the ground. People'd always sit around and catch, you know, and the last one finished would always get help from somebody else. That's the way it was. . . . In my day, when you came home from school, you know, you changed your clothes and done your work, and then you played. Was no such thing as you played and then you done your work. You worked, then you played. But I enjoyed it. I enjoyed it a lot.

When I first came to Princeton. . . . [t]here was a restaurant on the corner of Hulfish Street and Witherspoon called Griggs' Restaurant, and we used to spend a lot of time there on Saturdays or Sundays when we wanted to let

YMCA basketball team (1950s)

off steam and we wasn't in school. It was pretty nice. That was my favorite restaurant because Mr. Griggs he was one heck of a guy. They made big hamburgers, and if you ate a cheeseburger and got a bottle of Coke, that would last you all day, so you wouldn't have to go home and get lunch. That was one of my favorite spots.

Hank Pannell (1939–)

I guess everybody my age remembers Einstein from when we were kids. He used to give us nickels. And he used to talk to everybody in our community. I didn't know as a kid that he was *Einstein*. Who, Einstein? But I realize now that he came in that community just to get away and to talk to people who would treat him as a regular guy.

We lived on Jackson Street, one of the nicest houses on Jackson Street, that my grandfather and grandmother had purchased. They came here from Virginia in the 1920s. My grandfather, Henry Pannell—I only vaguely remember him—I think he was a bricklayer at the university. But my grandmother was a mainstay in the beginning of my life. In the kitchen, she had one long wall with nothing but big ovens. She was a baker, and she used to bake rolls for the whole town. We used to deliver them all over town and sell them on the side—two for a nickel—for our little hustle. I don't think she minded, but she must have known it. One time we were all jumping the fence around the Playhouse [movie theater]—it's long since gone—and my friend Sidney Moore missed and fell on the concrete and broke his arm. We took him to my grandmother's, and she set his arm and bandaged it, and put it in a sling. So, she was like the doctor up there.

We ate like kings. I don't remember cereal. We used to always have good food; maybe that's why I'm so heavy today. We used to have smothered pork chops and biscuits and real food—ham and eggs. I remember we used to have grits for breakfast with some sort of meat and gravy, smothered chicken and chicken livers, and my favorite, kidney stew, on Sunday mornings. [My grandmother] used to have these country hams hanging, and I used to get in trouble because they were cured and everything, but I used to sneak in and snatch little pieces off before it was even cooked. We used to go right around on the next block to Frasier's Fish Market to get porgies and whiting already cleaned and bring it home.

For all the church affairs, my grandmother used to bake rolls and pies and cakes, and our house was the center of activity. When my sister passed away, Rev. Arthur Lewis came up for her funeral and preached some of it. He said that when his father and his father's brother first came to Princeton, they stayed at Aunt Carrie's until they got situated. And other people have come up and told me that as well.

You know, there were such great people. We all grew up together. And it wasn't just all black kids. There was the Servis family, the Cavanaugh family, the Toto family—we were all family. They were part of our crew, our little gang, our club. We used to all be together. They used to come to my house. We were at their houses. I remember my mother or grandmother got sick, their parents were right there. The same thing when Mrs. Cavanaugh got sick—my mother and grandmother were right there.

I wouldn't trade one second of my childhood. I have so many fond memories of growing up here. We just did so many things. We had our little group, maybe a dozen of us, from uptown—from Jackson and Quarry Streets—that we used to call uptown. Downtown was from Maclean Street on down. We used to swim in Stony Brook and camp down there overnight. Up on Mount Lucas Road, where the glaciers had left just thousands of granite boulders, there was a place we called Devil's Cave. It was a big cave, and we used to camp up there and hunt snakes. Where the shopping center is, we used to have BB gun wars and pick berries. It was just like farmland over there.

We would go to the Italian bakery right across the street on Witherspoon and buy sticks of pepperoni and hot loaves of Italian bread, and steal butter out of the house, and go make a campfire and go camping. One of our favorite camping spots was on the university grounds across from the train station. There used to be a stream that ran down along there, and we could go down to Carnegie Lake. That and Stony Brook are where I learned to fish. We'd catch sunfish and bass, catfish and carp. Just about every day in the summertime, we'd either go swimming or fishing. And in the wintertime, when the lake froze, we'd go to a little island in the middle of the lake and camp and build a bonfire and skate on the ice and all. We just had so much fun.

Nobody bothered us. In the evenings, a lot of times, we used to go over to WPRB, the university radio station, and they used to let us get on the radio. So many things we did! We knew a lot of students from Princeton summer camp at Blairstown. The university had Blairstown as their football training camp, and they also used to invite kids from Philadelphia, Camden, and Princeton. Now, that was a real camp.[12]

Boy, we had a ball. I guess I started going to camp when I was ten. At fourteen and fifteen and sixteen, I was a junior counselor up there. I loved it so much. We used to compete to see if we could go up there for the whole eight-week period, which you could do as a counselor. I mean, it was four two-week periods during the summer, and we wanted to go for the whole summer, because we just loved it. Those students were tough. We used to swim, fish, go to the Delaware Water Gap, canoe, rowboat, arts and crafts— everything. That was in the late forties, early fifties.

I really didn't know anything about racism. I knew that we couldn't go into like the Balt, the big cafeteria up on Nassau Street right where Hinkson's and Burger King are, and Veidt's, and places like that, you couldn't go in. But we didn't want to go no way. We had to go upstairs in the Garden Theatre, but we liked it upstairs. On Nassau Street, there was a little store called Cleve's, and we used to go there, but we were treated like—you know. We knew we weren't welcome in that store. I remember several incidents—one where he said, "You niggers, get out of here." So we bought our candy at a little store right around the corner—at Mr. Ball's.

Hattie Black (1934–)

I think it was great growing up in Princeton. My experience was on Birch Avenue, you know, everybody's mother was your mother. So you didn't do anything wrong, because somebody was always watching out for you. When I was growing up everybody was your family. It was just great, like we were one big happy family. Princeton has changed. I just don't see it with the more integrated community. But I really enjoyed growing up [here].

Lamont Fletcher (1942–)

Being raised in Princeton, I would say that I really didn't know what it was—the full impact of what it was like to be black, in that the black community was very small. There weren't that many children in school—black children in school. It was a predominantly white society growing up. But when I went south to North Carolina, I got a completely different perspective. I mean, I got a completely different perspective in that I saw the full range. When I went to college, it was a predominantly black college, so I saw the full spectrum of students—those students who were struggling academically and those students who were really challenging the professors in calculus and all the math courses and science courses—challenging the professors. And when you grow up in Princeton, you don't get the full range. You get what your family's like. You get what your neighborhood's like. And, when I was growing up, there really wasn't too much communication as to the progress black folk were making. We didn't see—we didn't see black doctors in Princeton, black lawyers, black professional people. There were a few black teachers in schools, but very few. There are fewer now in Princeton regional schools. So we didn't have that many role models. So, going south and living in North Carolina gave me a completely different perspective as to what it's like to be black—and also being segregated. I had heard growing up that there was prejudice in Princeton, but I never—I could say I never experienced it.

Paul Mitnaul (1927–)

My grandfather was already here in Princeton, and so we came up [in 1933]—my two sisters and my mother and father. My father was a laborer and my mother was a housekeeper. My grandfather was a jack of all trades, I tell you. That's where I think I might have gotten it from. Anything you wanted done, call on him. He had a knack for that. Swords—sharpened the swords and lawnmowers—he grinded with a pedal. He had a sharpener shop. When I was in grammar school I took a correspondence course and got to learn all about radios and whatnot. . . . My grandfather had a little outhouse type thing in the back in order to sell hotdogs. And so he gave it up to me. And I wired it up and had a little shop when I was about twelve years old. I fixed a lot of the neighbors' radios in this town. I used to carry these big radios—in those days, radios were pretty big, as a matter of fact, they were heavier than I weighed. I would pick them up, take the chassis out, put them on my shoulder, and carry them back so I could work on the set at home. So my grandfather said, "I have to fix you up with something. This is too heavy for you." So he got a baby carriage—the wheels and whatnot—and you would see me running down the street there with this wagon, carrying these radios on it. Well, my grandfather got me started because he loved his radios. He started out with the biggest radio he could buy. Good old days. . . .

The Johnson Trolley used to run right in front of my house and went down to Trenton. Every morning Dr. Einstein and [another man from the Institute for Advanced Study] would walk down to the bird sanctuary. They would take two steps, look up to see the birds, and start talking about the birds and what have you. And I would be out there. Every morning they'd speak to me. I didn't know who [Einstein] was. He was just another man, and he'd pat me on the head. I didn't know who he was until later on.

Marilyn Yates (1935–)

My dad was a mechanic, an automobile mechanic. His name was Ralph Mitnaul. He was at Tuskegee for two years. He started out working with the army. He worked down at Fort Dix; he was an auto mechanic there at Fort Dix. When he retired from Fort Dix, he decided he wanted to start his own business, so he had a little shop—it used to be down here [by Clay Street]. It wasn't like it is now. There was no project or anything. People owned their homes. And then when they tore that down and decided to put the projects up, he moved up on Witherspoon Lane, which is just off of Spring Street. He had his shop up there. So, he did that for many years. He would do it in the driveway. He would do it anywhere. He was a plain old mechanic.

And my mother, Ethel Carraway Mitnaul, graduated from Howard University, where she majored in education and languages. But then she and my dad got married, of course, and started having a family. So, she couldn't teach, because at that time they didn't have women who had children teach. So, she still practiced substitute teaching, like if someone was out, she would teach.

So, then she decided to work in a private family, which she did for a long time. She worked [for them] during the summer, down the shore in Bay Head. And I know, because I had to go down with her during the summer to Bay Head. I was with her everywhere she went. That's what she did, because, as I said, she couldn't get a job teaching, because she was married and had children. And when that [restriction] finally lifted, she was doing something else. She had changed her profession and was involved at Skillman—the New Jersey Neuropsychiatric Institute that'd [been built] out in Skillman.

She's done a lot. She graduated from Princeton High School and then she went to Howard University, where she graduated. She was very well read, she spoke French, Latin, *and* German, and she liked to work. She used to tutor some of the kids. We lived up on John Street, and they used to come to the house, and she would give lessons there.

Eric Craig, three years old, with his dog, Chips (1937)

My mom was really a very smart woman. She went to school—to Rider at nights—and decided to take up shorthand and business courses, and she used to come home and compare her book cards with me. She was so smart. She had A+s all the way. She was really good. So, then she decided to go to Skillman, and she took up practical nursing, working with the patients and whatnot.

When she first went to Skillman, she worked in the building for patients who were really, really, really bad off. There were some who would just sit and do nothing or just sit curled up like in the womb. She just loved to work. And then she moved up from there to the office of the director of the institute—she was his assistant. So, she moved up. My mom was something else, she really was.

Jacqui Swain (1944–)

My mother was only fifteen when she had me and my father was nineteen. She was a model, one of the first black pinup models on the East Coast. I was born right here in Princeton. I was one of those lucky black babies who got to be born at Princeton Hospital because I was premature. My father moved the nuclear family out to Rahway, New Jersey, in 1950, about the time Princeton schools integrated. I did all my schooling in Rahway public schools, but I spent an awful lot of time here in Princeton because my mother worked for the Red Cross and my father was in the navy. But I was bonded with grandparents and great-grands, so I spent as much time as possible here with them until it was time for me to go to school.

I lived on old Clay Street. It was a very safe enclave, a very wonderful place for me as a young African American because I knew everybody on the street. There were all privately owned family homes on Clay Street at that time, and we had to be pretty self-sufficient because an awful lot of the services in Princeton weren't available to us. So everything that needed to happen in the community happened right there in the John Witherspoon community. There were shoemakers. There were candy store owners. There were grocery stores. There were barbershops. There were beauty parlors. There were, oh goodness, speakeasies. There were bars. There were churches. There were all sorts of craftspeople right in that area. But it was just a wonderful way to live, and as a child I had no idea that I was being deprived of something in Princeton.

Nana was very strict. She wanted me to read and learn and get an education, because she didn't want me cleaning some white woman's kitchen. So she allowed me to read anything and everything. But my favorite were comic books. My father taught me to read before I went to school. We used to read the Sunday funnies, and that's how I learned to read. Well, Mr. Ball had comic books, and Nana didn't really want me to read them. So I used to sneak and read these comics. Mr. Ball would tear them in half so that each half would only cost a nickel. And sometimes that's all I had was five pennies, so I'd go buy the comic. I'd buy the first half and when I got another nickel, I'd go buy the other half. If you didn't have the first half, friends of other friends of mine who read comics, we would switch, you know. When I finished the first half, and they had the second half, they'd give me the second half. Or if we went to the store together, one of us would buy the first half, the other one would buy the second half.

Joan Hill (1942–)

When we moved from Jackson Street, we bought a home on Witherspoon Street. Actually, it was a gift to my mother and father from my uncle. It was one of those fixer-uppers. I can remember that it didn't have bathroom facilities, but we were happy there. All of the people that lived in the neighborhood, whether they were Italian, Jewish, Polish, black, or whatever, we are still like family today. We lived next door to the cemetery. We used to have fun in the cemetery, there were cherry trees and all kinds of good adventurous things that you could do. I can remember my brothers making bicycles out of different parts. This year it might be a broken bicycle, but next year we would get a tire or something. We would even make our own scooters out of wood. We were very creative when I was growing up in the forties. Kids aren't creative now, but we were creative. They have everything for them now with computers. We always had a house full of people. Male and female, we always had parties in our backyard. We had games, horseshoes and other games that we would play. We started ice-skating when we were three, four, and five. I skated down at Lake Carnegie, and that was something to look forward to on Saturday. From hot-dog roasting to marshmallows, we were always active and doing things. There was always something to do. I guess coming from a large family you always have things to do, but along with our large family we interacted with people who, had, you know, we had friends who had large families and everybody interacted and worked together. Like it says, it takes a village to raise a family, well, we were all a village. And we raised and looked after each other.

3

School Integration:
A Big Loss for
Black Children

WITHERSPOON SCHOOL CHILDREN
1922-28, 1929 30, 31, 32, 33,

Students at the Witherspoon School for Colored Children
on Quarry Street (1922–29)

FOR MORE THAN A hundred years, the Witherspoon School for Colored Children was the treasured heart of the neighborhood. This was not just any elementary school. This was a school for *the children* of people whose enslaved predecessors had faced severe punishments for breaking laws that forbade them to read, write, or teach another slave to do so. These were the children of adults, enslaved and free, who, throughout their lives, had been barred from public schools, public education, and public libraries. And so it was that generation after generation of Princeton's African American residents had an inner fervor about the importance of education for their children.

This was *their* school—and moreover, its work was begun in the 1830s by a brilliant, highly educated, formerly enslaved woman from Princeton named Betsey Stockton. Betsey, born about 1798, was a descendant of the enslaved African Stocktons who first arrived in the area in the late 1690s. Her mother, "Celie" or "Sealy," was owned by Richard Stockton II, and her father, though unnamed, was white, which deemed Betsey a mulatto. When "Bet" was about six, Richard Stockton II gave her to his daughter, Betsy Stockton Green, and her husband, Ashbel Green, a Presbyterian minister and the eighth president of Princeton University. Green, who had graduated as valedictorian of his class in 1783 at Princeton, had studied with and been mentored by John Witherspoon. "Bet" joined the Green's household, which included three sons, and from the time she was small she did domestic work, such as cooking, cleaning, housekeeping, baking, and sewing.[1]

From the beginning, Bet was a mischievous, rather wild child, who was precocious and clearly very bright. Ashbel Green followed his youngest son James's lead in teaching Bet to read and write; he encouraged her and allowed her, along with his sons, to use his personal library. When Bet was nineteen, she joined the Presbyterian Church and began her religious studies in earnest. When she turned twenty, Green freed her from bondage and paid her wages for her housekeeping work. Eventually, when she had an opportunity to do missionary work, he highly recommended her to travel as a missionary with a group going to Hawaii (then called the Sandwich Islands), which she did in November 1822 on a sea voyage that lasted for five months. While in Maui, she created a school for nonroyal Hawaiians, the *maka ainana*, which became the first school for indigenous children in Hawaii.[2]

When she returned to Princeton in 1835, after teaching for a couple of years in Philadelphia, she likewise established the first educational system for Princeton's black community. Initially, *Records of the Morning Sabbath School of the Presbyterian Church (Colored) on Witherspoon Street*, kept by white male students from the Princeton Theological Seminary, details the work of long-term teachers, foremost "Aunt Betsey Stockton."[3] Parallel with her efforts in religious education were two secular schools Stockton created in Princeton before the Civil War. One was a "common school" for young children started in a wooden schoolhouse by 1840, and the other was a night school for adults. For many, this night school was the first time in their lives they had gotten to go to school. Over time, as the numbers of students she was teaching increased, she trained many of her star pupils as teachers, and also enlisted Princeton's college and seminary teachers to volunteer their time teaching courses that included algebra, Latin, history, and English literature.

In 1858, Stockton founded the first official home of the Witherspoon School for Colored Children, District School No. 6, the first public elementary and middle school for African Americans in Princeton. As the population of black children increased, the Witherspoon School was relocated into a larger building at Thirty-Five Quarry Street in 1908. The school in that location was attended by generations of black children, including most of the people featured in this book. One of them, Consuelo Campbell, remembers the day when she and the other children moved back into their school on Quarry Street after it was renovated in 1938 and 1939. For two years, she and the other students had attended classes in the Witherspoon Street Presbyterian Church and the Masonic Lodge. "I can remember each child brought his own chair up the hill. And it was just a good feeling. I still remember going up the hill with our chairs into our new building, our new school building and how proud we were."

The children's beloved black teachers lived in the neighborhood and knew them very well. At the Witherspoon elementary school, they taught reading, writing, geography, arithmetic, grammar, Latin, and algebra. It's significant that they also taught their students black history and prepared them to stand up against stereotypes, speak out, study hard, and go to college.

Prior to the integration of Princeton High School in 1916, black teenagers in Princeton had to travel ten miles to the integrated Trenton High School or attend the Manual Training and Industrial School for Colored Youth in Bordentown. A number of parents sent their teenagers south to live with relatives and attend segregated high schools so they could earn high school diplomas. When students at Princeton High School (PHS) were finally integrated, black students could live at home. But when they graduated, PHS gave them "certificates of completion" instead of the high school diplomas that white graduates received.

The younger children continued to be segregated for another three decades. The year 1947 marked the beginning of a dramatic change for both the borough and the township. That was the year New Jersey amended the state constitution to prohibit racial discrimination or segregation in the state militia and public schools: "No person shall be denied the enjoyment of any civil or military right, nor be discriminated against in the exercise of any civil or military right, nor be segregated in the militia or in the public schools, because of religious principles, race, color, ancestry or national origin."[4]

When the constitution was ratified, it opened the door for a new system called "the Princeton Plan" to integrate Princeton's grade schools. During the summer of 1948, Howard Waxwood, black principal of the Witherspoon School for Colored Children on Quarry Street, and Chester Stroup, white principal of the Nassau Street School, held open houses to let parents, both black and white, see the schools their children would be attending that coming September.

And so it was in the fall of 1948, prior to the landmark *Brown v. Board of Education*, with little to no fanfare, Princeton's elementary schools quickly and quietly integrated. White students entered the Witherspoon community and black students ventured uptown to the white community under the Princeton mandate that *all* borough children from kindergarten to fifth grade go to the Nassau Street School, which was previously all white. All sixth through eighth graders would attend junior high at the Witherspoon School, often referred to as "the Quarry Street School," where they took pride in their school newspaper, the *Witherspoon Herald*. A telling fact about Princeton's monumental school integration in 1948 is how—even though New Jersey was the first state in the entire nation to ratify a constitution that prohibited racial discrimination in both the state militia and public schools—the news was *not* reported. Princeton undergraduate Jenny Hildebrand

Beloved teachers of the Witherspoon School for Colored Children (about 1940)

noticed that when integration was mentioned in the newspapers, it was referred to as "centralization," "reorganization," or "change." She wrote:

In 1947 and 1948, only a handful of articles even mention integration . . . they merely skirted the issue. This is not so surprising when one realizes that the newspapers were written by white people for white people. The black community was usually left out of the current news. . . . The lack of reporting on integration demonstrates how members of the black community and racial issues as a whole were and continue to be overlooked by the white community.

Reactions were mixed. Many African American parents were concerned about the safety of their children leaving the neighborhood and walking busy streets of the uptown to get to school. They were also concerned that their children would no longer have the same teachers they had grown to love. Their African American teachers had not merely been people the children saw at school. They also saw them at church every Sunday or had them over for dinner. The new white teachers were strangers to the children.[5]

One benefit of desegregation was that black children, who had always gotten the cast-off books and supplies from the white school, were given adequate school supplies and materials for the first time. Black teachers were paid less than white teachers, and that did not change. As Doris Burrell said, "While it was not a racial utopia, it was a beginning of social desegregation."[6]

Many of the disadvantages of desegregation, however, invisible to most whites, were palpable to African Americans. At a 1996 reunion of the Witherspoon School for Colored Children, the coordinating committee wrote:

> Our teachers not only taught us the three R's well, they also did a lot of character building. The messages to us were clear:
>
> 1. Be a credit to your race. Racism will always be with us. Don't use it as a crutch. You have to work twice as hard and put twice the effort into what you do.
> 2. Anything worthwhile takes planning and effort.
> 3. No one is successful by accident. People who become successful are usually the ones who are the least surprised because they know how hard they've worked to attain these goals.
> 4. Create opportunities where they don't exist and take advantage of the ones that do.
> 5. Respect our girls and women.
> 6. You don't know where you are going if you don't know where you came from. We were taught African American history all year around and instructed that we came from greatness. If you need role models, our history is full of them.[7]

Once desegregation happened, life shifted for black grade school children in ways for which no one was prepared. Merely putting white and black children in the same classroom was not enough. No plan had been created to address the deeply ingrained attitudes of white superiority and black inferiority that white teachers in Princeton, like the majority of whites throughout North America, had been taught from childhood. They'd learned early from other children that Negroes and whites could not marry and that, if you had even one drop of Negro blood, you were a Negro. In whatever ways that white teachers had been indoctrinated, with rare exception, they did not call on their black students nor encourage them. As vividly remembered by today's residents, they ignored the hands raised by black students and often expressed little interest in their ideas, insights, or thoughts.

In fact, some white teachers belittled black children's aspirations, called them the n word, and separated young black and white children from playing or dancing together. Black students said their white teachers, for the most part, not only expected them to fail but also actively discouraged them from going to college. Hank Pannell says, "I just thank God for the wonderful teachers I had prior to the integration of schools, and that I got that basic education through third grade. Because when I went to the Nassau Street School, things changed. That's when I found out about discrimination. I really feel as though I was cheated."

It might be a surprise that so many African Americans felt betrayed by integration. Yet integration thrust them away from being center stage in their own lives. They missed learning at a school that expected them to succeed. They learned the hard way that some people did not want to give them a chance to prove themselves equal or superior to white students. African American teachers had pushed them to excel. Their white teachers, on the other hand, often saw them as "people occupying seats," remembers Frances Broadway Craig, now a grade school teacher in Princeton. "When I was [in fifth grade] I was reading better than almost anybody, but they would always try to push the white kids into the top group."[8]

Lamont Fletcher, also a Princeton elementary schoolteacher, understands that personal sense of loss that so many of the residents express:

What happened [at the Witherspoon School for Colored Children] was the black teachers went the extra mile to make sure the black kids learned more than the other kids were learning, so that they could have something to hang on to because segregation is based on "I'm better than you." So the black teachers would work with them extra hours. Made sure they knew how to read, made sure they took a foreign language, made sure their literature and their math was perfect, and the proper enunciation and pronunciation of words and things of that sort. And the whole racial pride thing—they got that.[9]

Principal Waxwood and other black teachers who remained in the system tried to make up for the big loss of self-esteem black children experienced. But integration took its toll. Prior to school desegregation, a majority of black eighth graders graduating from the Witherspoon School for Colored Children went on to high school and college. Of course, they were not allowed into all-white Princeton University, but a large percentage traveled south to black colleges, which included Bennett College, Spellman, Morgan State, Virginia State, and Morehouse, or attended Lincoln University outside Philadelphia or Howard University in Washington, DC. A good number of these students not only graduated from high school and college but also got master's degrees and continued in doctoral or postdoctoral programs in engineering, theology, law school, medical school, and other fields.

Within three years after desegregation, the number of Princeton's black students attending and graduating from college dropped dramatically. Unlike white students, who were automatically tracked into an academic or business curriculum at Princeton High School, African American students were assigned a "general," nonacademic track that did not allow them to take academic, college-bound courses. Black parents had to go to bat for their children to be placed on the academic track. If the parents were not assertive, it didn't happen. Most of these students, no matter their tracking, never saw a guidance counselor during their four years of high school. And if they did, the outcome wasn't necessarily positive. When one young woman asked for information about colleges, for instance, the counselor said, "What for? You're only going to be working in somebody's house."

"During this period [after desegregation], we lost a lot of institutions," says Clyde Thomas, who graduated from the Witherspoon School before integration, and had gone on to graduate from Princeton High and Pennsylvania State University. "We lost a lot of social clubs . . . and the Y and YW that had been the strength and backbone of this community. They had provided values for us. Our teachers and mentors used to tell us, 'The world owes you nothing. You have to work hard for everything you have.' In my opinion, they were very successful."[10]

Young Y basketball team (about 1936)

In the 1950s, a Princeton University student studying social class in the Negro community for his senior thesis found that thirteen of the sixty people he interviewed in Princeton had completed high school, while forty-seven had dropped out before graduation, citing finances as the reason. He concluded that economic factors requiring them to work to help out their families "make it impossible for Negroes to take advantage of free education on the secondary level even when this is offered on a so-called equal basis with members of the other races."[11]

Some of those unresolved issues still haunt Princeton's public school system today. Black and Hispanic students continue to be "tracked" in the high school and disproportionately placed in remedial or special education classes. High school guidance counselor and Witherspoon resident Shirley Satterfield says she's found that African American students are not surviving too well at Princeton High School. "There's still that concern about African American, especially males, being put in Special Ed classes, so you still have that stigma," she says. "It's very difficult. . . . They are struggling, but not to succeed, they're just struggling."

Black students from the Witherspoon neighborhood still say they feel discrimination on many levels within the classroom and in clubs, social organizations, projects, and other extracurricular activities. They don't take as many Advanced Placement classes as white students, nor are they going to college in equally proportionate numbers. "I'm trying to find out why they're not succeeding," says Satterfield:

> I don't know where the breakdown came, though I think it came when they integrated, because the level of education was different. We had black teachers who cared and black men who went on to study Latin and Greek at Lincoln University. They were just proud to have the opportunity to have an education, while its almost reversed now, with black males not valuing the system, and its not all their fault, because education for them has gone down. And a lot of it I think happened when they integrated [the schools].
>
> Now they have all these minority education programs, and they just dwell so much on it. We should just leave it alone and go on and educate everybody. Teach them in lower grades and let them know that they can learn just like everybody else, and by the time they get to high school, give them AP courses.[12]

> I just thank God for the wonderful teachers that I had prior to the integration of schools.
>
> —HENRY F. (HANK) PANNELL

Sophie Hall Hinds (1875–1974)

My father was determined that all of his children should get an education of some kind. None of us got what I think we ought to have had, but he provided the best he could. We were fed and clothed and all that. And always had a place to live and plenty to eat. We always had a turkey for Christmas dinner. The only time we didn't have much to eat was after I got married.

But I never suffered very much. The Lord's been good to me all these ninety-six and some years. And if I see December, I'll be ninety-seven.

When my father was down in the South, the master's daughter was teachin' my father some readin,' and her father said to my father, "How you makin' out?" And he said, "I'm too dumb to learn." And the man said, "Ain't nobody too dumb to learn." My mother taught him what she knew, and he passed her by in his reading and all that. He could converse with any of these professors in Princeton. It didn't make any difference to him who you were because he could talk with them. He was wonderful, I think.

Albert Hinds (1902–2006)

Where I first perhaps met segregation, I guess, was going to school. At the time, as I say, you didn't think of it. We had a black school, just a couple blocks up the street. There's a building on the north corner on Maclean Street and Witherspoon, across from the church—that was the original school for blacks, for colored, as they were called at that time. In fact, my mother went to that school, and I went to that school, until around 1910. [In] 1910 the school was moved to Quarry Street, but still called under the name of Witherspoon School.

We didn't think too much about segregation at the time, it was just it. You see, you went to the black school, segregated school, until eighth grade, then we went to high school, which was integrated, for quite some time. I guess my class, in entering high school, might've been the second class in the high school of integration.

It was in 1919 I finished grammar school. I finished high school in 1923. The only one thing that they did to the blacks when we went to high school, they tried to track us into a certain category: nonacademic. But four of us—black boys—we used to say, we're not going to be tracked! We're going to take an academic course! And we did take an academic course. In fact, we didn't have things the white kids had, like, for instance, algebra, French, Latin—we didn't have it in Witherspoon School.

But we went. None of us failed. We all went in 1919, we all came out in 1923. We coped with the French, and Latin, and everything else. In fact, one of the members of our group helped the white kids with French. Another one helped them in Latin and math. So, ya know, we were there, and they know we were there, particularly the blacks, and I mean the boys. So there wasn't no pressure.

There was racial tension, all that. I didn't have that time to know about it, because I was always doin' something. I played football the whole time I was in high school. I played left end. I was mentioned All-State. I guess maybe in sports, I might have—I don't know what you call it—but in playin' the other side would say, "Get the nigger, get the nigger, get the nigger!" And if a white team came and there's a black on that team, right away my guys would say, "Hiney, Hiney, Hiney, there's your man!"

You know? Now, he can't be my man, unless he's playin' right end, you know! Right away, they're telling me who's going to be against me, which they can't do! And I've had some experience—that's where every time I tackled somebody, I tackled a guy, hear somebody say—they'd hit me atop o' the head—boom! But at the end of the game, I was still there!

My team was supportive. We went to Lakewood to play, and we went to a restaurant to get a sandwich or something, and they said that we had to go in the back door, through the kitchen, so they didn't eat there. And another time, the last game of the season, we sorta had a banquet at a restaurant, in this town where we played. And we were treated—there were two blacks on the team—and we were treated very well.

A month later, I was playing with a black YMCA team from here, and we were going to Asbury Park. And on the way down, we said, "We're hungry. Let's stop and get something to eat." We went there [to the same restaurant], and they said, "Mmm-mm. We don't serve you." Because we were a whole black team.

Susie Waxwood (1902–2006)

My parents made great sacrifices to see we got an education. My mother used to say she did not raise her children, because we were always in boarding school. I went with my sisters and my brothers to a church school in New Orleans called Straight University, believe it or not. I was in the sixth grade when I went there, and I stayed in that school through high school. It is now Dillard University. I lived in the girls' dormitory, and my brothers lived in the boys' dormitory across the campus. But we saw our parents almost every second week. They would come and get us and take us home, and then they would bring us back on Sundays to be there for school.

Bessie Parago (1907–2007)

You know I've never had an Afro-American teacher in my life. My grandchildren said to me, "What?" I said, "Never." They said, "Nanny, you ain't never had?" Come out of school and ain't never had one in my life.

My children, in fact, what happened was that at the Witherspoon School, they had that one big room for the kindergarten, that Charlie Potter was teacher up there, so okay, well, that was alright. So, then they built this school down here, Community Park. And so they came to me and said, "Mrs. Parago, will you send Barbara?" They had just integrated down here. I said, "Not my child. By herself? No. Uh-uh."

So when she got ready to go to high school, Jean Wright—I'll never forget it—she said, "Well, we'll put her in general." And I said, "Oh, no you won't. I'll fill out that program, make that schedule out." They were putting all those children in general diplomas. I said, "No you're not. Not Barbara. Not in the academic."

Then she said, "What about for the language and the Latin?" I said, "Well, don't you worry about the Latin or the language. I'll take care of that." I had sense enough to have [my daughter] tutored in Latin all summer, she took her language, made the Latin club, got a B in language, and that's when I told her, "Don't you worry about it." So she did come out with [an] academic diploma. Other than that, she would have come out general. [But] when I told Jean Wright I would make out the schedule, Caroline Gates said I was making trouble for the teachers.

Harriett Calloway (1906–2005)

We went to school up on Quarry Street. It was a nice school . . . they were all black, no integration. The teachers were nice . . . Mrs. Rodman and Mrs. Ford. At that time, there weren't too many classes that they would offer to blacks. And even here at Princeton, I know when Blaine, my husband, went away from Quarry Street to Nassau Street School; he quit because what he wanted to do, the teacher didn't think he was qualified.

I went to Quarry Street School and then I left Princeton, for I guess five or ten years, and I went to school in Trenton for a while. Then I came back to Princeton, must have been 1920. When I stopped going to school, I was in tenth grade and I never went back. I don't know why. I think about it a lot of times, you know, but I've made it thus far with what little I got. You understand what I mean—I can read and write and count. I had intended to [go back to school], but I just didn't.

Emma Epps (1902–1989)

That was a mistake I think my parents made when the Bigelows moved back to Boston [and] wanted my parents to go with them because [Mrs. Bigelow] said there was no educational value for us in Princeton. She was right. Because, you see, at that time we couldn't go to the Princeton High School. That meant that anybody who finished the school on Quarry Street, where that nursing home is, you'd have to go somewhere else to school, which meant south. Now there was a difficulty in that. First, we were poor. Also, this school here was not an "A" school, and the prejudice was very high. I'm sorry to say it's getting back to that here now. I didn't ever think it would in my lifetime. But prejudice now here is getting to be pretty bad again. I don't know why. It kind of shakes me.

Alice Satterfield (1922–2010)

In my younger years, I wasn't so much aware of racial prejudices because at the Witherspoon School, we had such wonderful colored teachers, and we had a community where the people cared for us, and we had our own community affairs. We had the YMCA, and we had other groups that we'd attend, so we didn't really miss it nor feel it. The only time I really felt it was when the white kids went to school on Nassau Street, and you know, we weren't allowed to go there. And I noticed all the time all the old books from the Nassau Street School would come down to our school. They were worn, old and outdated, but still we studied. Our teachers, our wonderful colored teachers, saw the difference, and they worked hard on us. I'm telling you, at our school, our teachers taught us. They taught us manners and respectability and how to carry ourselves properly, and you knew that they cared for you, they went out of their way to help you.

I can see myself right now. I remember so vividly coming out the front door in the afternoon when we were dismissed from school. The teachers would stand right out that door, and we had to march out two by two. They would say, "Alright, you go directly home, and no foolishness, you go right home and study." I learned to read and study, to get my head in the books and just do a good job of everything. The main thing was respectability, good manners, and how to carry yourself in a ladylike way, and the boys in a mannerly way. If you didn't go straight home, and the elderly people, if they saw you doing something on the street which you knew was not right or not proper to do, they would reprimand you and then call your parents to tell your parents. And your parents would also look into it and reprimand you. See, that's where "It takes a community to raise a child"—that's an original African saying. And it does. It didn't have to be their child, it could be their neighbor's child or someone down around, but they knew because it was a community where people cared, they knew the people. And they knew the rights and wrongs, and they knew how far to go with them, you know, but when they saw you doing something out of order, ha ha, watch out!

In the year 1947, they decided to break down the barriers so there wouldn't be a segregated school system in town. So the coloreds who lived in the borough were sent to Nassau Street School, and those who lived in the township, they went then to the township school. We lived in the borough, this is the borough here, and so my daughter Shirley went to Nassau Street School. But she didn't get the education there because there was still prejudice. And she had a gym teacher who was as prejudiced as he could be, and they were learning one day, you know a little dance thing. So when one of the white boys was dancing with Shirley, this teacher, this gym teacher made them separate: "Oh, you're not supposed to dance with them, with those coloreds." So that was one of the things that hurt Shirley very much because she didn't think of prejudice at that time, and kids—kids are taught prejudice.

Witherspoon neighborhood children (1933)

Most times younger kids are not really prejudiced, they have to be taught or they have to see it happen, or they see their parents or some of their peers doing it. But kids grow up caring about each other until they're taught differently. Most of the teachers were very prejudiced at the time. And they didn't care whether you got it or not. And anything nasty was said, they didn't try to correct it. When they desegregated the schools, they went uptown to the Nassau School, and there weren't any colored teachers at Nassau. They were all white teachers. They sent the middle school children, whites, to the John Witherspoon Middle School. I have to go back to give our own teachers all the credit for what the students learned during those years that they were there. It has improved a little bit through the years, but not much. There's still a tendency to push you aside in a lot of ways.

Clyde (Buster) Thomas (1934–2004)

They were doing renovations in the Witherspoon School for the Colored up on Quarry Street around 1938 or '39, and the school was not quite completed when I was going into the kindergarten, so we went into what is now the Masonic building on the corner of John and Maclean Streets. We were there until around Christmastime, and then we moved into the new kindergarten. I remained there until June of 1948. I was sort of fascinated by some of the history or achievements that they were telling us of African Americans and people from the African Continent. I guess we were a pretty much closed society at that time, and that's all I ever really knew about our people.

My mom worked for a family on Princeton-Kingston Road, shortly before I was born up until around 1965. She worked for the Ira Wade family. He graduated with Jimmy Stewart's class [in 1924] and was a professor of modern languages at Princeton. Because my grandparents and my mother did domestic work, occasionally they would take me to their jobs, and at a very early age, I started observing the difference between their homes and my home and what they had and what I didn't have. I never really talked this over with my friends, although I sort of sensed that I had a different take on what was happening, because nobody else mentioned it, and they never really discussed it. I became very bitter about a lot of different things that I sensed were going on, but nobody explained to me.

Joan Hill (1942–)

I went to elementary school in the all-black school, which was the Witherspoon School. I went as far as first grade there. From there I went to the Nassau Street School, after the school system integrated with the Princeton Plan in 1948. My friends said that they experienced a little racism. I do not remember feeling different [from the majority]. It could be because I was a leader and not a follower. I was very good in sports from running to baseball, basketball, whatever, so I was always a team captain. Everybody wanted to be on my team.

I was also inclined to be, for want of another word, a good student, so I did not have the problems that my other friends had, being tracked. They [teachers] did not want you in academics. Of course, that was to go on to college. I remember one of my girlfriends leaving one of the classes because a teacher wrote "Nigger" on the board. This was history class, and the teacher was saying that in the South, in the days of slavery, that white people called black people what he wrote on the board. I went up and told him that I didn't appreciate that. He said, "If it offended you, I apologize."

Hank Pannell (1939–)

I went to the Princeton Nursery School as soon as it started. I remember the snacks and lunch and having fun. I went to kindergarten at Quarry Street School through third grade. That's when the Princeton Plan came in effect, and the schools integrated. I just thank God for the wonderful teachers that I had prior to the integration of schools, and that I got that basic education through third grade. Because when we went to Nassau Street School, things changed. That's when I found out about discrimination. I really feel as though I was cheated. Just an example—I'm only five years younger than Clyde Thomas, and his friends all went to college. His class was the last group that graduated out of Quarry Street School. And that's a perfect example of how many students who graduated from that school went on to college and had such excellent careers.

At the Nassau Street School, we were pretty much ignored in the classroom and just geared toward general education. We weren't pressed to ask or answer questions. Even in high school, we used to sit [in] history class and compete among ourselves because the teacher never called on us. I never got another African American teacher until high school—and then only briefly.

I remember one incident in seventh grade when Mr. Horner, the music teacher, singled me out—I don't know why—to sing "Shortnin' Bread." I refused to do it. We got into a little thing, and I got sent to Mr. Waxwood, who was the principal. He [was supposed] to expel me or suspend me, but he sat me down and told me what racism was and how some white people think and all. He really gave me a lesson. He said that I shouldn't have reacted the way I did, that I should have gone to him. He said that things like that are going to happen—that's just the way the world is—and there's other ways to get even rather than physically. I think it was the first and last time I'd ever been directly insulted like that by anybody. But Mr. Waxwood tried his best to help all of us understand and deal with society as it was. He was a *great* man; he looked out for all of us.

Estelle Johnson (1919–2011)

After you finished the eighth grade, then you went to the high school. And in high school they selected your courses for you. Now, you could say you wanted a business course, but they would certainly tell you that blacks wouldn't need a business course. The counselors told you the studies and things that you ought to take. And the general course is what they really want you to take. If you were going to go to college, which they thought you weren't going to do, your parents better come over there and fight about that. Well, I didn't need to fight, because I knew doggone well that I was not going to college, because we were too poor. I didn't object when they had me take the general course. As long as I got out of high school, it didn't matter that much, you see. Some kids were able to take college courses. Their parents went there or had some white friends go there and say it's all right for this child to take, you had to know somebody or something. So, you got what you could.

Simeon Moss (1920–2007)

Princeton tried integration on a small basis. I remember that I was supposed to go eighth in the Witherspoon school and they picked three of us out and sent us over to the high school, which was a seventh through twelfth. It was a small school, 550 kids in the high school. And they put us in the middle track unit, and a couple years later they put Evelyn Craig and my sister, Lydia, and another girl in the same thing. They were trying this, with three or four people, integrating it at the eighth grade. The biggest problem was that most of the blacks were put into general-type courses rather than into academic-type courses. You know, "tracking" students. The teachers were prejudiced in my opinion. It was my opinion that they tolerated blacks . . . and it went that far. If you were in a confrontation with a white student, the white student always won so far as the teacher was concerned. In the other school, we gained equipment and knowledge—scientific knowledge. I think the science programs were much better in the high school than they would have been in the segregated school. But the leadership was lost. We had to develop that all over again, what little we had at the very beginning. See, our leaders were the stewards at the clubs, the restaurant owners, the guys who pushed the brooms in the schools, the janitors. They were the leaders. They produced kids who became leaders. Then all the sudden come World War II and it wiped out a lot of good people who said that Princeton is too small for me. A lot of black people said Princeton was too small and they went out and did other things. Opportunities were not here.

Eric Craig (1934–)

I worked for Grover Lumber Company for six years. There was a student at Grover Lumber Yard when me and Howard Sweeney worked there. I swear, we were in the truck with him, and he had a dictionary and asked him the definition of words. I don't think he got one wrong—very smart fellow. He was a student at Princeton University—white student, very nice boy. And I don't fool with the dictionary. If I hear something, right away, I'm at the dictionary. I do a lot of reading, but the best I've seen, the best in the business has got to be Edgar Allan Poe. He's deep. I love reading him.

Our mother taught us well. She was smart. She had a command of the English language you wouldn't believe. Crossword puzzles like nothing. She was quick, too. In the nursing home, the doctor asked her, "Have you lived here all your life?" She said, "Not yet." She used to always say, "Look it up." That was her expression. If you look at a word and don't know it, you go to the dictionary to see what it is.

Consuelo Campbell (1929–2013)

The old Witherspoon School building had what was called the Annex. It housed the seventh and eighth grade with a potbelly stove and a floor that a couple of kids' foot went through. Now eventually, the borough decided they needed to do a little bit better for the students. And not only for the students but for our community, period. And in order to get any of this going, our parents had to go and vote. "Yes, we need Witherspoon School to be remodeled so our kids don't go through the floor when they are in seventh grade. And yes, we need a community building, which could house the YW and YM."

Now the reason why I remember that was that there were only a few cars in our whole neighborhood. And those men went around and picked up people to go vote. I'll never forget that. 'Cause they came all the way over to where my mother worked to get her, to take her. And she was so pleased. She was serving dinner, and she stopped serving dinner and went to vote. And that's how we got that building there that's on Witherspoon [Street] that's called the Arts Council and Witherspoon [School], which is not the Annex but became really classrooms. We had to go vote for that. Even though it was needed, we had to go prove to the powers that be. I'll never forget that, that yes, we wanted, and yes we needed. The people went and voted. They might not vote anymore, but they voted then, which was most important as far as I'm concerned.

So that's the story of Witherspoon. We started out, kindergarten through fourth grade was at the Witherspoon Church Building. And the Masonic Temple housed the rest—fifth, sixth, seventh, and eighth until the Annex and Witherspoon was ready. And when I started out, I was in fourth grade. I started out at the church and ended up down at the Masonic Temple. And the day when we moved into our new building, I can remember each child brought his own chair up the hill. And it was just a good feeling. I still remember going up the hill with our chairs into our new building, our new school building and how proud we were.

Burnetta Griggs Peterson (1931–2013)

As a family, we loved Princeton. We really did. We had a heartache here, but we loved the town. It's a beautiful town, and it's a wonderful town in which to raise children because of, you know, the facilities that are here. The facilities were closed to me. The schools were segregated, the YMCA, YWCA, you know, all those things, the churches, even the cemetery, they were all segregated. And so I would say, if you're asking me some of the favorite things I liked to do then, it would be very simple. Like ice-skating down at Carnegie Lake, or riding my bicycle in town. But I was very much a person to be at home. Our home was the center of our life.

It was a normal growing-up. My early years were spent at Witherspoon School, which is where my mother taught. And I can't speak, you know, I speak very highly of my teachers there 'cause they certainly motivated us and prepared us for that which was to come, you know, in later years, and they all were excellent. Mrs. Gates and Mrs. Harris, Mrs. Sarah Harris had, they gave

Principal Howard B. Waxwood and his wife Susie Waxwood (1980s)

us lessons in regard to our own people, you know, black history, and particularly during Negro History Week. In fact, one of the things that I lost I looked for so many times, we started a booklet in Mrs. Harris's grade just in cardboard and covered and so forth, and then we had pictures of outstanding African Americans and little essays underneath. [I]t was something that I treasured, and it was well done, and it was shared, you know, in other words, each student might have taken someone that they particularly wanted to write about, and we had pictures of them in that book, and it was compiled. Mrs. Gates certainly gave us a background of outstanding African Americans. You know, I don't think we encountered it except in those grades, I don't remember it being taught in the high school at all at that time, about African American history.

In high school, I was on like the basketball team, on the paper staff, you know, there was some theatrical group I was part of, and I participated. I enjoyed my friends. My parents had friends both, you know, white and African American. But it was unusual when I thought about it, that I had friends at the high school, but I don't ever remember going to their homes, nor do I remember them being invited to my home. It just didn't occur. I was all for desegregation. You know, I found it unusual that an enlightened town like Princeton happened to be, that they could have permitted this all these years, that they could pay to send their township African American students into the borough of Princeton to be educated. You know, that just seemed so ridiculous really.

My daughters went to Stuart. Stuart is a [private] school that imparts values, and it gives young girls and young women an excellent opportunity for their personal development. They didn't have any racial problems over there. [However, previously] my youngest daughter was on this bus, and she was going to Littlebrook, and three boys, they just hurled racial comments at her, and to the extent that one evening, the African American bus driver came by our home, and he said he stopped because he wanted us to know that Kim was encountering problems on the bus, and he did not think that we knew of them, and we didn't.

Well, the following morning I was at Littlebrook School, in the principal's office, Mr. Lory Taylor's office, I told him, you know, that we had been told about what was happening to Kim prior to coming to school on the school bus, and that I did not consider it a privilege to ride on that school bus, I thought it was her right to do so, without these derogatory things being said to her, but that I was going to solve his problem as of that day, she would never ride a school bus again, I would take her to school. And you know, but I wanted him to know that I thought any other African American child should be able to ride that bus without encountering the problems that she had. And oh, they naturally wanted another opportunity to solve this problem, but I didn't give it to them, and I transported her to school, and then the following year, we left and went to Stuart. I think all families have to teach them what they might encounter and what they can expect, and if they encountered, you know, a problem, we would discuss it. But our girls were coming up when those barriers were breaking down.

Joe Moore (1941–)

I went from the Quarry Street School, which was the all-black school, to the Nassau Street School in the first year of the Princeton Plan. As best I can remember, it was a little intimidating, because it was the first time that I was leaving the comfort of the neighborhood and going to school with white kids I'd never seen or known before. But the transition was not that bad. Eventually, it grew into a positive experience. It was the first time that I met new friends outside of the John Witherspoon neighborhood, the first time I met new white friends. And some of us remain friends to this day.

Education in the John Witherspoon Street neighborhood was always important; the families always made sure that education was a part of your expectation—that you were going to complete high school, whether it was integrated or not. Education was a critical part of our growing up. So, regardless of whether it was the Princeton Plan or not, we were going to complete high school. There was no way we were going to escape that, whether it was an all-black experience or an integrated experience.

I think that in terms of expectations, the integrated experience was quite different than the non-integration experience. Back in the Quarry Street School, everybody had the expectation that you were going to succeed. And they demanded from you more than the integrated schools did. The downside of that was that the teachers, particularly the white teachers, did not expect a lot from us unless you were just blatantly, innately intelligent. There was not a lot of encouragement.

Clyde (Buster) Thomas (1934–2004)

When I was growing up, in the fourth and fifth grades, I knew some kids that were getting involved in some negative things, because they were really internalizing so many things that I was internalizing. They really felt inferior, but we had teachers who would try to give you just the opposite. That's why they were feeding us the contributions and achievements of blacks and Africans. I think our teachers were really very dedicated and committed to us. They tried helping us bridge that gap in what you're really experiencing and what you really could be. They tried to inculcate that you had to be twice as good as the others, and you often heard the "Be a credit to your race" kind of thing. They tried to develop responsibility and that you had to have some kind of plan for success. One of the things that personally helped me was that even though we were in a pretty segregated situation in Princeton, at the time, our conduct and behavior was always being monitored. By having a black YW and YMCA, you had mature adults who would pull you aside when you did something wrong. You got it from the school from eight to three and when you went into the recreational play after school, you got the same kind of guidance, telling you that you're heading down the wrong road and that, granted things were bad, but they were gradually getting better.

When I was in the sixth or seventh grade, the Jackie Robinson situation was just beginning, but I was still embittered even with that because of the way his own teammates treated him. I mean, they wouldn't socialize with him, and Larry Doby was experiencing the same thing. I couldn't understand that. Here you are, supposedly in a democratic country, and you fought a war that was supposed to be making the rest of the world free and democratic, and people were coming back and they couldn't find jobs.

My best friend's mother graduated number one in her class at Howard University, and she couldn't get a job in Princeton. Yet I think the thing that helped me again was the advice that we got from the African American adults who were supervising at the Y. So, you constantly got this talking to whether at home or at school. I think that is the missing link really with a lot of our youngsters. They don't get that kind of counseling and guidance that is so badly needed. Ever since they did the integration of the Y in the 1950s, my guess would be you probably can't find a kid on Clay Street that belongs to the YM or YWCA. I don't really know why we have such a big dropout rate among kids in the high school. I think we need, as activists, to find out answers to some questions. If you are going to address the situation, you have to find out why.

I feel that I was treated better than a lot of my friends in high school, but that was mainly because of sports. The first year, I went into commercial business, but because of my achievements in sports, I was approached about going to college and taking academic courses. Generally, they would accept one or two and be open and friendly, but it was not the whole group of African Americans that they were willing to accept. I'm not saying that I was accepted on their level, but I was invited to a lot more things and encouraged to do a lot more things. My whole attitude sort of changed in high school—but I think it was primarily from the effort of these teachers that I had in grammar school. By the time I got to high school, I mean, they told me where I was headed. And being older, I think I sort of had a little more maturity, saying I did want to become something and I really wanted to do something in life. And if I wanted to do that, I realized that I had to change my whole attitude. It wasn't that really difficult, but it just happened like that.

I did have a couple of white teachers that had an interest in me in high school. There was this one coach—Mr. Weiss—we had a couple of games where, because I was like the outstanding player, I was called nigger. The coach was talking to me about not having that bother me. He said it didn't mean anything, you know, "Don't let that get under you. There's always going to be people like that." I dealt with that part a little better, because of the way this coach was talking to me about it. . . . "You know, we're winning and they're trying to get you upset, and they figure if they can get you disqualified or out of the game, they have a chance to win."

So, you don't want to hurt your team. You want to help your team. And, although I don't think those players were telling me, "I'm going to personally hurt you," you shouldn't have to deal with that kind of thing. Some people out here are just like that. You don't want to govern yourself by the way that they're acting or behaving. You don't let their attitude govern what you do. And you know, those kinds of things made sense to me when I thought about it, so it didn't really bother me when I had to deal with it elsewhere. And there were a couple of places where I think the coach wanted to take me, and when they found out I was black, they wouldn't allow me in. He did try to make the change to get me in, and then he explained to me about it. I never really spoke to anybody about how I felt when I was growing up. I learned how to mask my true feelings, so a lot of people never really knew how bitter I felt when I was growing up in Princeton and seeing the difference in treatment.

Kathleen Edwards (1924–2000)

I liked school. Loved it. I didn't care where I was, I liked school. But the black students were not prepared. Because we were not taught the subjects that were taught at the other schools. Personally, I don't think they expected any of us to succeed. They were simply shocked when we did succeed in spite of all adversity. We had some teachers we would tell our dreams and everything, and they would tell us, "I don't know why you are wasting time with that because you are not going to amount to anything" and "They don't hire blacks for so and so." Your teachers were something like your parents. They could build you up or they could knock you down. I graduated from Princeton High School in 1942. Two other black students graduated with me. A lot of 'em started off with me, but they didn't graduate. For other reasons, for one or the other, they either dropped out or just didn't want to do it. I knew I had to make it so I did.

Romus Broadway (1939–)

Segregation ended while I was in high school in Princeton. But there was still the attitude of racial superiority. We knew it, because we grew up within an earshot of Princeton University, and we could sense the superior attitudes of the white students there. Even the white low-class had racist attitudes. How the hell could we expect any better? We understood that, so it didn't bother us. It bothered the white kids more than it bothered the blacks.

In high school, I really didn't try to carry white friendships any longer. That's because white friendship never really tried to carry me. That [philosophy] took me right through to the military, where I encountered some hard bastards from the South. We had to be on our toes all the time, because we could have made some mistakes which would have been very costly— through rank, promotion, or court-martial. There were guys looking for a chance for us to mess up. That's what made us really sharp.

I have a fond memory and a very bad memory of Princeton High School. The good part was that I graduated. Also, the friends that I grew up with, the African American ones, have remained friends. The bad part was that once we began high school, the white people I went to school with [earlier] didn't speak after high school. I figure that it was that the homes, the white homes, did not want African Americans and their children to socialize.

Princeton High School was integrated in 1948, the year I came from the segregated school. There were a few fights, and when there were parties, we understood that we wouldn't be invited. But we took it in stride—at least I took it in stride.

There were white kids that lived near me on Birch and Leigh Avenues who I considered to be my friends from the time that I was in nursery school. There weren't a whole lot, but there were some guys that really stood out. Guys like that kept me from putting a blanket over the whole white race. They helped me accept a person as an individual, rather than for a particular racial group.

Fannie Floyd (1924–2008)

Before Princeton High went mixed, which happened in the later part of the twenties, I think, black students had to go to high school in Trenton or somewhere else. It was quite frightening, going to a mixed high school from an all-black school. At our black school, we had only two physical education teachers, a music teacher, a nature studies teacher, and a home economics teacher who were white. One PE teacher and the home ec teacher, they were prejudiced and we knew it because of their remarks. They didn't care how they talked to kids. And then when we went to the mixed school, Princeton High, there was such a difference, especially with so few of us in a big school; some of the teachers didn't make you feel too comfortable, so it was kind of a frightening experience.

In high school, I didn't have any black teachers. Some [of the white teachers] were fair, and some were just, just terrible. They weren't interested in black students, and very few black students were guided into the academic and college courses. We found that maybe two blacks, or maybe sometimes one, in a class of thirty kids would go to college. I guess there were about thirty black students in my class. There were a few blacks from outside of Princeton, so maybe there were forty. They still have problems in the school system, especially the high school. It's all because either the leaders are not open to seeing the problem [or] willing to recognize what's going on.

Before going to high school, there was very little contact, except those who lived in the black neighborhood like the Irish and Italians. We played together and were neighborly. They would send their cooking over here and we would send our cooking over there, so we played together like that. Once they moved away or once we got to high school, it was different lots of times because they started going with their race, not associating with the black kids. Some of the white students were very nice. There was not a lot of tension; we simply did not bother with each other. But some of us were friends and are still friends. Some were very nice; it all depended on where they came from too. And your own experiences had a lot to do with your reactions as well. [With time,] I found it got easier at Princeton High, as far as speaking out in class and things like that. But I took the academic course and went on to college and came back to Princeton.

In the civil rights days, it was pretty trying times. On the March on Washington [in 1963], it was a thrilling experience to see so many people gathering in Princeton and passing through so fast. It was interesting in Princeton too because the whites and blacks in Princeton had such an active human relationship. It was quite an experience.

Jay Craig (1930–)

When I was in high school I played sports with a couple of local teams in Princeton—basketball and football. The football team was called the Hawks and the basketball team I played with was called the Cobras. But they weren't affiliated with the schools. We practiced out of the YMCA, and we actually played games in the Witherspoon School. They had a beautiful basketball court there. The school was new, you must bear in mind.

I was educated by black teachers in the black elementary and middle school, as opposed to the way I was not educated—at the very least, not encouraged—by white teachers at Princeton High School, which was integrated. I was bright enough, sophisticated enough to tell, just to tell right here in my gut what was going on. And I could see it. I mean, I was in classes with some white boys and white girls who weren't exactly bright, but you know they went on to college later on in life. They were encouraged, and the teacher would be leaning over them rather than leaning over us. I knew enough then to know what was happening at Princeton High School when it comes to being discouraged.

William Johnson (1938–)

I think I did the right thing by staying here on the East Coast. . . . The other right thing I think I've done is try to carry myself as a professional educator, but more importantly, a role model for the children of Princeton, because I am the *only* African American male administrator in the district. And there has only been one other in the twenty-five years that I've lived here. So, it's kind of interesting that over a long period of time, I've been able to do that. It's kind of interesting to think about that—that's a long time. A quarter of a century. I've been working this job longer than some people have been on earth.

Now I'm seeing the children of my children come back. I had a Back-to-School Night this year, [and] a bunch of young women who came in with their children . . . and then they saw each other for the first time and . . . they ran to each other, and their kids were [saying], "Why are they acting like that?" I said, "They haven't seen each other since they were in middle school." They said, "You were their principal?" I said, "Yes." "And you're *my* principal? . . . You're really old!"

Now, with new technology, we're going into the information age. We've gone through the social revolution of the sixties, we had the craziness of the seventies, the eighties, and the nineties. The schools are still trying to prepare young people for society. . . . [T]he schools used to be able to prepare them, because it was pretty predictable. Now, there's so much stuff out there that how do you prepare everyone to be successful in "the future"? And how do you make certain that all the students get equal access to it? So, that's the struggle.

4

The University:
A Place to Labor,
Not to Study

James Everett Ward and Arthur Jewel Wilson Jr. (1944). Both entered
Princeton through the US Navy's V-12 officer training program in 1942.

FOR MOST OF ITS life, Princeton University has earned its description as "a northern institution with its spiritual heart in the South."[1] From the time the tiny "College of New Jersey" moved to "Prince Town" in 1756, the all-white, all-male Anglo-Saxon school was a refuge for the Southern aristocracy. Not only did the first eight presidents own slaves, but the trustees were also slaveholders—including Israel Read (who served from 1761–93), Jeremiah Halsey (1770–80), and Richard Stockton (1791–1828).

From the start of this small Presbyterian school, which was called a "Union of Religion and Learning," at least 40 percent of the student population came from the South up until the mid-1900s. In 1848, the percentage of Southern students was 51.5 percent.[2] For them, Princeton was a home away from home, a place where their proslavery, Confederate, anti-Negro sentiment was pervasive for nearly two hundred years. As Paul Robeson wrote:

> Traditionally the great university has drawn a large part of its student body and faculty from below the Mason-Dixon line, and along with these sons of the Bourbons[3] came the most rigid social and economic patterns of White Supremacy. And like the South to which its heart belonged, Princeton's controlling mind was in Wall Street. Bourbon and Banker were one in Princeton, and there the decaying smell of the Plantation Big House was blended with the crisper smell of the Counting house. The theology was Calvin: the religion—cash.[4]

Standing apart from the college's Southern way of thinking was Joseph Bloomfield, a trustee in the late 1700s and early 1800s, who was a prominent abolitionist and president of the New Jersey Society for the Abolition of Slavery. As governor of New Jersey from 1801 to 1812, Bloomfield presided over legislation enacted in 1804 that provided for the gradual abolition of slavery for women after their twenty-first birthday and men after their twenty-fifth.[5]

After the American Revolution, Princeton University had remained loyal to its Southern mind-set. As its Presbyterian leadership distanced itself from the churches of New England and New York, the college became the intellectual center for conservative, Old School Presbyterianism. And while the Old School Presbyterians did not officially condone slavery as an institution, they were opposed to the radical abolitionist fervor that was on the rise in the 1830s.

They, like many if not most whites, were also uncomfortable with the numbers of free Negros who would not let America's racial inequities get them down or defeat them. Not only were Negroes sending money to free their loved ones from slavery, but they were also founding organizations of their own to fight for justice. Most whites feared insurrection and rebellion from free Negroes and agreed they must be kept in check. One approach to solving the "problem" was to deport the entire Negro population. For members of the Witherspoon neighborhood building their families and lives, this was an abhorrent idea. "The discriminations faced by the free Negro were numerous and varied, [but] as Americans in a booming country with great natural resources, they were optimistic, given to hope that tomorrow would bring a better day. Because of this faith, most Negroes were cool toward schemes to send them out of the country."[6]

Among whites, the notion of deportation began gathering zealous advocates in the early nineteenth century. In December 1816, a group of eminent white citizens, including Henry Clay and Francis Scott Key, founded the American Colonization Society (ACS). The organization, largely made up of Southern slaveholders, proposed sending Negroes to Africa to avoid the unrest they might inspire at home. That same year, Princeton's College of New Jersey became the state's branch headquarters for the ACS. Robert Stockton, the grandson of Princeton's founder, Richard Stockton, was the New Jersey chapter's first president. The colonization members raised funds from individuals, churches, state legislatures, and the US Congress to finance the exportation of free Negroes and to spur the voluntary freeing of slaves in an effort to rid the United States of a population they considered volatile and racially inferior to whites. With these funds, in 1822, the ACS, with Robert Stockton as its chief negotiator with Liberia, founded the colony of Liberia, where emancipated slaves and free blacks were to be sent.[7]

In *College As It Is*, based on an 1845 memoir by Edward Shippen, editor Jeff Looney notes that Southern students in the 1800s found Princeton especially congenial because many faculty members were colonizationists. John Maclean Jr., president of the College of New Jersey from 1854 to 1868, was a member of the ACS and fervently sought to "repatriate" Negroes to Africa.

In spite of its religious and political conservatism, the college was not immune to the competing forces that eventually escalated into the Civil War. Scholar Sean Wilentz writes, "Princeton also helped produce a few individuals who would stand among the most forceful antislavery activists of the era—including a seminarian [who graduated from the Princeton Theological Seminary and became an ordained Presbyterian minister and journalist] named Elijah Lovejoy, [who,] in 1837 became the first white martyr in the abolitionist cause."[8]

The number of students enrolled in Princeton from Southern states peaked in 1848,[9] and even the most conservative Princetonians were being won over by the Union's cause. During the Civil War, student enrollment from Southern slave-owning families declined. Yet Princeton's ongoing ambivalence is immortalized in the fact that it is still one of the only institutions of higher learning that honors students on both sides of the conflict.

In the 1870s, when the eleventh president of the college, the Scottishborn Reverend James McCosh, allowed four black seminarians from the progressive Princeton Theological Seminary to attend his lectures, several Southern students protested and demanded that the blacks be barred from the campus. Rev. McCosh refused. The white students quit the college but were soon back, without further incident.[10]

Despite more openness and sympathy for integration on the part of some faculty and students, Woodrow Wilson, as thirteenth president of Princeton University, made clear that the university's long-standing commitment to segregation was as solid as ever. In a 1909 letter responding to a black minister's inquiry about attending Princeton University, Wilson understated his prejudice toward African Americans when he wrote, "It would be altogether inadvisable for a colored man to enter." And as one alumnus from the class of 1928 put it when he wrote to the university's then president John G. Hibben: "Princeton is popular through the south because it is the one eastern school which does not enroll Negroes."[11]

In 1912, the scholar and intellectual leader W.E.B. Du Bois criticized Princeton University for its segregationist policies and urged it to integrate. His message stayed alive and controversial. Three decades later, in 1942, students at the *Daily Princetonian* urged the integration of the university and started an open dialogue on the subject. They drew the anger of students, alumni, and administrators who accused them of "promoting racial disunity" and "trying to do the impossible."[12] An editorial in the *Princeton Herald* asserted that admitting black students to the university might be morally justified but would simply be too offensive to the large number of Princeton's Southern students.

As it happened, a year later, because of World War II, Witherspoon residents saw what they had been waiting for. For generations, they'd watched the university turn away their own high-achieving young scholars—not because they lacked brilliance but because of the vicious lies about black inferiority. The time had come for the truth. The four African American men who officially broke Princeton's color barrier arrived on campus after the navy opened a training school at Princeton on October 5, 1942. John Leroy Howard, Arthur Jewell Wilson, James Everett Ward, and Melvin Murchison Jr. were admitted as part of the US Navy's V-12 officer-training program, which selected only the most highly qualified naval men to become commissioned officers.

Witherspoon residents watched with pleasure as the four young black men excelled. They took pride when John Leroy Howard, class of 1947, was the first black man in the history of the university to earn a Princeton undergraduate degree. They also loved Arthur "Pete" Jewell Wilson Jr., class of 1947, the first black athlete at Princeton and a key player on the basketball team. Neighborhood kids sneaked into the bleachers to watch him play for the Tigers in 1944–45. "You can't imagine the joy I felt watching a black man playing basketball for Princeton," Hank Pannell recalls. "I was a kid, and I could hardly believe my eyes. When Pete Wilson became captain of the team, I was over the moon."[13]

The door had opened, but only a crack. In 1947, the university admitted another black student only months after Jackie Robinson integrated professional baseball. He was Joseph Ralph Moss, a Witherspoon resident, and the first African American to enter Princeton as an undergraduate during peacetime. He graduated in June 1951. Two more men from the neighborhood, Robert Rivers and Simeon Moss, were admitted in the late 1940s and earned degrees.[14] In the 1950s, each undergraduate class included only one or two black students. "My social life had to be tolerated," Robert Rivers, class of 1953, told a reporter for the *Daily Princetonian* in the 1990s. "I had to live in two worlds. My social life was not on campus." Royce Vaughn, class

James (Jimmy) Johnson outside East Pyne Hall,
next to Nassau Hall (1890)

of 1953, told the same reporter, "If it had not been for Bob and his family, I wouldn't have made it at Princeton." He said that the Rivers family gave him a sense of belonging.[15]

In 1955, the university named an assistant professor in the English Department—the first black scholar to hold a professorship at Princeton. In 1959, the university conferred an honorary degree upon the celebrated opera star Marian Anderson, and in 1960, the Reverend Dr. Martin Luther King Jr. preached in the university chapel as a personal guest of the university chaplain, the Reverend Ernest M. Gordon, a Presbyterian born in Scotland. As a former prisoner of war during World War II, Rev. Gordon had suffered greatly; he felt very strongly about the importance of civil rights for all people. Rev. Gordon hosted Dr. King at his home several times and also brought other black friends and leaders to campus to talk about ending segregation and dedicating themselves to working for equal rights.

Among Princeton University's students and alumni, however, opposition to full integration remained strong. By 1960, only two blacks were enrolled in a student population of 809. As reported in the *Daily Princetonian*, it was a painful time, when a white student would get up and leave the room when a black student walked in, when sometimes students hung Confederate flags from their dorm windows. "Some white students would throw away the silverware after a black student used it, or would sometimes toss garbage or urinate out their windows on black students. . . . Much of the discrimination, however, was more subtle."[16]

While these things were going on at the university, Witherspoon residents welcomed black students into their homes and also worked to raise consciousness among the larger white community of Princeton about the impact of discrimination. Witherspoon residents had formed an inclusive Princeton Association for Human Rights and another organization, the Elizabeth Taylor Byrd Scholarship Fund, which worked to develop leadership in African American youth. They were pushing for fair housing and nondiscrimination policies in hiring. Among other things, they set up events and speakers not only to inspire African American young people, but also those from all walks of life, including black and white Princeton students, faculty, and staff.

At one such community event, the guest speaker was former Witherspoon resident Bruce Wright, a professor of law at Yale University at the time, who would later become a judge on the New York Supreme Court. He told a story, which he tells later in this text, of being admitted to the university on a full scholarship in 1938, and then being turned away on his first day because admissions hadn't realized that he was black. Consuelo Campbell, an organizer of this event, said, "When this story was carried back across Nassau Street, Princeton President Robert Goheen and several other people on staff were aghast."[17] This incident, along with others, spurred Goheen and his staff into action.

They decided that Goheen should address the issue with townspeople. Before a capacity crowd of 1,200 at the Princeton Playhouse, which no longer exists, Goheen appeared on behalf of the Princeton Association for Human Rights. He said, "The revolution of 1963 is both a real social force and a long-deferred claim for fair and fruitful opportunities, which every American must recognize." Goheen called on the entire town and university community to work "for equal and open opportunities in all areas" for blacks. He declared that the university would no longer list rental properties where there was evidence of discrimination; they would open opportunities and make concerted efforts to attract more black applicants to the university.

In 1964, Goheen appointed Carl A. Fields as assistant director of student aid, making Princeton the first Ivy League college to appoint a black administrator. Four years later, Fields's promotion to dean of the college made worldwide news. Under Dean Fields's direction, Princeton University's administration began recruiting African American students. The office of admissions actively reached out and began inviting prospective black students to the university for tours and interviews.

Eight African American students were admitted to the class of 1964. Neighbors were excited when James Floyd Jr., son of their own James and Fannie Floyd, was admitted as an undergraduate to the Princeton class of 1969. Fourteen black students were enrolled in this class. "We were sort of like an experiment," Jim Floyd Jr. said. "The fourteen of us in our class knew each other and were in touch with each other. All of us graduated in our class, which surprised people. They expected us to have academic difficulties."[18]

The Witherspoon residents knew how lonesome it could feel to be black in a sea of traditional whiteness; James and Fanny Floyd and other neighbors worked with Fields to set up a "Family Sponsor Program," which paired local black families with black students to give them a home away from home. In 1969, black undergraduates had staged a sit-in in Nassau Hall to address changes they wanted on campus. With the university's cooperation, they also set up a storefront tutoring program for children from the Witherspoon neighborhood. Residents welcomed the presence of the students, the tutoring, and the new relationship that connected them more closely with the university.

From the midfifties into the early sixties, Princeton—and many of its faculty, administrators, students, and alumni—were jolted by the civil rights movement. Many white Princetonians had witnessed the violence of segregation for the first time as television cameras showed the police using dogs, fire hoses, guns, batons, and their fists against peaceful demonstrators; they were moved by those injustices to a new awareness of what it meant to be black in America. They were further inspired to action by speakers invited to campus, including Malcolm X and Stokely Carmichael, and entertainers Odetta, Miriam Makeba, Marian Anderson, and the Freedom Singers, who performed at the McCarter Theatre.

This progressive shift was demonstrated when the Princeton Association for Human Rights chartered buses that carried 250 black and white Princeton residents and university students, faculty, and staff to the 1963 March on Washington. Others traveled to Mississippi to help register black voters in 1964. In 1965, several neighborhood residents were joined by two university professors who also made the journey to Selma to march with Dr. Martin Luther King Jr.[19] Even more university students and faculty traveled to DC for the Poor People's March on Washington in 1968, as did Witherspoon activists.

The Association of Black Collegians (ABC) was created in 1967 at Princeton, and that same year, ABC held a university-sponsored conference that was attended by two hundred black students from major colleges and universities in the northeastern United States. When Princeton became co-ed in 1969, twelve black undergraduate women were admitted to the school. That same year, the Program in African American Studies was created and more African American faculty were hired. In 1970, Princeton named Larry Ellis head coach of track, field, and cross-country, making him the first African American head coach of any sport in the Ivy League.[20]

By the time Princeton University's class of 1970 ceremoniously unlocked and permanently opened the university's front gates at their graduation,[21] a transition away from slavery, segregation, and decades of oppression had begun. At that graduation, Howard Bell, class of 1970, was the first black student to receive the Moses Taylor Pyne Honor Prize, the highest general distinction conferred on an undergraduate. The open, unlocked gates became a new symbol for the university, and, for its nearest neighbors in the African American neighborhood, an avenue of hope. Finally, Princeton University, led by President Robert F. Goheen, was actively seeking black students, staff, and faculty to change Princeton's story and set it on a new path.

Since that time, the numbers of black and Hispanic students admitted to Princeton have increased every year. Of the 1,911 members of the class of 2020, 152 students are black, 95 are multiracial, 171 are Hispanic, 382 are Asian, and 229 are international students. Eight hundred of the class are women—the powerful consequence of Princeton's admission of women in 1969. The leadership of the university, including administration, faculty, and staff, has also become much more diverse. While many issues around race, class, and gender still need to be addressed on campus and in our culture, they are at least out in the open and up for discussion. At the university's annual "P-Rade" for Reunions, a witness to the university's progress is palpable as the oldest alumni, all white elderly men, lead the procession in their orange and black class jackets. They are followed by more lively groups of male and female alumni of mixed races and ethnicities from more recent classes, moving together in their class jackets with small children on their shoulders, turning the parade into a joyful event expressive of the diversity of America today.

> I think people have a false idea about people that lived in Princeton
> and education. Some people thought that you just got it by osmosis.
> It floated down from the university.
>   —ESTELLE TADLOCK JOHNSON

Sophie Hall Hinds (1875–1974)

My father worked at the university . . . for a while. A lot of men did work with the clubs in them days. And they got paid $25 a month. And that's all they got. The families just took what they got in those days and times. My father worked for [Professor] Gerry Lambert for a while. And my father had the pleasure of planting a magnolia tree right where you got up from Nassau Street up to the chapel. The tree came in late one evening and everybody wanted to go home, so nobody would stay. But President McCosh had the pleasure of holding [the tree] while my father planted it.

Joe Moore (1941–)

The university represented a way in which you could expand your activity beyond John Witherspoon Street area, so that whenever there were activities going on at the university, we would check it out. We were not supposed to be over on the campus. So that also became sort of a game with us. Our parents did not approve of us going across Nassau Street. The university was not an area that wanted us. It was a privileged place—not for us. But we often would go over there, to go down to the old Brokaw Field to watch a baseball game, or just to walk through on our way to the train station. So the university provided a certain amount of youthful exploration. Sneaking into football games was a regular for us.

It was sort of an unwritten law that you didn't go across [Nassau] Street. That was filtered down to all the families in the John Witherspoon Street neighborhood. It was a general cardinal rule. In fact, sometimes it would be enforced by the local cops. We would sit on the wall in front of the library just on a Sunday afternoon, just eating ice cream, and we would be told to move— because anytime you crossed that side of Nassau Street, you were suspect.

Estelle Johnson (1919–2011)

I think people have a false idea about people that lived in Princeton and education. Some people thought that you just got it by osmosis. It floated down from the university. If you lived in Princeton, you thought you were richer than anybody else, which was not so, because if we were richer, I wouldn't have been going through the stuff that I had been going through. But trying to get that across to other people was kind of hard. We had a better understanding of white people in particular, I think, than maybe some people in Trenton because we tried to live up to some of the standards that they did. And it looked

Firestone Library's maintenance and janitorial staff (around 1940)

like we were living above our means to people who did not know what to do with whatever it is that they were handed. My mother always said, "It's what you do with what you got." It might just be junk, but it looks like it's got value to it. So, it looks as though we thought ourselves better or something. Not so. We were just using nice things that people gave us, and we knew how to use them, because we worked around a private family all the time. We served tea parties and cooked and helped them with their children and all those kind of things. So, we knew how to do and what to do with things.

Marilyn Yates (1935–)

My mother worked for one of the deans of the university, Dean Brown. She worked for his family—did housework—down on the lower part of Mercer Street. They had a house there. And she used to take us with her to work, and we just mingled with the kids, did things with the children. It was good growing up. It was a very good experience.

One time we went to go swimming at this club on Washington Road—it was a swimming club. Mrs. Brown got us all out and was taking us in together—her kids and my brother and me—and they wouldn't let us in. So, she would not go in either. She said, "Well, none of us are coming in." That's the only time I really experienced any prejudice; I just never have. And that's the honest truth. I can remember that one time. Golly, I was a youngster. I had to be no more than nine years old. It was during the summer and Mom was working. Whatever job my mom had, the people were very nice and they always took us in with theirs. We just all had a good time together.

We never talked about race. We never had to stand outside anywhere because any place we couldn't go to, we didn't go. We never went to the Nassau Inn or any place like that, because we couldn't afford it. That wasn't our thing. At that time, it was just all white, of course. But we never went anywhere we weren't supposed to be. And it didn't cross our mind at all, why we should go there, because that was more than we could afford anyhow.

Leonard Rivers (1934–)

Probably one of the most ominous things I can remember about growing up in the shadow of the university is the gate. You go [up] Witherspoon Street [to the] University, and that gate was always locked shut, it was never open. Never. We had the John Witherspoon area, that was our community. We knew that when you crossed Nassau Street and you went to the university, that was not us. You see, every once and a while we would go over there and try to sneak in the stadium and see a football game, or we would go down and try to bum some tickets to go to a basketball game. Or [during] reunions, we used to sneak over there and take a look at what was going on. But in our mind, we knew that there were no people of color at Princeton, and because there were no people of color at Princeton, that was not us. And if you happen[ed] to wander through, or even walk in, campus security would stop you and want to know where you're going, where'd you come from, what direction you're going. . . . If we were with our Italian friends, campus security would send us back home, but go get tickets for these other Italian kids. And we['d] sit there like, wait a second, why are they chasing us off campus?

When I was a kid, during the war, the [US] Navy V-12 Program brought naval officers to town to train them on the university campus. And the word ran around Princeton like crazy, "Princeton's got a black football player!" They'd never had a black football player before. Now this kid, Mel Merchison, was a black football player. We all snuck in the stadium and climbed up to the top to see Mel Merchison play. And that was like a phenomenon.

For a period of time, I worked in professional sports, and we spent an awful lot of time trying to get an attachment with the United Negro College Scholarship Fund, mentorship programs, Big Brother programs, and that type of thing. When I came back to Princeton, I coached at the university for over ten years, but not much had changed. I can remember when I was coaching football over there, and we started an all-black backfield, except the quarterback. Bob Casciola was the head coach. The next week, he got over a hundred letters from alumni: "What are you doing with an all-black backfield?" So that's the Princeton that sticks in my memory.

I was the head baseball coach at Princeton, and, you know, I have no attachment to the place at all. They have a "Friends of Princeton Baseball" group at Princeton. Every year they have a big fund-raiser. The alumni come by, the old ex-coaches that bring the ex-coaches in and the ex-coaches and the alumni, they play each other. I was head coach there for five years, I won over one hundred games in five years, but I've never been invited back for that game. What's that tell you?

My father, if you saw my father, you would think he's probably German, he had straight hair and he's light-skinned. And when I was the head baseball coach at Princeton, we played a doubleheader against Yale. My father used to come down and watch the games all the time. My uncle, at that time, was a policeman in town, Ted Lewis. My father used to come down and he used to put a chaise lounge chair behind the backstop. And this time, he brought two lounge chairs because my uncle was going to come down when he got off from work and watch the second game of the doubleheader. So I saw my father walk in, I saw him sit in the chair and I'm down on the field. This guy asked to use the extra chair and my father said sure. For the last half of the game this guy was telling my father about how bad it was that Princeton hired nigger coaches, and that they don't know how to coach and shouldn't be on the field. My father just sat there and listened to him.

In between games, my father went like this to me; he said, "C'mere." So I hopped over the fence and went up on the hill and when I walked up to my father, my father said to this guy, "I'd like you to meet my son." And the guy looked at me like that, and looked at my father, and looked at me like that, and he got up and almost ran out of the gate. And my father's answer to him was to introduce me to this guy. So when I went up there, this guy just took off. It's funny, but at the same time it's not.

When I was coaching baseball, I heard people make comments in the stands. We'd play a single game on Friday, a doubleheader on Saturday. I took the baseball team, we played Harvard on Friday up in Cambridge, then we got on the bus and went from Cambridge to White River Junction, and we were going to check in [at] the Howard Johnson's in White River Junction. Well, I fell asleep on the front seat of the bus and we pull into White River Junction and Prosima, who was white, was my trainer. When you pull in the motel, they got all your keys ready for you. So Pross jumps off the bus and goes in the lobby, and he's got the box of keys and the kids are getting off the bus and he's giving them their room keys. So I walked in and I'm standing behind him while he's giving the keys out. And the woman who worked behind the counter hollered across, and said, "Hey, coach, hey, here's a key for your bus driver over there."

Pross said, "That's not the bus driver, that's the coach."

Bruce Wright (1917–2005)

I had gotten a full scholarship to Princeton University. They didn't know I was colored, but as soon as they found out, they reneged. When I received word of the scholarship, in the midst of the Great Depression, it was wonderful because my father had no money. I mean, we were joyous and happy. And it solved a problem, because I was very sad before that. I had no idea what I would do. I knew I didn't want to be like my father working two or three jobs.

[On the first day at Princeton] I stood in the registration line, as I was told to do. Some of the people there apparently accepted my presence without a question. I was approached by an upperclassman who was there to help freshmen, who asked me my name, disappeared, came back and said, "The dean of admissions would like to see you." Not the dean of freshmen, the dean of admissions. I followed him into the office of Radcliffe Heermance, then the dean of admissions, and that's when he confronted me, looking at me as though I was a disgusting specimen under a microscope. He said, "The race problem is beyond solution in America, a Christian country." He said, "And if you're trying to come here, you're going to be someplace where you're not wanted." He encouraged me to go to "a college *of my own kind.*" I was shattered, and I became more so as time went on.

For some reason, I persisted in writing to Heermance to demand to know why. Was I a menace, a danger to a great university that had existed since the colonial days? [His letter of response is] dated June 13, 1939:

Dear Mr. Wright,

Princeton University does not discriminate against any race, color, or creed. This is clearly set forth in the original charter of the college, and the tradition has been maintained throughout the life of the university.

Now let me give you a purely personal reaction. And I speak as one who has always been particularly interested in the colored race, because I have had very pleasant relations with your race, both in civilian life and in the Army. I cannot conscientiously advise a colored student to apply for admission to Princeton, simply because I do not think that he would be happy in this environment. There are no colored students in the University, and a member of your race might feel very much alone. There are, moreover, a number of southern students enrolled in the college. This has been a tradition of longstanding in Princeton. And, as you know, there is still a feeling in the south quite different from that existing in New England. My personal experience would enforce my advice to any colored student, that he would be happier in an environment of others of his race.

Very sincerely yours,
RADCLIFFE HEERMANCE

Exclusion from Princeton of blacks—over a century and a half during that period—meant for me that the university was betraying its mission.

There was a neighbor of mine, Jim Yelson, he said, "Listen, I can get a scholarship for you. After all, you were the state champion in the mile run." I went there [to Virginia State College for Negroes] and I lasted almost a full semester. Katherine drove me down there in her Oldsmobile and she said, "Well, this looks like a pretty nice place, Bruce." But it wasn't. It was not for me. It was run by a dictator who was the president. I didn't last there very long. Fortunately, I got into Lincoln University, where most of the black guys from Princeton seemed to go if they went to a university at all. Lincoln was founded for blacks in 1854 but it was integrated. It was all for guys and they had a few white students there from the locality. I had the most marvelous time in my life at Lincoln. . . .

So I eventually graduated from New York University [law school] in 1949. And I was admitted to the bar in 1950. I was a member of the bar for fifty years, then stopped paying dues. That was my goal, to be a member of the bar for fifty years.

I lived in Harlem at the 135th Street and Fifth Avenue project there, developed by the Jim Crow Metropolitan Life Insurance Company, called Riverton. And I was about three blocks from Langston Hughes. Somebody wanted us to meet, because my first book of poetry had been published in England while I was still in the forces, and I was always agitating for integration. That's how I met Langston. We became good friends and neighbors. We both went to Lincoln University and we used to talk about it all the time. Now there's a big display there in the library honoring him. He was such a joyous guy. I was certainly sorry to see him die. I'd hoped he would live a long, long time.

Mayor Lindsay appointed me to the [New York State] bench. He and I had had conversations when I was general counsel to one of his agencies, a city agency. I became general counsel to it, which meant you ran it. So he appointed me to criminal court for a ten-year term. Then I got elected after that to the civil court for a ten-year term. And from the civil court, I didn't stay there ten years. I got elected to the New York Supreme Court. You have to run for that one. You have to hit the hustings, get out in the street and tell people you're respectable. Even though I'm a Negro, you can imagine how respectable I am.

It's a fifteen-year term for the Supreme Court. At seventy-something I had to step down to retire for age. After that, I became a professor. I loved teaching. Nowadays I read to little kids who are barely old enough to understand anything beyond, "I have to go to the toilet, Mr. Wright" at the library in Old Saybrook. Just emancipated, I think, from nursing at their mothers' breasts.

A few weeks ago, I went to the sixty-fifth anniversary of my graduation from Lincoln University. Those four years really were the most wonderful experience I'd ever had. I have an honorary doctorate degree from Lincoln, so you must call me Dr. Wright. But I've never forgiven Princeton for what they did. I had also applied to Notre Dame, and they said the same thing that Princeton said except that I had sent a picture, so they refused me and they knew. I got a letter of apology fifty years later from a rector at Notre Dame. He said he didn't know about it. He was snooping through some records. I got an apology from various Princetonians, yes, but not from the university itself. They made me an honorary member of the class of 2001 and I got this jacket that holds a six-pack of beer, and I don't even drink beer, never did, just Scotch.

Emma Epps (1902–1989)

The Robesons lived right across the street. When we went to Green Street they went to Green Street. [Paul Robeson] has one sister, Marion, who I saw two weeks ago. He lives in Philadelphia now. Paul's not well, and he won't see anybody, really. We're really disturbed about that. He just stays in his room, mostly hurt. He says that this country turned him down, turned their back on him, which it really did. His getting on the stage—his getting on the stage in *Othello* and all that was not fostered by America. It was done by Russia. And when Russia offered him the medal, I think it's pretty hard on somebody that's helped you with your music and your drama to say, "I can't accept." That doesn't make sense. And, of course, when he visited Russia, the United States government branded him as a communist.

When they were discussing the integration of the university here, they had Paul here at the clubs a couple times, at big games, and big affairs. And that hurt him. Although he put on a good face. Because he had tried to get into Princeton, and he was born right here, and they turned him down.

Paul Robeson was good at everything. He's a darn good lawyer, yeah? His voice, as Dr. Penoski said, "I'd never heard him. He walked on the stage and I knew I was in for a grand evening." He had personality. He was the football, the reason for Rutgers and Princeton breaking for a long time was Paul. He was on the football team at Rutgers, Princeton then had no colored. [They were] against the colored, intensely so. . . .

I remember what the [Princeton University] students used to do, because for the bonfire, the victory bonfire, they'd come down in our neighborhood and tear off our porch to burn up for their bonfire. They'd come down and steal everything for their bonfires. They were terrible.

And we had a curfew just for that reason. You'd see us running. Mr. Kilfoyle'd go, "Run Emmie, run!" And that curfew bell would ring. That was for nine o'clock. Sometimes, you know, in the early spring, it was still kind of light. Oh, no, they [the Princeton students] were terrors. A big circus came here once. I remember. And those students broke the circus up. They took their horses and ponies and everything else and put 'em over in the college.

The university has always dominated the town. Where the Community Park School is, and so forth, you see Taylor Pyne gave that lot back down there where the township hall is, too. He gave that lot to the colored. 'Cause we had a colored YMCA where now the Community House is. But the university didn't want it then, and so they persuaded some of our folks who just didn't have enough brains to see what was going on, when the old "Y" burned down, to let them put a community house which would be more "modern." I said, "but then we'll lose the ground" because Taylor Pyne said that when this cannot be used, the colored YMCA, it reverts to the college. So when they put the Community House up, it belonged to the community and then we lost this field. Negroes have owned a lot of things here. We were all over town. This was all there down on Palmer Square—all these houses. It was very funny because the paper said that there was a slum. And I said, "Isn't that funny? They just move the houses and it's not a slum." . . . When they were talking about housing for lower-income people, [the mayor] said that, well, they didn't have to worry about Princeton 'cause Princeton just took care of its own. That, to me, was a joke. 'Cause they didn't take care of their own then, and they certainly aren't doing it now.

The university isn't what it used to be, I must admit. But that's one good thing. We do have some new commissions that we had to fight. How far it will go. And we do have some wealthy people that go along with us, from the other races. I think if anybody had told me just five years ago we'd have a colored mayor in town I think I'd knock him down. I'd be so disgusted with him. But here it is.

Robert Rivers (1931–)

The town of Princeton and the university were always pretty much joined at the hip. Service people that worked at the university lived in the community across Nassau Street. It was pretty hard to separate one from the other. You can do it now, but in those days, a lot of blacks worked over there, and they were really desirable jobs considering what was available. I thought they were pretty honorable jobs. Take, for example, all those folks that worked over on the Avenue, for all the clubs on Prospect Street. Most folks really prized when they got jobs over there as doormen, or janitors, or whatever.

Another thing that tells you a little bit about some of the bridging that was going on is that there was a bit of a thing buzzing on campus about why don't we have black students here. And one of the ones who really kicked that off was Frank Broderick, who was the editor of the *Princetonian*. He was also the director at Princeton Summer Camp at Blairstown. And they were bringing the kids from Dorothea House and the Italian kids and everybody else to the camp, but they wouldn't take the black kids there. And this was run by the Student Christian Association. So they agreed to do something experimental and have a bunch of us go up there.

That gave you another side of Princeton. The camp was run by students and all the counselors were students. My counselor was a fellow named Lou Baglioli, and he was a football quarterback. I felt the camp was a great place. That first summer, out of the blue, something I never expected or tried to get or anything else—I was named the best camper. I think that probably impacted me as much as anything. I didn't even know there was a best camper. I still have the glove. I know the building's been torn down now, but I know what table I was sitting at when I got it. It was just the most shocking thing that had ever happened to me. I said, "Well, gee whiz.

Something's got to be good about Princeton." From then on, there was a whole series of blacks that won best camper. Buster [Clyde Thomas] was one of them, amd Robert Burrell was another one. Also Ronald Taylor, who went to Harvard Dental School. I have a long history of being there. I went back as camp doctor, and then I missed a few times and came back again. I'm on the board there now.

My first year at Princeton University, I lived at home. The reasons why I chose Princeton included that I was offered a job and a scholarship. And I also had places to eat, including Princeton's McCosh Infirmary where my aunts, Bessie and Mabel Hillian, prepared the food. Considering cost, it was probably the best option I had for continuing my education. I may have been one of the few students who never ate a meal in the Commons. That was probably one more reason why I never really bonded with the student community. That club system was so dominant then. People very quickly went off to their pigeonholes, and there wasn't really an awful lot of ways to interact.

The shot across the bow for me was bicker. I didn't like the system. I mean, I'd worked parties at the Tiger Inn on weekends for several years before I went to Princeton. I shoveled coal at Dial Lodge when they closed down during the war. I just didn't feel like I would be too comfortable there, with the people I knew from the community. It was an exclusive system, and I just didn't like exclusive systems. I picked a club, the Terrace Club. I didn't know anybody working there and I was admitted. Then the governing board decided that I shouldn't be a member of the club. The student president of the club resigned because of that decision. Years later, I finally obtained a more complete story about the ugly behavior that took place back in 1951. But the thing that really bothered me was that I had classmates that went into that club with me. Near as I could remember, nobody came to me to talk to me. Nobody from the administration came to talk to me and say, "Hey, something's wrong here."

I remember when Walter White, the executive for NAACP, came here in about 1947, students pelted him with snowballs. I don't remember reading anything about anybody apologizing or whatever, but those things happened. So I went through the social scene at Princeton with my antenna way up in the air. I probably had a wall that was too high for me, and it

The Hill House on Green Street (1914).
Booker T. Washington is fourth from the right on the front row.

probably had a lot to do with the fact that I really had not developed a congenial bond with that class. The only social thing I did was my job. I worked for four years at the Student Center at Murray-Dodge Hall. I got to eat over there too. I got to know some people that came through there and worked with them.

I would have to say that my academic experience over there was excellent. I don't know what it is to have drugs and be on a high, but I really just felt that there. I had an appreciation of music because of these crazy things I had done—organ, piano, trombone, and the rest of it. I took a couple music courses with Edward Cohn. That sort of lit my fire, because I got an A in one and an A+ in another. I think I got too brave because then I took a composition course with Milton Babbitt, who has gone on to be very famous. He turned me on, but let me tell you, I decided that I was not a composer.

When I got into my area, the science area, Aurin Chase is one that I remember that was very supportive. And I wrote my thesis for Elmer Butler. The experience of doing a thesis is the height of whatever Princeton is all about. Mine was about growth and development. I became an associate member of a scientific research honorary society (Sigma Xi). There was never any friction that amounted to anything. I never had a feeling that some white professor was going to lay it on me. The faculty was sort of apathetic about blacks, but they were supportive more than nonsupportive. At that time, all the students had their grades posted in Alexander Hall. And for me that was a plus, because I knew what the other students were doing. And they knew what I was doing, so they couldn't tell me I was coming in the back door.

Romus Broadway (1939–)

Princeton University has always been viewed, at least to my knowledge, as not antagonistic, but not a voluntary participant in leveling the playing field. As a matter of fact, what the university may have done may have been more destructive in terms of employment at the clubs. When you finished high school, there were jobs waiting for you as a waiter or a dishwasher or a cook, but not as a student.

Arthur Lewis (1931–2013)

My cousin, Andrew Hatcher, he was secretary to John Kennedy. He grew up on John Street. Some of the fellows around his age who grew up here were clamoring to get into Princeton University, which was turning them down. The first blacks eventually came in through the V-12 program in the military. I felt so good about that. You could go on that campus and see some faces of color. There was one of the fellows who came, his name was Mel Merchison, he was a football player. I remember when he got discharged and he didn't stay and graduate. Some people told him, "Why don't you go back to Virginia and go to school?" That was the story I always heard. Only John Leroy Howard, Pete [Arthur Jewell] Wilson, and Jim [James Everett] Ward graduated. Pete told me that when we was getting discharged from the navy, that they asked him to stay for basketball and he said that there was no way he was going to stay on the campus as the only black person. So he told them that if they gave Jim Moore the same kind of scholarship they have given him, he would consent to staying. And so he did. When we were growing up, Pete Wilson was our Michael Jordan.

Burnett Griggs (1888–1977)

Mr. Woodrow Wilson was a different type of man. I remember Mr. Woodrow Wilson when he was president of the university. A poor man couldn't approach him, let's say. Princeton was really a rich man's school then. Most of the students that came here, their families were wealthy people. There was a man named Sport Moore, he handled secondhand clothes, you know; he'd buy students' clothes. I've known students tell their parents they wanted a suit or something, and the parents would send them the suit, and the best of suits—Brooks Brothers and all those big men furnishing stores in New York—and by George, they never wore it. They'd take it and hock it to Sport Moore for little or nothing and go into New York for the weekend. I had some very good friends among the students at the club. I think Princeton at that time drew largely from the better class of people from the South; most of 'em were Southern boys.

I've seen tremendous progress in Princeton. The biggest change since I first came here is the students—Negro students in the university. You have Negroes on the faculty, and that was unheard-of when I came here. They have Negroes in these banks now; they have jobs that they never held before. So, I think there's been progress. Of course, it's never fast enough. I don't know why I should say that, but . . . I never went to any college or never even finished grammar school, but I would always like to think of Princeton as being a man's institution. I never favored having girls here, but it seems to be the trend everywhere now; they're all co-ed. So, "Time marches on." I'm just an old-timer, I guess.

Eric Craig (1934–)

My father never discussed racism unless it came up in the conversation with my mother, not with us. But one of my father's favorite words was "cracker." He'd come home from the club and count out his tips, saying, "Goddamn crackers, Goddamn crackers." I've been in the Cap and Gown where he worked—I was probably running an errand—but I never spent much time there. I can't recall any incidents in the clubs, but the clubs are fantastic architecturally . . . the street is gorgeous; you'd think you were in another world. My dad would bring home these cans of food and that's how we had food on many occasions and the best, because they ate the best of food. It came from the best of butcher shops, the meat, the vegetables, and that was a good help to a lot of families.

Jay Craig (1930–)

My dad was a waiter, and he worked in the most exclusive clubs on the East Coast. He worked in one of the most exclusive clubs in Charleston for quite a few years. My mother went down to meet him once, to come back with him. And they were sitting in the Jim Crow car, and that is when this conductor came up and told my father that he didn't have to sit there in the segregated car, because my father looked white. I think his father was white, and his mother was Native American. And I think my father said, "This is my wife, and I'll sit where I want to sit."

I've spoken to my own kids more about racism than my parents spoke to me. But I could *see* racism in Princeton. We would go into Princeton University on the campus. I can remember the occasion of being asked what I was doing there. I will never forget these words: "You have a place." It was one of those cracker proctors at Princeton University, who said, "You have a place to play downtown," while my white contemporaries were playing right next to me on the lawn with a ball.

Jacqui Swain (1944–)

Princeton University used to run these ads where they needed help. I would come over and apply for a job after I graduated from Rider. But they were always full. They finally found a job for me, washing glassware and tending animals down in [the] Biochemistry [Department]. I did this because the League of Women Voters wanted to show the university some of the racist practices they had. But strangely enough, one afternoon I suddenly was miraculously moved from the laboratory washing the glassware to the office.

And I decided that someone finally figured out that this was part of a civil rights exposé.

The League of Women Voters and the Princeton Human Rights Commission wanted to expose realtors, barbers, beauticians, eating establishments, doctors, just all sorts of prejudice in the town. And they wanted to do it in such a way that Princeton couldn't cover it up, nobody could cover it up that you had to do twice as much work as the next person, and make half or a quarter of the money.

I came back to the Woodrow Wilson School, and Lord knows, it was the School of Public and International Affairs, and these folks couldn't deal with folks in their own community. I was the only black secretary. I integrated the school. There were a couple of black janitors. I remember being called by the librarian. She wanted to notify me that somebody had barfed in one of the carrels. I didn't quite understand what she wanted me to do about it. And she said, "But you don't understand. He just threw up all over the place." And I said, "I don't know what you think I can do about it." So she had to back down.

Then, oh, just crazy assumptions. I was in the elevator one day, and someone got on and they had a tray with all this trash on it. As I was going back down, they tried to put the tray in my hand. Needless to say, the tray went all over the place. My alertness at Woodrow Wilson School became number one. I learned that politicians have the best knack of being very subtle about the things they expect that you're going to do, especially if you're African American.

There was a gentleman here who asked if I could help with a Fulbright conference. It was summer, I didn't have a whole lot to do. So I did the work, and I had to do it from home because there was so much. So the day of the conference, the man from the office came to pick up the conference materials and I said, "Now who's going to pay me?" It hadn't dawned on him that somebody would have to pay me. Then he whipped, leapt into this thing like I was a fool. "Well, do you realize how important Fulbright is? Now, can you imagine that the university is going to be embarrassed in the face of the world if this conference doesn't happen?"

I said, "Well, I'll tell you what. You're just going to be embarrassed in the face of the world." He wanted to strong-arm me, but I was married then, and my husband came out of the dining room. So this guy said, "Oh,

I'll give you my personal check." So my husband said, "Just have a seat, my man, because you are not taking out of this house until I come back here with my wife's money." And he went to the bank and cashed the check. Because in our hearts we knew that this man was going to cancel payment on that check.

Another time, I was over at a party in Maclean House and someone very influential kept telling me about a sandwich that he had dropped on the floor. Finally, I went to the kitchen because I knew the caterer. And the man came into the kitchen, and he was belligerent about the fact that the sandwich was being ground into the very, very expensive Oriental rug. One of the caterers said, "Do you know these people would literally perish in their own filth if we weren't around here to clean it up?" It's little things like this.

So Princeton is my home, but I see it very differently than folks who were born in Princeton, grew up in Princeton, went to school in Princeton, married in Princeton, had children in Princeton. Part of having had a marvelous life is having had this duality of not going to school here, and only living here part-time, and then coming back, and being totally immersed and actually knowing what I'm being totally immersed into.

Joe Moore (1941–)

In December 1968, I got a call from a guy named Bob Goheen. He was president of Princeton University. It was right after Thanksgiving 1968. Fact of the matter, I'd just gotten married that August. He said, "Joe?" I said, "Yes, Dr." The reason why we were personable was because his oldest daughter, Elizabeth, and I were classmates at Princeton High together. And I had been over to his house several times. So he knew me. He said, "We need a minority dean at Princeton, and everything I hear about you and your work is exemplary. So I would like to offer you a deanship at Princeton." I hang up the phone and I said, "Whoa!" So I go and I say to my dad, "Daddy, guess what?" I say, "I was offered a position at Princeton." And my father says, "That's a plantation, son. Why would you want to work there?" You have to remember, my father is now retired. He had spent forty-three years as a groundskeeper cutting grass, clipping the hedges, and making sure people didn't slip on the snow when it snowed. He didn't tell me not to do it, but he just reminded me of his experience and what his perception was. Eventually, I said yes, I would do it. I started Princeton on March 10, 1969, as the assistant dean of students. Neil Rudenstine, who is now president of Harvard, was the dean of students.

That was the beginning, the advent of increased minority enrollment at Princeton. The university was full of tension at this time, because there was a climate in which change was taking place. It was a critical time in the university's history. The minority students were looking for a way to express themselves creatively, both inside and outside the classroom. A lot of the black students were really intimidated by the environment. Although they had the ability, they weren't very comfortable there. So I spent a lot of time, in addition to putting out brushfires, encouraging students, particularly minority students, to hang in there, and providing support for them to make it through.

I was also concerned that we do something in a larger place, in terms of the university's acknowledgment of the culture of the minority students. One was the need for the black students to work within the black community and have some meaningful relationships with families within the black community. I supported the development of Harambi House Players, which was a cultural and theatrical expression on the part of minority students at Princeton.

I also designed and made a presentation to the board of trustees for the Third World Center. Most people don't realize that. But the Third World Center was my administrative response to the need for Princeton to address the minority issue. But instead of calling it—on other campuses, you have a black center—we called it the Third World Center. And the university acknowledged it from that point. I couldn't go to the university and say, "I want to have a black center." A guy named Conrad Snowden and myself went to New York one day, and I think we put it together over four glasses of Jack Daniel's. We came back and presented it to the university. We were invited by the board of trustees to make the presentation. That's very rare, because the board of trustees very rarely allows anybody outside of the board to come to their meetings. During that period, black students, in their concern for the black community, created something called the Community House Program, to come across town and work with the youngsters in the community.

The deans at the university used to rotate positions. We didn't do the same thing every year. And the first year, I did student organizations and room assignments. And you know how difficult that is, right? So I made the room assignments for the incoming freshmen. And I had this white kid from Florida living with this black guy—I think he was from the South, too. But it was a threesome, so there was a third kid. It was freshman week and the third kid hadn't shown up yet. When he did, I get this call from security. "Dean Moore, Dean Moore, we have a problem." He gave me the phone, and I talked to the father. I said, "You have a problem?" He said, "Yeah. My son is not living with this nigger. There's no way."

I said, "Excuse me?" Then I went over to the room, and the father says again, "He's not living—not living with this nigger. I am not leaving this university until he gets another room. I called the dean."

I said, "You're not getting another room." He said, "Who are you?!"

"Hi, I'm Dean Moore. You remember?"

He says, "I'm not leaving. I demand to see the president."

A few days later, President Goheen calls me up and says, "Joe, I just wanted you to know I said if they didn't like this living arrangement, they could take their son out of here." I said, "Thanks for your support."

Leonard Rivers (1934–)

My father worked in Tiger Inn, oh thirty-five, forty years. My brother and I, when we were kids, used to go over with him in the summertime and cut the grass and do all the rest of that stuff. During house party weekends, we'd go over there early Sunday morning to help him wash glasses and clean up the bar. When he retired there was no pension, nothing.

Before my father passed away, one of my nephews belonged to Tiger Inn. Well, some of the old alums, when they found out my father was terminally ill, they invited him over for a dinner and presented him with some things and stuff like that. Well, I walked in the front door with my mother and father. And I felt funny walking in the front door of the place. I mean, it's a conditioned reflex: "I don't belong walking in the front door. Let me go around the side and go in the kitchen."

Robert Rivers (1931–)

Another reason for going to Princeton was that I wanted to see at close hand how these national leaders worked, how they act, how they behave, what kind of things they have to deal with. I had to deal with different kinds of people all my life. I really did. So you have to learn not to be afraid of them. You have to learn what their strengths are. There are good people and there are some that are not so good. You learn to work with the good ones and deal with the bad ones. That was part of the thing that I learned at Princeton.

On the other hand, when I finished Princeton, I was ready to leave the country. Socially, it hadn't been comfortable, and it wasn't just Princeton. It was the times. I was just tired of being around a place where I couldn't go to a restaurant and I couldn't swim in a swimming pool or do things. You couldn't buy a house—all kinds of stuff was going on. This whole business of segregation and discrimination—I couldn't resolve that in my mind. I couldn't figure what the problem was. I think it was a lot of different reasons that people bought into segregation and discrimination. Some of it was a selfish thing about job competition. Another side of it had to do with not wanting black guys around white women and all that. A whole bunch of people thought that blacks—however you define a race, which they're having an awful lot of trouble with these days—are more stupid than somebody else. There were people that actually felt they were superior.

After I left Princeton, I was just tired of holding the antenna up and living in a sort of phony situation and performing all the time. I wanted to go to medical school, and the first thing I thought about was Dr. Charles Drew, who set up a plasma program at Columbia during World War II, but they wouldn't take his blood because he was African American. Anyway, he had trained at McGill, and my intention was to go to McGill University [in Canada] just to get away from all this nonsense. At that time, Canada was thought to be a place that was liberal and all the rest of it.

I applied to a bunch of other schools—you have to remember that there weren't many medical schools open at that time. The medical schools in the South were not admitting blacks. We're talking about 1953 here. In the fifties, they were still lynching people. For some reason, I didn't apply to Harvard. I think I was admitted to all the schools in this country I applied to,

Robert J. Rivers, graduate, Princeton
University class of 1953

including Northwestern and Rochester. But not McGill—the only school I didn't get into. I was crushed. So I'm all set to go to the University of Rochester, when out of the blue I get a call from E. Lang Makrauer, a Princeton alumnus from the class of 1923. He said, "Would you like to go to Harvard?" I said, "I really hadn't thought about it."

He flew me up to Boston—it was the first time I'd been on an airplane. I met Dr. Hinton—he was the one who developed the big test for syphilis—and he was a black faculty member. The thing that astounded me when I went up there was that it wasn't like I was busting in on anything. I said, "They're treating me a like a human being. I'm here because they want me to come here." And so I went to Harvard. I met a lot of good folks there. Harvard was a good experience; I just felt warm there. . . . In medical school, you know, you're always concerned about what if you have white patients or black patients, and whether you're going to have problems—but I never had any problems with patients. And that was a good feeling.

A lot of blacks that graduated, even from the Ivy schools, had difficulty finding jobs. When I courted my wife, I remember getting on a ferry boat going across to Norfolk and they still had the "Colored Only" signs where you could drink or go to the bathroom. That must have been somewhere around 1957. We got married in 1958.

When I went into medicine I was always concerned about what kind of practice I would have and what kind of impact I could have on whatever community I served in. I kept asking myself, if I came to Princeton and practiced, could I practice the kind of medicine I wanted to? This was when the town was still divided. So I kept looking for a way to come back to New Jersey. I actually did my public health paper on Princeton's health facility. I came down here and went through Princeton's hospital and spent quite a bit of time. One of the things I looked for when I did the survey was to see how many black physicians and nurses there were—but obviously, they didn't have them. Somehow I [didn't] feel comfortable that I could do, without severe limitations, what I wanted to do in Jersey. Blacks couldn't find houses; black doctors weren't allowed in the hospitals—they wouldn't give them privileges. In a way, I've regretted it, but I just didn't feel I could grow here.

I'd gone through this phase where I really wasn't that happy about Princeton. But I started to become more positive about Princeton in the sixties, when Robert Goheen became president and Carl Fields appeared on campus. Goheen was very courageous for some of the things he did. He got me involved—I was actually one of the first board members on the Association for Black Princeton Alumni. After Martin Luther King [Jr.]'s assassination, everybody started to move—I don't know where they thought all these talented blacks were before this, but everybody was interested. . . . Before I knew it, I was on the board of trustees. That was 1969.

Those first four years, I was down in Princeton all the time. It was an exciting time. I loved coming down here and talking to all these wild students about what they were upset about. I'd never really felt a strong bond up until that point with the university. But I felt it was great just to be a part of all that. Not only were blacks coming on the board and coming into the university in greater numbers, but women were coming in, too. It was the first board I'd been on where there was a wide range—young ones were coming on, and you had all this mix of people, this diversity. You had all these different ideas and people respected it. Those folks were just class, class folks. It was just amazing to me how the bottom line was not, "What's in it for my constituency?" but, "What can we do for Princeton?" Compared to some of these folks on the board, who was I? But they listened to me. I really enjoyed those eight years, and I think that's what really tied me into Princeton, although there were still problems.

5

—

Every Day,
You Work
to Survive

Princeton Rug Washing and Carpet Cleaning Works,
23 John Street (about 1925)

THROUGH MANY GENERATIONS, CHILDREN in the Witherspoon neighborhood learned how to work and work hard. They saw their grandparents and parents doing whatever was necessary, and they, too, pitched in to help with jobs and tasks that needed to be done. As they matured, they learned that when any crack appeared in the facade that barred them from meaningful, intellectually satisfying work, they had to seize the moment. If they managed to squeeze through the cracks, however, they faced continuing challenges from whites who had been culturally trained to look down on black people as less capable, less intelligent, perhaps menacing, and less worthy of a living wage than they themselves were.

Up until the 1970s, African Americans who persisted through discriminatory obstacles to earn higher degrees more often than not found that the jobs available to them in Princeton as college graduates were indistinguishable from ones they could get as grade school dropouts. Whether they were engineers or artisans, carpenters, photographers, chemists, language teachers, economists, painters, mathematicians, inventors, or singers, they, along with everyone else in the neighborhood, most often had to take low-paying jobs unrelated to their capabilities or their interests.

These jobs were as housekeepers, valets, gardeners, janitors, butlers, cooks, drivers, bellhops, dishwashers, gardeners, and laundry workers. As longtime Princeton resident Kathleen Edwards said, "There were no opportunities then. I mean here we had people graduating from Tuskegee. I mean you got people graduating from Howard. What was they doing? Going over to the Avenue slingin' trash, or washin' dishes, or whatever have you. I mean, you got to live. . . . All these people who have worked, cooked, scrubbed floors, scrubbed venetian blinds, washed windows. They took those nickels and dimes and half-dollars and made those monies work, so that he went to school, she went to school, she had a new dress, he had a new pair of shoes. It might take a little time to get it, but they got it."[1]

In 1948, a senior thesis by James Whitehill Funk on "The Pattern of Negro Labor in Princeton" pointed out that Italians and Negroes filled janitorial jobs in Princeton, along with other "menial, unskilled and sometimes disagreeable jobs." The thesis stated that in February 1947, twenty-eight Negro janitors worked at Princeton University, which was "a significant change, in that before the war there were no Negro janitors employed."[2] Out of a total of sixty taxi drivers, only three blacks had been granted taxi licenses. Occupations beyond domestic service jobs open to African Americans included cooking, hauling, hack driving, truck driving, storage, and delivery. Small businesses employed blacks as stock clerks, cleaners, and helpers. Gas stations employed black attendants and lubrication men. "The coal companies' trucks use Negroes, while the oil trucks do not."[3] According to Funk, "In 1946, the telephone company hired its first Negro operator. Since then it has increased the number of Negro operators to seven." In all of Princeton, there were eleven barbershops, and three of them were owned and operated by Negroes. Out of seventeen beauty parlors in the town, ten were owned and operated by Negroes.[4]

In Princeton restaurants and clubs, African Americans got jobs as dishwashers, pantry men, bakers, butlers, coat-takers, stock clerks, or janitors, but not as hosts, hostesses, or top line waiters. In his thesis Funk advised, "An adequate idea of those unskilled laboring jobs may be quickly gained by seeking out the backrooms of stores; the kitchens about town; those drivers of trucks; the men behind the broom handles; and generally those men behind the scenes performing those jobs which are physically the hardest and least tasteful to the average worker."[5]

"That's the way Princeton was," says Leonard Rivers. "Despite all that, because of the type of community we lived in, in the John Witherspoon area, I mean, we survived it. . . . Back in those days, we were all in it together. When I say we were all in it together, I'll give you a good example. My mother worked as a sleep-in maid. My father worked three jobs. My father worked at the university and then he cleaned a couple of taprooms. . . . And for about thirty years he cleaned the taproom at Nassau Tavern. But come dinnertime, we sat down at the dinner table at six o'clock. And come Sunday, as a family, you go to church in the morning. And then the neighbors, when our parents were doing all this work, the community took care of us—Mrs. Sperling across the street, Mrs. Hill. . . . My father used to wait a lot of cocktail parties, and everybody in the community used to help him. My mother would take in somebody's ironing or do cleaning for somebody, aside from her regular job. That's the way the black community was in our childhood. And the amazing thing is, I never felt poor. None of us ever felt poor. We had each other, we had clean clothes, we had food, and we had everything else we needed."[6]

Back in the era after the Revolutionary War, when the neighborhood included nearly five hundred people,[7] there were even fewer opportunities for black residents. One of the best jobs was to work as a servant at the small college across the street. For each student they served, a servant was paid forty-four cents a month—or $4.40 for the ten-month session.[8] In the early hours of the morning, they started up the coal fires to warm each bedroom and filled pitchers with water. According to Thomas Jefferson Wertenbacker, the servants also had to "black the students' shoes and boots before breakfast, sweep every room and make up the beds before noon, to take the soiled linen into the dining room and then deliver it to the washerwomen, to ring the college bell and sound the rouser, to eject from Nassau Hall all vendors of apples, nuts, etc. They were permitted to earn an extra penny by running errands, provided they did not connive with the boys to break the regulations."[9]

At the turn of the twentieth century, the university, beginning its transformation from a small, rather insular college to a major university with more national and international clout, provided a growing number of jobs for African Americans. The town itself was attracting wealthy businessmen, financiers, and industrialists who built large mansions on their country estates and hired maids, butlers, cooks, caretakers, waiters, and drivers.[10]

More entrepreneurial opportunities also sprang up within the black community to provide needed services for residents and, sometimes, for students. Residents worked as carpenters, plumbers, seamstresses, stone masons, trash haulers, mechanics, and child caretakers. From Nassau Street to Birch Avenue, the active business community of the Witherspoon neighborhood provided car services, restaurants, taverns, grocery stores, convenience stores, liquor stores, a live chicken store, and clothing stores. William Moore, known as "Sport," had a successful business as the owner of a clothing and antique furniture store. He bought new and slightly used clothes from students for the cash they needed to finance their trips into New York and then sold them to residents.[11]

Black-owned businesses of the past and present are a source of pride in the neighborhood. The very first black-run business we know of in the neighborhood was owned by a free black entrepreneur named Cesar Trent, who purchased a lot on Witherspoon, just above Nassau Street, in 1792. Trent sold firewood, and later opened a confectionary store.[12] Many other black businesses have existed in this neighborhood, and though their numbers have shrunk in recent years, they still play a vital role in community life. "These businesses provided a safe, intimate atmosphere in which people of the community were afforded the opportunity to avoid the white-owned establishments uptown," writes Lauren Miller. "They also kept the community closely linked in daily interactions, which fostered a familiarity and closeness."[13]

Residents speak fondly of black businesses, like Mr. Ball's confectionery, which they frequented as children and adults; Miss Van's Ice Cream Parlor; the artist Rex Goreleigh's studio, where he gave art classes; Jimmy Mack's barbershop; and William Gale's Cleaners, which was the first black-owned dry cleaners in Princeton. They also recall Christine Moore Howell's beauty salon, called Christine's, with its interracial clientele; Andrew Teague's two ice companies; Dickerson's Funeral Parlor, owned by James Dickerson; and Barclay's Ice, Coal and Wood Plant, whose owner, George Barclay, was known as the "Singing Ice Man."[14]

Doris Burrell, who opened Burrell's Salon in 1944, said she was about thirteen years old when she started doing people's hair in the neighborhood. "On Sunday mornings I really was busy getting people ready for church. . . . On Saturdays, I'd walk all over town, doing people's hair for fifty cents. The job took me two hours and I charged fifty cents. That's when I knew what I wanted to do. . . . I wanted to someday own my own business and that's what I did. We've had wonderful experiences on Leigh Avenue. There's no two ways about it."[15] For many years, Fred Burrell, Doris's husband, also operated a florist shop out of their Leigh Avenue home.

Perhaps the best-known businessman in the history of the neighborhood was Burnett Griggs, who ran Griggs' Imperial Restaurant for forty-two years until he retired at eighty-three. "Out of all the people in my childhood, I remember Mr. Griggs and his wife especially well," said Hank Pannell. "They were like family. . . . Mrs. Griggs was my first grade teacher at Witherspoon School. She used to give us ice cream from the restaurant. I was very close with Mr. Griggs. He was the guy who taught me how to fish, and that's my passion." Griggs gave Pannell a hand-painted wooden sign that hangs in his house to this day. The sign reads:

God grant that I may live to fish until my dying day
And when it comes to my last cast, I then most humbly pray

When in the Lord's safe landing net I'm peacefully asleep
That in his mercy I be judged good enough to keep.

Griggs' Restaurant was huge, and black and white people ate there. "Everybody from Nassau Street ate lunch, breakfast, everything there," Pannell said. "He used to sell these great big hamburgers and they were thirty-five cents. We used to look forward to getting thirty-five cents so we could get those hamburgers. And if you didn't have thirty-five cents, you know, people took care of each other in those days."[16]

> Rich Princeton was white: the Negroes were there to do the work. . . .
> Under the caste system in Princeton the Negro, restricted to menial
> jobs at low pay and lacking any semblance of political rights or bar-
> gaining power, could hope not for justice but for charity. . . . From an
> early age, I had come to accept and follow a certain protective tactic
> of Negro life in America and did not fully break with the pattern
> until many years later. . . . Always show that you are grateful. (Even
> if what you have gained has been wrested away from unwilling pow-
> ers, be sure to be grateful lest "they" take it all away.) Above all, do
> nothing to give them cause to fear you.
> —PAUL ROBESON, *HERE I STAND*

Johnnie Dennis (1903–2007)

I came to Princeton to work. I was a young woman. I was in my teens. You had to go where they had jobs. You haven't read your history. You *had* to go. Read your history, because you went away to work when you could because that was after slavery time—nearly one hundred years ago. And I worked in Princeton all my life. Sometimes it's the washing and ironing, sometimes it's taking care of the children. Sometimes it's clean the yard, sometimes clean the house, sometimes do the cooking, and all like that. Somebody has to do it. I worked for different people—there's some of them living and some of them dead.

I worked for professors and lawyers and doctors—educated people, people who had better jobs than I did. Some were schoolteachers, mothers, fathers. I worked for families with children. Never got married but I raised up a lot of children, a lot of young people. Boys and girls, they grew up wonderful. You must've been to a blind school and raised in a blind world, because Princeton is open to everybody to see what they can learn from others right here. They don't have to go to college or see anything like that. Like I worked for doctors—I learned things from them—how to do for children. And I worked with the nurses—with people who were real trained nurses—I learned from them. Because when you're born in this world, from the time you can talk, you're learning. You can learn things from other folks, other people. You always have to have principles.

Nobody's born on a flowerbed. I remember living and work. You work every day you're living—every day to live, you work. You just do what you can. Learn what you learn, and you get your job. I had no significant mistreatment. Life goes on, you know. You got other things to think about. You took the hard bumps and did what you did and got over it. You like them, you just go ahead. If they don't like you, you can't help that.

I like—I love—everybody. And I never found nothing that one did so much special, so much for me that I have to like them special. They helped me. I've been to Washington, Massachusetts, I think Boston. They [my employers] traveled, a lot of them. And they didn't leave me behind. When a movie or anything come to Princeton that you hadn't seen, they made a way for you to see it—I'd go to see it. And Einstein was here. They didn't leave us behind. Well, they had different meetings with different things, people and all, but they just wanted to see what Einstein looked like.

People raise each other and we never suffer for anything. They was kind to me. They took you on. They taught you what they knew and you helped them. I didn't ask them for more education. I'd get an education from what they was telling, teaching me. When I was working, I was learning right then.

Sophie Hall Hinds (1875–1974)

So I know something, a little bit about farming because I had to do it. We had cows and geese and chickens. [From the time I was a young girl] I had to get up early in the morning and milk the cows before they went to pasture. I had to take the cattle to pasture and go after them at night. We slaughtered chickens and like that, but any big animals that had to be killed went to the slaughterhouse. There was a slaughterhouse here in Princeton near where the trolley used to come in.

People used to cut their ice from the pond. They had what you'd call springhouses. It must have been a stone thing built in the ground and closed up on top. You pushed back a door and went there and got your ice. And it stayed cold down there. And we used to make ice cream. That was a job every Sunday, and they had this old thing you'd turn, an ice-cream freezer. I had two ice-cream freezers.

Leonard Rivers (1934–)

When you were a kid, see, you got to understand, back in those days, there were restaurants on Nassau Street that black folks didn't go in. You didn't go into Balt; if you went into Balt, you'd better go in there and go to the bathroom and run out. There were other restaurants up there that didn't make any secret about the fact that, hey, you didn't belong up there. And they would tell you that, "You don't belong up here."

Thomas (Buddy) Phox (1920–2008)

We had discipline to survive. My father would say, "Okay, you can play sports, but you've still got responsibilities at home." My job was to keep the furnace supplied with coal. There were no questions asked, that was my *job*. My sisters, my brother—we all had jobs, and if they weren't done, you had to answer to *him*.

My mother, now she was very low-key—she hardly ever raised her voice. I don't think I ever heard my mother yell. She didn't have to. 'Cause when my father spoke, that was the law. But she, she was very soft-voiced, very sweet. Amazing, the things my mother used to do. She was a domestic, worked for a family that lived halfway to Trenton. Practically raised their three girls. She left in the mornings, then came home in the evening to cook our meals. She was a seamstress and made our clothes. She used an old foot pedal sewing machine, and it was my job to stand there and pump the machine. So after dinner, she'd sew, then she would have to make the bread for the next day in the coal stove. She cooked our breakfast then, too. We ate oatmeal

Phillip Diggs, first African American police officer
in the Borough of Princeton (1920)

like it was the only thing available 'cause you could make it the night before
and it'd be warm in the morning, so when you got up to go to school, you
just went in and got your bowl of oatmeal and you'd be out the door. And of
course she also made our lunches. How she could do all that, and still smile
and be pleasant, I just can't imagine . . . it's incredible.

Kathleen Edwards (1924–2000)

People did a lot of things here to survive. The younger ones don't realize it,
or they don't believe it. Because we said that the indignities and the hard-
ships that we went through, my children will not go through. You make

that promise to yourself. But then the only thing you had was the service. And it wasn't until the war came that we had a chance really to break out. Even the ones who became educated, you couldn't get out and go no place because there was nothing here. I remember vividly my girlfriend, Livy, she went through all this. She went to college and everything else, but what could she come home to? She had to go to Bammon's for a job. So when they left Princeton to take advantage of the economic opportunity, they didn't come back. What did they call this—"a one-horse town." See, our loss was the other towns' gain.

In spite of all the adversities and all the roadblocks put in [our] way, people have still excelled. And the ones who were putting us through those wringers, they cannot get it into their heads how come—because they could not survive that. Because they could not survive like we have under the circumstances. They would be up there in Twelve Sullivan Way, which is the crazy house, Trenton Psychiatric Hospital. But we have our sanity.

There are more opportunities now. But then, if there were opportunities, we just had no way of getting to them. See, we had no cars. And if we had cars, we had no gas to put in. And if we had gas to put in, then we didn't have any money for tires or the license. There was always something to stop you. But now we have been very fortunate enough to know that if you have the right education and motivation and everything else, the sky is the limit. Now every once in a while, you are going to run into those bigots, but that's life.

Alice Satterfield (1922–2010)

My mother taught at the school on Quarry Street, called the School for Coloreds at that time. She taught there, and then a few years later, the town fathers thought that my mother didn't know enough to teach here. So they wanted her to go south to teach and leave her family. My mother said no. She said, "No, I'm not leaving my children." There weren't that many kinds of jobs in those years that colored people could do, so she became a domestic. But she was a wonderful, beautiful Christian lady, and through the years, with the church and the community and the neighborhood, she got to know everyone around, white and colored.

James A. Carter, Negro Baseball League,
Newark Eagles (1949–50)

James A. Carter (1928–2000)

I played in the Negro League, and the name of the team was the Newark
Eagles. We had fellas like Larry Dobe, Monty Irvin. And we played different cities. We traveled a lot. It was all new to me because I was only
eighteen, and [it] was fun for me. It was a fun day. I lived in Princeton. I
commuted back and forth. Except when we went on, like, long trips, and I
just stayed in hotels like everybody else. I was eighteen, and I loved playing baseball. I loved playing all sports really, but I think baseball was my
favorite.

We did a lot of traveling by bus. Was no airplanes for us in those days, everything was by bus. Syracuse, Rochester, Albany, Jackson, Mississippi. You
know, places like that. Like I said, it was fun, and I met a lot of nice people.
Right now I still have contact with a couple of fellas from Elizabeth, and we

go around to different schools or to Shay Stadium and sign autographs for the kids, which is pretty neat.

Then after I got married I worked for the university. I kind of thought that the town people and the university got along pretty good. There's always room for improvement, but always we got along pretty good with the university and it got along pretty good with us. I worked in the boiler room where they make steam. I worked in the boiler room for eighteen years, that's where I retired from. You know where the hockey rink is? Right in back. So you walk right out the back door and into the rink. That's what I used to do in the afternoon shift, go and see a hockey game or whatever, and if there was a night game and we were on the night shift, that's what I'd do, go and watch a little bit of hockey. It was a job. The boiler room pay was a good pay. 'Course the only thing I didn't like about it, I had to go to work at twelve o'clock at night and work till eight o'clock in the morning, what they call the night shift. That was only maybe once a month. I had a lot to do. I had no regrets about it.

I've had a good life here, and I'm still having a good life here. Princeton is Princeton. That's the most I can say about it. It's had some changes. We've had our ups and downs in Princeton, and it's a nice town, nice town to grow up in. Nassau Street, I can remember, on a Sunday, it was kind of quiet on Sundays. But now on Sundays in Princeton on Nassau Street, it's like a little New York. In that way, it's been changed.

Florence Twyman (1916–2001)

My first job, my sister, the one who was four years older, got me, was as a domestic worker for a professor's wife. You had to do everything, including all the stuff that maids now don't do. I had to cook, feed and teach the kids, clean the house, and do anything I was told to do. I got thirty-five cents an hour, but if I worked fast, she'd pay me fifty cents. I had to wear what we called monkey suits to serve dinner in at night. My first job was live-in, and I stayed there until I got married. When I was married to my first husband, Walter Harris, I was walking home and saw a man in my room [in which she lived in her employer's house] looking through my things. My sister taught me you don't keep anything like nice clothes in the home of your employer. If they thought you were doing too well, they'd fire you; they didn't want you to have something. You know, "What do you think, you're too good to eat in the kitchen?"

There wasn't any public transportation then—you either walked or got picked up. Taxis were too expensive. Mostly you walked. If your employer picked you up, you had to sit in the backseat. And when you went to the house, you couldn't go in the front door. I bought a car—just a little old used one—after my first husband died, but the woman I worked for asked me not to park in front of her house. Because people'd think she had company, she said, but that wasn't the real reason. But you know, you really saw how other people lived. I saw things that—and most people do—were things that people didn't want known . . . whether people were getting along, if they were gonna get a divorce. We knew more about them than they ever knew about us; they don't get in our homes, but we get into theirs.

One day I was going to Sears, and there were a bunch of white women outside the door, all these women's lib people out there boycotting Sears. They didn't want me to go in there, but I told them, "I won't stop coming here until you liberate me from domestic work." It seemed to me that those were mostly women who didn't need help. They didn't help black women, they weren't fighting for women on the bottom of the totem pole, it didn't seem. But money follows money, and I guess you just got to fight your own battle.

Alice Satterfield (1922–2010)

In the summertime our schools would close and most times our parents would keep working. The girls would get together with their dolls and play. There used to be a grass growing—I haven't seen it for years. It had long leaves, and the roots were long, long roots. In the summertime, the girls who had dolls, we'd play with dolls, and those who didn't would go pick those weeds and pretend, fold it down and wrap it with a piece of cloth, and the long stems you'd braid and make into braids, and that was hair. The boys would find old wagon wheels and build wagons, and just have a good time playing baseball. We'd play hopscotch, and games like Tiddlywinks and pick-up sticks.

Helen Wooding and I were the best marble players goin'! We had that kind of fun and entertainment. How often today do you see kids playing Tiddlywinks, or jacks, or hopscotch? We saw a bit of sidewalk, we'd mark it off and play hopscotch or play baton ball on the street. We made our own fun. We didn't lack for anything in those days, in the way of making our own pleasure. We never locked doors, never had a key. We could go away for a week, go to school, go anywhere. You could go to a person's house and borrow things, and nobody said anything. That was all right. We didn't know about locking up. That's what bothers me today. Every time you step out the door, you gotta lock it up. Geez, well these times, you know, it's quite different than it was fifty years ago, quite different. Everything is material [nowadays]. But those were happy days as far as I'm concerned. You always had some place to go and somebody to look after you. We didn't have a lot, like wealth, but we had love and we had caring.

Romus Broadway (1939–)

During high school, I washed dishes at the Tower Club. It was extremely difficult for African American youth to get jobs anywhere else but in a university kitchen. In fact, I cannot think of any other employment that was available for black youth. But you never saw any white kids working in those kitchens.

After high school, I went to the military in 1956. My first job out of the military was working in the Princeton Laboratory. They called me a technician, but that was a glorified term for "jack-of-all-trades." I worked there for four years and then became disenchanted, and I was forced to quit. And then I just decided that I didn't want to do anything else in Princeton. So in April of 1965, I packed up and started heading west. I ended up in Los Angeles about two weeks after the riots out there. Because of the climactic conditions, companies were pulling black men off the streets and offering them jobs. So I worked for American Airlines, and a year later, in 1966, transferred to Washington, DC. I worked with them a few years until I was involved in a motorcycle accident in 1969 that changed my career. I came back home for four years. While I was recovering, I worked in the Princeton community, trying to get my feet wet again. I then went to school, at the University of Massachusetts, in 1973. I graduated in 1978.

Live Chicken Store at Witherspoon and Spring Streets (1919)

While I was away, I always had the *Town Topics*, Princeton's local weekly newspaper, sent to me, so that I could maintain a link with the community. I really didn't miss much of what was going on. I had a sense of the changes, social and economic, that were taking place.

We were all aware [of discrimination]. We discussed the discriminatory practices of white people, and why we couldn't get jobs on Nassau Street. We all knew what the deal was, but we couldn't do anything about it. I think that it kept us on our toes.

At the same time, we all saw our mothers and fathers working equally. From what I saw there was no division of labor in the black community. I saw men cook, clean, and mop floors. I also saw black women go out and work with their husbands.

[I first noticed a change in the type of work] African Americans were getting about 1963–64. While I was employed by Pepsi-Cola, the company sent a guy out to recruit blacks. Around the same time, the university began to send out people to find qualified blacks for the trade unions. Before then, the only work available was on Prospect Avenue in kitchens and as janitors. Then in '63, things began to change. This lessening of discrimination in employment was probably triggered by the March on Washington or the Vietnam War.

In addition to the change in jobs available, I noticed a change in the income of African Americans. I remember when we worked for fifty dollars per week in 1960. I can remember my mother working for thirty-five dollars a week for years. She didn't make a hundred dollars per week until she was in her sixties. There were a lot of African Americans who did not make a hundred dollars a week until 1964. Another change was that more black women started going to college. Before the sixties, black women would usually get married straight out of high school. There weren't a lot who went to college. But during the sixties, you began to see more black women go to college.

The African American community could not blindly accept these changes and forget the difficult past at the same time. We always had faith that this change would occur. Even a little change, when compared to what black people have faced, was positive. I tell my nieces and nephews, though, that this isn't the end of change; it is only the start.

Lois Craig (1927–)

I took a commercial course at Princeton High School, which involved typing. I didn't have any problem. But some of the black kids that went ahead of me said that they weren't encouraged to take it at all. The teachers came right out and told them, "You know you are never going to be hired as a secretary, so why are you taking this course?"

When I came out of high school in 1945, I cleaned houses. I graduated when I was about seventeen, and I cleaned houses up until I was about twenty-five. And I was cleaning for a professor and his wife on Jefferson Road and they were getting ready to move away. And she knew that I had had a commercial while in high school, and she just also knew that I was fairly intelligent. They decided that they would get me a job at the university before they moved. And they set me up for an interview, and I was like maybe the third or fourth black at the university that went in as a secretary. Let's see, I say that was 1956, 1958, somewhere in there. And there were only like four of us. I was in the Registrar's Office. You know, when I first went to work at the university, everybody was saying, "You notice that every one of those girls that they picked were light." And that was true. [Before that] there were no black anything, besides the janitors over there. There were only men.

Let me tell you one interesting thing about the university while I was there working in the Registrar's Office and I keypunched. I keypunched every student that applied to Princeton, every student. And it was one day, one day was called "Negro Day." And that was the day they took all the blacks' applications; we were called Negroes then, all the applications. And that was the day they picked those that were coming, and they picked six or seven and threw the others away. And that was called "Negro Day" up until around 1970.

I left the university in 1968. I was offered a better job with a private company. At that time I was keypunching, which led right up to computers today. Eight years ago I retired from Princeton Bank & Trust Company on Nassau Street. That is still there. And then after I left there, I took a course in childcare. So then I worked in a private school, the Waldorf School of Princeton, as a nursery kindergarten teacher. And I did that for about nine years and I retired last June.

Doris Burrell (1919–2015)

I had teachers who really wanted me to be an artist. But hairdressing is art to me. When I graduated that's what I did. . . . I took a job doing housework and saved my money and then after a year, I enrolled in Simplex Beauty College in Newark, New Jersey.

I was twenty-five when I opened my shop in Princeton. I've been in business for fifty-six years. It's still in its original location at Twenty-One Leigh Avenue. There's a green canopy over the steps and it's called Burrell's Salon. I wanted to expand and get larger. I really wanted to go to Trenton, or Chicago, or some big city. But, we thought and thought about it. The important thing really was to raise the family. It was all right. I don't regret it, I really don't. . . . In a way, because it was so segregated, blacks really had a very wonderful social life here. There were so many things going on here. All kinds of clubs and things because we weren't able to branch out. . . . I really enjoyed that part a lot. . . . You see, human nature is like that. I mean, you want to live even though you might be segregated or confined in some way. You could be in jail, but you have to find what you're gonna do with your time while you're there, under these circumstances.

Arthur Lewis (1931–2013)

I can tell you an incident that stands out in my mind after I came out of high school. My senior year I took the post office exam and got the number one score you can get. And I went up to the post office and I talked to Charlie Murray, he was the postmaster at the time, and he told me that they wanted me to start working the fifth day of July, 1949. When I got there, they told me that [I was] going to be a carrier. I said, "Well, I signed up to be a clerk." Four blacks passed the exam. They were all made carriers. Three whites passed the exam. They were all made clerks. Two of the whites wanted to be carriers, but they would not change. So I went up to New Brunswick to sign up for classes at Rutgers, and I made the mistake of saying something to the superintendent of mail that I would be going to college in the nighttime. The next day he told me that he changed my schedule. I didn't get off till 8:30 at night. I still started at 5:30 in the morning, but I was getting off at 8:30 at night. What it was is they were trying to keep me from getting an education.

And then during the Christmas holidays, I was driving a mail truck, and the truck broke down right in front of 144 Mercer Street. So I locked the truck up and walked to the door of this house and knocked. The lady came out and said, "Let me get the phone so you can call the post office." She had a long cord on the phone and she brought it to the door. I didn't want to go too far from the truck. They said they would send another truck over. They said, "Okay, we'll take all the mail from your truck and we'll call down to Floron Johnson's Garage and have them come pick the truck up." The next morning, when the superintendent of mail came in, he told me I wasn't going on my route that day. He was switching my job. Probably a couple weeks later, I got a letter in the mail at home saying I was being terminated on the 29th of December because I had abandoned government property. I left the truck unattended. Now these same fellows who told me to leave the truck and take the mail out and whatnot, they didn't come to my defense.

Sophie Hall Hinds (1875–1974)

My father worked for twenty-five years in a grocery store up on Nassau Street in Princeton. He ran groceries for a while and then after a while he became clerk in the store and they depended on him a lot, 'cause if they wanted the truth, they could get it out of him. The store ran from about seven in the morning 'til about eight or nine at night. He didn't have all this fun time to play around in. If you worked you *worked* in them days and times.

And another thing my father used to do is put out the lights on the streetlamps. We had oil lamps in those days and times and some man used to go around and light the lights and when it come dark enough, on my father's way coming home he would put those lights out on Nassau Street. People might pick up their groceries on a Saturday night because they wouldn't have much time during the day. And he was the janitor of the white Methodist church here on Vandeventer Avenue and Nassau for about twenty-five years. And there was other work he done before he got those positions.

Hank Pannell (1939–)

My grandmother died when I was twelve, and my mother sold the house on Jackson Street and we moved to Clay Street. When I was a sophomore in high school, my mother passed away. She had a tumor of the brain. I don't know what we would have done without the help of the community.

I was like the head of the household. At home, I cooked. My brothers cooked. My brothers and sister were each one a year behind me. All the neighbors just helped us immensely. People brought food to the house—and we were allowed to stay on Clay Street. We didn't lack for food or anything. I worked a night job at Mary Slee's restaurant for Phelan DeShield, who was a chef. His wife was one of my mother's best friends. I worked from 3:00 until 11:00 six nights a week to support my brothers and sister. I started out washing dishes, and I was assistant chef. There were a lot of times the chef wasn't in, and I'd take over. I had learned to cook from my grandmother. In the summers, I used to go away with the chef to work at camps, like Golden Chain was a camp right up in Blairstown. I would go up as his assistant chef. This was when I was sixteen. I couldn't be a counselor anymore since I was working then. And because I was working in the restaurant, Chef always made sure that the next meal was there for us.

My brother, Roderick—he's an artist—he had a job with Rex Goreleigh. He worked at his art school. Then he graduated high school and went on to the University of Southern Illinois-Carbondale. My other brother, Linwood, was sort of an adventurer. He went off to see the world. When he was sixteen or seventeen, he just decided to up and travel. He went to Europe. He didn't graduate from high school. I don't really know where he is right now. The last time I heard from him was eight or nine years ago. RoseMarie went on through school, got a job, got an apartment in Trenton, and then a year or so later, she married a gentleman from my mother's home in Maryland. She moved to Colton's Point, Maryland, and bought a house there. She passed away two years ago of cancer. She was really sick for eighteen months.

My father died after my mother, but he had sort of moved away when he and my mother separated. He and my Uncle John were both waiters, and my father used to go all over with a group of men to the shore and other places. Sometimes they worked at the Nassau Inn—but they were really popular.

They traveled all over. Later on, he found out my mother had died, and he moved to Trenton, and my sister lived with him for a while. Then she got her own apartment. He still worked with the same crew of professional waiters.

Burnett Griggs (1888–1977)

To tell you the truth, I would say that 70 percent of my business came from white people. There was a noted crew coach—I'm trying to think of his name—he coached at Penn, and out at Washington, and whenever he was going to New York to race Columbia, he'd call me up and tell me to arrange to have the crew stop here.

There was an Italian man who used to work in the university, and he used to come in the restaurant all the time. He had a daughter that was getting married, and he said they were having a few friends in and he wanted to know if I'd prepare something for them. And I asked him to give me an idea what he wanted and all. So I prepared it, and he came for it, and he said, "How much do I owe you?"

And I said, "Well, I'll tell you when you bring my dishes and things back."

And when he brought them back, I said, "How was it?" "Oh," he said, "just wonderful; everything was lovely."

I said, "Well, the bill is paid; you don't owe me anything more."

And I met him on Nassau Street one day (laughs) about a year ago, and he brought that up. He said, "People don't do those kind of things for you." But I was never afraid to do something for someone 'cause that's been my life, and people have been wonderful to me.

So many people are afraid to do something for someone; I never was. And you know, that's the best advertisement in the world—the cheapest advertisement. I don't know what those meals cost me to make, but I'll bet you I got ten times their value for what it cost me. Because when you do things like that, people talk about it. I never was afraid to do things for people because Princeton has been wonderful to me. I tell people, "All that I am and all that I ever hope to be I owe to Princeton." I love it.

When I opened my restaurant, Du Pres had a restaurant up on Nassau Street. And I remember when the Baltimore opened up here. And Renwick used to be big, but I couldn't tell you very much about that, because

I never was in there. You see, years ago the lines were pretty strictly drawn in Princeton, and I never went where I wasn't wanted. I don't like to spend money that well, and I won't give it to someone that don't want it.

I remember when the Balt used to be up on Nassau Street. Balt-i-more; that's why they called it the Balt. I remember when they wouldn't serve Negroes in there. If you got anything, you had to wrap it up and bring it out. And during the war—the Second World War—a Negro officer came here and he went in there, and they refused to serve him. They wanted to wrap it up for him and he wouldn't do that. He sued them. That's what broke that up. He beat 'em. And then they started serving Negroes in there.

Eric Craig (1934–)

I worked for the borough, became a sewer inspector from '61 to '68. In '68 I went to the university, was a carpenter for thirty-one years and retired from the carpenter shop at Princeton University. That was a great job, I pretty much was a troubleshooter. On my own, single work orders, kitchens, bathrooms, cabinets.

There were campus carpenters and real estate carpenters, and I was the only African American in real estate. I think I might have been the second or third African American mechanic to enter the shop. There was a certain degree of prejudice. Little names called here and there, you would hear them mentioned in lunchrooms. We didn't get the promotions that some of us deserved. But you just had to get around that.

There was a little bit of the other way too. We used to work on space heaters; when they would blow out, we'd put the little parts in them. I don't think we really had any business doing that. But there was this black fellow, for some reason, hated white people. He rented in the Butler tract. So me and Joe Zuba went. Zuba knew more about the space heaters than I did. So we got to the house, but when he met us at the door, he said to me, "You can come in but your brother can't." And Joe didn't know what to do. So I had to straighten that out. I said, "Look," I said, "I want to tell you something. See, Zuba knows more about the space heaters than I really do, and if Zuba don't come in, see, you're gonna freeze tonight." And he hurried up and changed that tune.

Jacqui Swain (top) and the Rosebuds (about 1960).
Left to right: Joyce Gillette, Sonya Massey, and Jacqueline Beasly

Jacqui Swain (1944–)

While I was in college, I sang with a girl group called "The Rosebuds." We made a record called *Say You'll be Mine*. A gentleman named Buzz Taylor, he lives here in Princeton, taped it and on my fiftieth birthday, that's what he gave me. It was Joyce Gillette, Jackie Washington, Sonya Massey, and myself. We had the absolute best time. We sang with Jackie Wilson and Gene Chandler and just every girl group and boy group that was around. Some of the things we encountered were racist. You know, we'd go someplace where the white groups would get dressing rooms, and they put us in the basements with the beer kegs and hang up sheets and all for us to dress. But we had a ball; we just thought we were the cat's meow. We'd go on TV shows, we were on a TV show with Marvin Gaye and Tammy Terrell down in Baltimore.

We were called into community service, and when I think about this, it makes me shudder. We would perform on the back of these flatbed trucks that would go through the city of Newark at twilight, you know, to keep things jumping, to keep fires from breaking out, and keep people from rioting. And I think about it now, but Lord, we could've been shot off the back of those trucks. But we were young and skinny, and we wore these dresses sometimes that were suede. I think about that all the time. Here we are on the back of flatbed trucks, just carrying on. Now, suppose somebody had been so disgruntled and just didn't give a darn that it was a free concert or free entertainment through the streets of Newark that are still smoldering from the fires last night.

The First Baptist Church didn't have a choir that they wanted to go public, so the pastor asked that the four of us sing some gospel music. "The Rosebuds" now became "The Prince-Tones" and went to travel up and down the East Coast with Reverend Edward Smith. We built into another group called "The United Voices of Princeton," which was an integrated group. Goodness I love to sing.

Albert Hinds (1902–2006)

During my times, there wasn't any jobs open for people who were with education. Most anybody who had any, had to leave Princeton. Until, I guess, what was World War II, is when what little openings there have been for blacks perhaps started. But prior to that, I mean, anyone had to leave Princeton to accomplish whatever was their profession. Since then the doors have been opened wider than at that time, but before then, most the jobs were just built around service, both for men and women. Domestic, waiting, and at the clubs along Prospect Avenue, doing house service for wealthy people. Construction work. That was about all.

Jimmy Mack (1935–)

I had an uncle who had a barbershop in Philadelphia. I also had an uncle who opened a barbershop in 1937 called Mack's Sanitary Barbershop on Witherspoon Street. After I got discharged from the navy [in 1960], I planned on going to the Naval Yard in either San Diego or San Francisco, California. [My uncle] needed a barber and wanted me to work for a couple of weeks. I stayed in Princeton two weeks, then three weeks and finally, I never did make it to the airport. So I'm still here . . . In this business, I've met a lot of friends. All types of people. Ninety-nine percent of my clientele are good people. That 1 percent don't bother me.

Thomas (Buddy) Phox (1920–2008)

Well, about me. The first job I ever had was as a caddy at a golf course Princeton University owned. School'd get out and I used to go down there and make a dollar or so. But later on, I went to work at a dairy on Witherspoon Street. Milk was delivered every day in glass bottles then, so I used to get up at two in the morning, run my route, come back around 6:30, quarter to seven, then go to school. That would be a start for the day. When I was working for the dairy, no union was on, so you had to do everything. Oftentimes you'd come back and help wash the cans that all the local farmers brought their milk in. After high school, I worked there full time until 1942, when I went into the army.

I went back to work at the dairy after the war, but after a while I started thinking, "Gee, I gotta do something else with my life." I went to work at the General Motors in Trenton for about three years. One summer, they closed down for two weeks to take inventory. I was looking for part-time jobs then, and my wife had just answered an ad in the paper for secretary-type work for a small operation, a two-man film company that was just starting in Princeton. She got the job, and they wanted to know if I'd be willing to take the film to New York at the end of the day to get processed. So I said sure, great. At the end of the two week period, they said, "We like your attitude, we like you, and we like your wife. Would you be interested in coming to work with us?" [One of the filmmakers] said, "I can't pay you much, I'm sure not as much as you're getting at GM, but if you'd like to give us a chance, I think we'll grow."

So we talked it over and I decided I'd take a chance. The company was called OM Film, Inc., and it grew rapidly. We were taking on big contracts, and I learned a lot about film. Anything I had an opportunity to learn, I would take notes, and I became very interested in the film end of it. I had a chance to go to technical school under the GI Bill—so I went nights to the New York Technical Institute, which was on Grove Street in Newark. The company grew so much that they could no longer operate in Princeton, so they moved to New York. That meant I had to join the union there, so when I got there, the person at the desk goes, "What area do you want to concentrate on?" In film there are different responsibilities and categories, but I had always liked the lighting aspect, so I said, "I think I'd like to try for electrician." There were no black electricians in the union in New York. They tried to give me another area, but I said, "No, this is what I like. Type it up." My case was appealed, but eventually they had to let me in.

I became a member of the Directors' Guild of America, as an assistant director. I was one of the first African Americans to do that. I turned sixty-five, and I started getting a pension from them, but I kept working as a freelance electrician. That's right, I went back to my first love, which was lighting. I worked for ABC, CBS, NBC, and Channel 15, but mostly I worked for ABC on the *20/20* program. Used to light Barbara Walters. She had the kind of coloring and facial contours that needed a lot of film light. If you watch *20/20*, you'll notice there's a light under her chin. We had to fill that in. It took a while to light Barbara, and she's very fussy. She would only want certain people to work on her, and she would request that I light her. She's a real pain in the neck, but a very bright woman.

The hardest person I've ever had to light, I should say, the most impossible person was a woman who had almost like a double chin. When you're doing commercials, facial tightness is very important because you're really selling the product with the skin, the face. It took a long time to fill in all of those areas she had on her face—very funny-shaped face. It would take almost two and a half hours just to get her ready before we could let the hair person take over. After they would do that, they would sort of pull everything up and hold it into place, and hopefully it wouldn't sag before the camera came out. It's a lot of responsibility, being an assistant or lighting director, but it's also a lot of fun. When you see something materialize that you worked on, well, that's just something. Of course, sometimes I'd be sitting watching the end of the film to see the credits, and finally you see it and it moves so fast you can't read the names.

Oh to be eighteen again, and not even know what's coming in the next year. It's mind-boggling.

Kathleen Montgomery Edwards (1924–2000)

The loss of the black businesses has affected the community because we don't have a sense of community now. Mr. Griggs had a restaurant. That was a very, very profitable business, black-owned business. You passed the corner of Witherspoon and Hulfish Street—well, that corner belongs to Mr. Griggs. Mrs. Mills, she had a beauty shop. And Mr. Gale had a cleaning business. Right upstairs was Dr. Thomas. He was our dentist, and he was the school dentist. At Seventy Witherspoon Street there was a black beauty shop. That was the first black beauty shop uptown, even before Mr. Gale went up there. Christine [Moore] and Mrs. Mills opened up at the same time. You know that cigar place you see, right there before where the frame place used to be? You see a little door right there, if you aren't going past real fast. You look to your left and see a door. Right there was our first black doctor, Dr. Gibbs.

There was a lot of black enterprise. I remember the first corset that I bought out of my own money without going to the rummage sale, I bought out of Darrell Lewis's mother's house. Mrs. Lewis worked for the Clothesline, and naturally we couldn't go into the Clothesline to buy anything or try nothing on. But they would give all these clothes to Mrs. Lewis, and let her bring them down here into the black community. She would try them on, and size them, and sell them.

But we didn't turn around and support a black enterprise like we should. You can take that for what it is worth. Everything was borne out real fine, but we didn't support it. And a white person came right along and set up the same thing, and we would flock right to it. Just couldn't get anything done. You couldn't get anywhere. Like my father said, "If you owe a man seventy-five cents, he owns seventy-five cents of you. Don't owe anybody nothing, especially across the fence." He meant the white folks across the fence. Not just in Princeton but in the world at large.

Jay Craig (1930–)

When I graduated from Princeton High School, I knew I had to go out to work. College was never mentioned. I knew I had to get a job and have some money in my pocket. [Around that time] I had an incident at one of the clothing stores in Princeton. Basically it was a great clothing store, and a friend of mine told me about an ad for a job. He worked in the basement section of the store. . . . The ad in the paper said, "a chance of advancement." So I went up to see about the job, and I talked to the owner or general manager. I said, "Now if my work is satisfactory, it said in the paper, 'a chance of advancement.' I'd like to come upstairs and take a crack at selling." "Oh no, no, no, this is not about that," he said. So I said, "Then this was false advertising. You've probably seen the color of my skin, and when I mentioned coming upstairs, you said, 'No, no no.'" I said, "Well, no thank you for the job offer. No thank you. I know what's going on here." And I just left. As Cornel West said, race does matter in all things. . . .

My daughter Sydney and I went by ship from Montreal to Rotterdam in 1985, eleven days across the North Atlantic through the Saint Lawrence River, up through where we could see both the coasts of Newfoundland and Labrador. Oh, beautiful! And then when we broke through into the open Atlantic, icebergs galore, absolutely beautiful. There were a couple of people that we met on the crossing. One person, I could see what he was driving at. I said, "Sydney, sooner or later this fellow's going to ask me what I do for a living." He always looked so perplexed. We were only seven blacks out of seven hundred people on the ship. You'd get these stares. "What's he doing here, what's this guy do for a living, where's this money coming from?" So eventually he asked me, "Oh, by the way, what do you do for a living?" And I told him I work with the film industry. But actually I was here. And I don't know why I was ashamed to tell him that I was like a custodian or handyman or maintenance person. I shouldn't have been ashamed to tell him. But I said, "Oh, I work in the film industry," and let it pass at that. But he could see by the expression that I didn't like that, because he wasn't a friend. If it had been with friends that I have met, it would have been, "Oh, how are you? What do you do?" you know, but it wasn't that at all. I could see where he was coming from.

Quarry workers in the Old Quarry on Spruce Street (about 1890)

I've been asked by a couple of people here, millionaires, "How did you manage that?" going to Europe or wherever. And that didn't go over well with me at all. If I can do it, why don't you do it? I believe in working and living, and you believe in just working and amassing a fortune. That's your business, you know. I think the least paid and the least appreciated people in the United States are the hardest working people. One of the greatest myths in the United States is people of color being lazy, because people of color have worked harder throughout the years than white Americans have ever worked, and for far, far, far less money.

And along those lines, if you want to come right down to it, when we speak of affirmative action, there has always been affirmative action in the United States of America, unsung, unheralded, undocumented, unnamed affirmative action. The biggest beneficiaries of affirmative action in the United States have been white American males. No matter how stupid, they got the job. How else could Ronald Reagan ever become president of the United States? His qualifications were that he was over thirty-five, he was born in America, and he was white. And no matter all these superb, superior, intellectual African Americans who could not have obtained that position. But Ronald Reagan did. Richard Nixon did. And now George Bush Jr. I get swept up. I get emotional. And it does my stress no good, but nevertheless, I feel it. We feel it. African Americans feel it.

Hank Pannell (1939–)

I started working a long way before high school. As kids, we had all kinds of home jobs. There used to be a trolley that ran right down Witherspoon Street that delivered coal, and one of our jobs was to go along the trolley track, and if any coal had spilled over, we got it. We had a coal stove at home. We'd have to take the ashes out of the cellar. We sifted through the ashes with a screen and got the unburnt coal and took it back in the house. Another job was that we had to empty the tray from beneath the icebox—we had iceboxes then, not refrigerators. Lonnie Barclay, the singing iceman, used to wake everybody up in the morning. He'd be singing out there, delivering ice. We also had milk on the step every morning. The milk bottle had two parts to it. There was the cream up top. Mom or Grandmom took the cream off, and then you drank the milk. They used the cream for cooking.

When I was small, there was a lot of money to be made. I used to go over to the university and shine shoes at night for fifty cents. We had a lot of students; we'd knock on different dorm rooms. They usually gave us a dollar, so we made really good money. I guess there were a lot of rich students at that time. Also, they would have parties, and I used to wait tables and serve drinks at their parties. And football games—we made a lot of money there. One of our favorite things, Joe Moore, a good friend of mine, and myself used to rope off the entrance to this huge parking lot across from the back of Nassau Inn and charge anybody that wasn't from town three dollars to park there. All the townies we'd let in free, so nobody would bother us. We used to make a fortune. We had all kinds of little ways to make money in those days. I used the money to buy clothes, bikes, to save toward cars, and to help out at home.

Romus Broadway (1939–)

In the time that I have lived in the community, I have noticed many changes. One change has been the migration of people from Birch Avenue, which was full of Italians and blacks. Once the Italians moved out, they were replaced by African Americans. And now you have a trend of white people coming back into the community. On Birch Avenue, houses that were once inexpensive now sell for two hundred thousand dollars. If a house is sold, it is mostly a white person buying it. Most of the young blacks today are going elsewhere. Before the eighties, there was hardly a choice. Now there are choices.

I began photographing after I won a five-dollar camera during a crap game, shooting dice, in the military forty-five years ago. Now, I look at photography from the point of a social historian capturing a moment of Princeton, preserving it, and putting it on display. I am the main social history photographer in the community.

Photographs tell the stories, if you look at them over periods of time. I've got collages of people in the neighborhood from the fifties, sixties, and seventies. As a matter of fact, I now have a collage in a restaurant in Trenton. When children see their own parents on the collage, they are shocked. All of a sudden, they see their own parents as teenagers thirty years ago.

In total, I have probably photographed about 15,000 people. If I put all my collages together, there are probably about 2,000 or maybe 3,000 people depicted in them. Of those, there are probably only three names that I can't remember. When people see my photographs, I hope that they will think of preserving their own moments in time, for their children or for the community. Or for whatever use that might come from it. My collages also help show how much children in the neighborhood change when they come back.

My main focus now is capturing the neighborhood residents. That wasn't the initial intention, but that is what it has become. I have gone to nursery schools in Princeton for years, as well as church gatherings, and I have captured some of the only times that people have. So, actually, a lot of people hope that I come to these social gatherings with my camera. In particular, I get a very good feeling out of taking photographs of children.

Because other than those photographs taken in school, people have virtually no photographs of their children. There are still very few cameras in the neighborhood.

Rev. Judson M. Carter (1938–2009)

Mr. Pleasant Macon, my grandfather, and his brother were [among] the first African Americans to have a business here in Princeton. Mr. Macon was the first one to have a store down here on Leigh Avenue in the twenties. His store sold milk and eggs and was the first to have electricity. His brother George Macon was the first African American to have a taxi license in Princeton. Pleasant had a bar and a restaurant with a hotel upstairs because back in those days it was hard for blacks to rent a hotel or motel along the highway. Pleasant lived upstairs on top of the business so he didn't have to worry about paying rent. It took him almost twenty years to pay off his mortgage. He always told me, "I'll pay on the interest if I don't have anything." Back in those days they were determined. A man's word was his bond.

[My grandfather] also had a lot of pigs. He would have duck dinners and chicken dinners and the community would go over and support him. He moved out to Route 1 when it was a dirt road. When he had a Model T, he told me that I could go twenty miles an hour and [I] thought I was speeding. When they cut US 1 through his land, he had seven acres on one side and three on the other. He had a lot of opposition out there on Route 1 because nobody expected a black man to be out there. They put a jug handle around his place to try to discourage him, but he just stuck in there. My willpower and all my adrenaline come from him. He was a mentor to me. Maybe that's why I'm doing what I'm doing now.

My sister and I used to go out there every Saturday to help him get his truck and feed the pigs on the other side of the highway. Pleasant would get the food for the pigs over at the university. The clubs had garbage and we would use the truck and go get it. We had a bad snow one winter. There was about thirty or forty inches of snow that season. Pleasant called me up and said, "Would you bring some boys out and go over and feed the pigs in the pen." Everywhere we went we had to shovel because you couldn't walk in the snow. After we shoveled up US 1, we shoveled across US 1 in the southbound lane. Then we had to shovel inside where the pigs were—that was another five or six hundred feet. I'll never forget that. I think we are the only African Americans that ever shoveled across US 1. Amen.

6

A Neighborhood
under Siege

Baker's Alley, looking south toward Nassau Street (1925),
later displaced by Palmer Square

IMAGINE HOW IT WOULD feel if you were the offspring of enslaved people or free Negroes who had never been able to purchase land or own a home. And now you have done it. You own your own home on your own land. Your own refuge. Your own place to raise your children and build a family. It's been hard won—bought with your hardscrabble wages, which are radically less than what white people get for the same job—or built by yourself. Since you couldn't get a loan, you couldn't get a mortgage, you may well have constructed it paycheck to paycheck—with the help of relatives, friends, and neighbors.

This was the situation for many of the elders speaking in this book, as well as for their parents, grandparents, great-grandparents, and great-great-grandparents. Robert Walker Sinkler was one of them. He'd earned a degree in economics at Rutgers University but could only get work as a waiter. Later on, he became a full-time athletic trainer at Princeton University. But despite his steady work and his regular income, not one financial institution in Princeton would give him a loan since the vast majority of banks in America made a practice of not giving loans to African Americans. Even if you were a GI after World War II, you couldn't get the Veterans Authority (VA) to approve the Federal Housing Authority Loan (FHA) guarantees for a mortgage they consistently granted to white soldiers.[1]

From the 1930s to the 1960s, as some 15 million white families in the United States procured homes with FHA loans, black families in Princeton and in the rest of the country were excluded from those programs. Sinkler, like other blacks, had to make do. "He couldn't get any money from the bank," says his daughter, teacher and librarian Joyce Sinkler Robinson. "So over a number of years, he built his own house from scratch. He'd get the lumber and cement he needed [for that week], and then pay later. That's how he built the house."[2]

Many of the Witherspoon homeowners were the first in their families to actually own a home. Their homes provided sanctuary, but they always had to be defended from real estate expansion. Too often, the contests weren't fair. On a significant number of occasions, residents seemingly secure in their homes, strong and well built as they were, heard from officials that their houses had been condemned and would be taken from them. Again and again, the seizure of their Witherspoon properties were initiated for purposes of redevelopment, but labeled as part of an effort to clean up "urban blight."

Even murder was resorted to for a land grab. One such time was in 1899 in the Princeton area along Route 1, when a white man murdered his black neighbor after the black man had refused on several occasions to sell his land to him. An article in the *Trenton Times* said friends of the slain man were hoping the white prisoner would be charged with the highest degree of murder, while the white man ("quite cheerful in his conversations with the keepers") was sure that his claim of killing his neighbor in self-defense and in defense of his two brothers would allow him to get off on all charges, which it did.[3]

Of course, in the early years, most Witherspoon residents, not having the funds or the possibility of bank loans to buy their own homes, rented apartments or houses—many of which were owned by exploitive landlords, including Princeton University. An investigation of living conditions in the neighborhood early in the 1900s examined fifty-four rented dwellings where the greater part of Princeton's unskilled laboring population lived. The majority were university employees—cooks, domestics, and laborers—living in houses found to be decrepit. In forty-five instances, the roofs leaked. In thirty-one cases, there was water in the cellars. Cold, damp, poorly protected houses were shoddily built, dreadfully maintained, and unsanitary. A good number of them had no source of running water or, the study said, the condition of the toilets constituted a menace to good housing and sanitation. Thirty-six of the toilets were in the backyards of the houses. Some were on back porches, and eight of the houses had no toilets, so neighbors had to use the toilets of neighbors or shared toilets in sheds.[4]

The borough advised the university to build inexpensive but clean housing for its employees to avoid the health hazards, especially tuberculosis, caused by these poor conditions. The university's response: it fired its Negro employees and replaced them with Greek workers. The university said they'd brought in the Greeks, for whom they built "a commodious and clean building . . . to take the place of the Negroes."[5]

At the request of the Town Club, a social welfare organization in the community, graduate student Arthur Evans Wood began a new study of neighborhood housing that was published in 1920. Wood was informed by one of the landlords who owned a great deal of property in the neighborhood that the way to make money in Princeton was to "get a shack in the back part of town and rent it out to [Negroes]." Woods found that landlords, by charging high rents and neglecting needed repairs and maintenance, made as much as a 40 percent profit on each house.[6]

Woods urged that the board of health, sanitary inspector, and police should be responsible for inspecting housing and responding to complaints by the tenants, but he added that this might require "a greater degree of social intelligence than is possessed by the present Chief [of Police] who has the distinction of owning [and renting out] a dwelling which, for weeks, was found to be in a condition of intolerable filth."[7]

Woods had noted that the "high fences and hedges form[ed] effective barriers between this neighborhood and the west end of town where the best residences of Princeton are located."[8] The Witherspoon neighborhood may have been well hidden from sight, but that did not stop developers from wanting it. After the crash of the stock market in October 1929—which was especially devastating to the underpaid, underserved black community—the town of Princeton decided to enlarge the business district as a way to raise revenues. The expanded area would begin directly across Nassau Street from the university and eliminate several entire streets of mostly black housing.

Edgar Palmer, a 1903 Princeton graduate, formed a company to turn Nassau Street into an appealing business area that would enhance the student experience, and the powers involved pressured black residents to sell their homes. According to NAACP documents:

> It appears that the Negroes of Princeton all live in a very small area which is now being sought for business purposes as well as residential sites for whites. They are being offered, I am told, excellent prices for the property. They would be glad to sell if after selling it would be possible to purchase lots within the city, but it appears that they will not be able to do this. The only available site offered to them, they say, is five miles out of the city.[9]

From the 1920s to the 1960s, the neighborhood was progressively downsized and pushed back from Nassau Street by the expansion of Palmer Square. Over the protests of black residents, the Palmer Square Project fulfilled its objectives to clear the way for more commercial stores and restaurants.

The process had the effect of shifting dozens of African American families away from Nassau Street, making them more "invisible" in the community. . . . [R]e-settling African Americans from the Borough to the Township also diluted their ability to influence elections to demonstrate their dissatisfaction with what was happening to them. Although the original idea was that the newly relocated African Americans could ride the trolley down Witherspoon to work, the trolley in fact ended operations in 1931.[10]

Palmer purchased multiple lots along Nassau, houses on Baker's Alley, and also several lots on Birch Avenue. He decided which buildings should be retained, moved, or demolished. In the 1930s, he moved a row of African American homes (referred to as "rainbow houses" because they were different colors). Contractors literally picked up and moved the houses en masse to Birch Avenue on logs pulled by horses along the trolley tracks on Witherspoon.[11]

Housing continued to be an issue as the town grew, as veterans came home after World War II, and Princeton underwent an increase in its population. In the early 1950s, a low-income housing project, with garden-style, two-story structures with one to four bedrooms, was built with the aid of federal funds in the Witherspoon neighborhood. Property owners who were unwilling to negotiate with the Borough Housing Authority for their land faced hearings and likely condemnation.

On the legal basis of discrimination, black residents were able to stop certain "slum clearance" of "blighted areas" tied to redevelopment plans, but they lost other battles, including the urban renewal efforts of the 1960s that destroyed dozens of beautiful homes built by black residents on Jackson Street, which significantly diminished the size and integrity of the neighborhood.

In the late 1960s, an organization called Princeton Community Housing (PCH), formed through the initiative of black men and women of the Witherspoon neighborhood, with the help of Presbyterian ministers and church members. PCH was able to use state funds provided for nonprofit housing to desegregate neighborhoods and create affordable housing. They were instrumental in constructing forty homes for middle- and lower-income households. "They pressured realtors who refused to show homes in white neighborhoods to African Americans. And they made cold calls throughout the community asking homeowners to sign an Open Housing Covenant stating that they would welcome members of any race as neighbors and as buyers of their homes."[12]

A group of young black men and women who were dedicated to saving their neighborhood created the Witherspoon-Jackson Development Corporation (W-JDC) to keep black-owned homes in the black community. "We wanted continuity in the neighborhood," said Joan Hill, a founding member of W-JDC. "We also formulated an operating board and an advisory board. We were interested enough or smart enough to know that we needed an advisory board that could not only advise us as far as banking and industry, but we knew we needed fund-raisers who could raise money. We had people who were multimillionaires on our advisory board who contributed; they put their money where their mouth was."[13] Altogether, the W-JDC bought twenty-three homes and made them available for people in the neighborhood.

Despite these groundbreaking and effective efforts, however, the black population of the Witherspoon neighborhood has been shrinking since the 1980s. For the younger generations, the prices of their parents' and grandparents' homes—the ones that survived urban development—have become out of reach in the increasingly gentrified neighborhood. The appeal of moving "back south"—especially to Georgia, North Carolina, and Florida, where the cost of living is lower, job opportunities are inviting, kinship ties exist, and racial relations have improved—draws an increasing number of young black families as well. Dubbed the "New Great Migration," this demographic shift to the "New South" is significant.

Older Witherspoon residents on limited or fixed incomes keep watching their tax bills go up and become more difficult to pay. The offers, which come in regularly on their properties, can be tempting as they approach end-of-life decisions.

The neighborhood, still under assault from gentrification, is now an eleven-block area bordered roughly east to west by million-dollar condos on Palmer Square to the tennis courts and Community Park School, and north to south by the Princeton Cemetery and the Princeton YMCA. Across the street from

Community Park, a deluxe 280-unit apartment complex has taken over the land that used to be the Princeton Hospital and Medical Center.

As young African Americans have departed and older residents have died, the numbers of Hispanic residents, particularly from Mexico and El Salvador, have increased in the neighborhood. The black population is much smaller now than it was at the turn of the last century when blacks comprised one-fifth of the town's population. In the 2010 Census, the number of blacks in the borough and township (now combined) was 5.8 percent of the town's population. In that same census, the Hispanic/Latino population was up to 8.4 percent of Princeton's population. And so a new shifting has begun in this neighborhood that has absorbed and welcomed new people over the centuries.

> The whole area—they were getting ready to wipe it out. They didn't care if we had anyplace to go or not, because they wanted it, just like they want it now.
>
> —KATHLEEN MONTGOMERY EDWARDS

Emma Epps (1902–1989)

Princeton had loads of good things, but we had so many bad ones, too. I guess they only want to tell the good parts. In the Master Plan, you see, Negroes were not supposed to be living in the houses here, but only on jobs. They didn't tell us. And I said to a woman the other day, "You know, maybe that plan has come around. They're beginning to squeeze us now."

Susie Waxwood (1902–2006)

When we moved up to Princeton in 1935, one of the main things that struck me was the prejudice in this town for housing. We had an awful time finding housing, and the restaurants were prejudiced. Black people didn't go into them. There were no signs, but they wouldn't wait on you if you walked in. In some ways it was worse because you didn't know what to expect. In the part of Louisiana we were from, there were quite a number of French and

Burnett Griggs' home next to Griggs' Imperial Restaurant,
64 Witherspoon Street (late 1940s)

Spanish people who came to live. A good number of them were Catholic, and while it was segregated and prejudiced, it was not as violent as other parts of the South or the northern part of Louisiana. Where I lived, you were told you were black or Negro or whatever they called you at the time, colored, but you were not treated in such a mean manner. As long as you didn't bother them, then they didn't bother you. And they didn't do things to really hurt you. Surely, they would not have us in their schools. They would have thrown us out. Prejudice was there, and it was very evident. When I came up to Princeton, I found prejudice but in a subtle way.

Fannie Floyd (1924–2008)

The real estate brokers were blatant. They weren't rude, but they wouldn't show you the houses. The houses were "sold," or "someone had a holding on it," or sometimes they would just say the owners don't want to sell to blacks. So a number of the churches, especially the ministers, including our minister, Reverend B. J. Anderson, really got things moving. They formed the Princeton Housing Group and pushed for open housing in Princeton. They got people to put up money—and that's how a couple of developments got started, one on Walnut Lane and on Alexander Road. That's how Jim and I were able to get our piece of property; these were all fields. So we got this land to build on, with the stipulation that they wouldn't sell us the lot across the street because it backed up to Jefferson Road, which was all white, and we would have to buy on this side. And then they sold to our black neighbor a lot that was next door to ours, but they didn't want too much to rock the boat. Our kids went to public school here, and they had a lot of white friends. They would go over and play at their houses. They belonged to the Cub Scouts and Boy Scouts of the Nassau Presbyterian Church. I was a den mother with the Cub Scouts, and they had a lot of white friends, and they still do have white friends from elementary school. They were active in high school too; they were in the choir, played football, played lacrosse. That's another way of sometimes mixing because it creates contact with other people and helps you form relationships.

Burnett Griggs (1888–1977)

So I came to Princeton in 1909, and I went to work at [the] Campus Club. I brought some money with me, and I put it in the Princeton Bank & Trust Company. In 1917, I went in the service [World War I] and was in France for over a year. Toward the end of 1919—shortly after I came back—I got a letter from the president of the bank, Edward J. Howe. He sent for me and I couldn't imagine what he wanted to see me about. He said, "I guess you were surprised at my sending for you." I said, "Yes," and he said, "Well, I know that you're a young man that's saved your money, and I want to help you. We've got a piece of property down there on Witherspoon Street that's not being taken care of properly, and if you'll take it over, I'll always stand back of you."

"Well," I said, "this is something I'll have to think about."

He said, "I want you to think about it and you come back and see me." Well, ten days passed, and I hadn't been back, and his secretary called me, and said Mr. Howe wanted to see me. I went up to the bank, and he said, "I've been looking for you in here every day. What's wrong?"

"Well," I said, "this is something that I had to give serious thought."

"Don't think about it anymore," he said, "I want to tell you something; we like to have people put money in this bank, but you'll never get anywhere until you invest your money. Any money invested in real estate in Princeton will never be worth any less. I'll always stand back of you."

And I accepted it. The first piece of property I bought was on the corner of Hulfish Street. Hulfish Street was just an alley then, and there was a house next door that I had my eye on, and when I got to the point where I thought I could have it, I went up to the bank to see Mr. Howe about it, and he said, "Go ahead, you can get the money." And those two properties stood me in $9,500. I opened a restaurant on the corner and I lived next door.

When the borough came along and tried to take my property for urban renewal, I fought them for almost three years. In order to get federal money, they had to make all the property owners an offer, and they finally got all of the houses along what used to be Jackson Street, except my property and Toto's [Grocery]. They offered me $109,000, and I told them I wouldn't sell it to them for a million dollars. You may think I'm kidding, but if someone came here right today and said, "Griggs, here's a million dollars for your property," I'd say, "No deal. I never intend as long as I live that anyone else shall ever own it. No one knows what I went through to own it."

I saved the pennies. I've seen the time when I'd go down to the YMCA down here where this Municipal Building is now, and on the way home I'd think I'd stop and get a little box of ice cream or an ice-cream cone, and I'd get right to the door, and I wouldn't spend that 15 cents or whatever it cost; I'd take it home and drop it in a bank till I got enough of them to wrap them and I took them to the bank. So, no one's going to take this away from me without a fight. It's mine; I earned it.

When the borough tried to take my property, that was just like waving a red flag in front of a bull, because this is something that I made up my mind no one was going to take away from me. I didn't go out of business because I wanted to, but [because of] the help [employee] problem and the long hours I was putting in, and I had this arthritis. When I'm on my feet, I'm in trouble. So I had to get out. I sit here and look all the way up to Nassau Street, where I spent so many years, and I wouldn't live anywhere else. I love Princeton; I love it.

Albert Hinds (1902–2006)

Blacks lived in areas, years ago, that they can't live, or don't live in now, like Chestnut Street—my mother lived on Chestnut Street. She lived on Williams Street. Most of the blacks, of course, lived in this area because the churches were here, you see, and of course they wanted to be close to the church. And so that is how this area became a concentrated black area. Perhaps you could call it the ghetto, but I see nothing wrong with the ghetto—nothing wrong with it. People have a bad connotation to the [word] "ghetto." Nothin' wrong with the ghetto, but don't make the ghetto a slum. You know, there's a difference. You can be wealthy and livin' in the ghetto.

So we lived other places, years ago, and more recently hadn't been able to live there. Now, of course, we could live anywhere. At that time, I don't think expense was the determining factor. In those days, it was race, ya know. But now, later on, it became too expensive to live in those places.

Joe Moore (1941–)

There were things happening in Princeton that, for the most part, very few blacks were paying attention to. Everybody would talk about the inability to secure homes. You could get a loan to buy a car, but you couldn't get a mortgage to buy a house. And if you did get a mortgage to buy a house, it was only in a selected area—you were forced to live in the John Witherspoon Street area. There were some blacks who paid attention to it—Kathy Edwards was trying to make us conscious of what was going on in this community. She was the first person, from my point of view, in becoming aware of civil rights, the first person I could identify who was always bringing these issues forward. But as a collective community, we weren't always paying attention to it.

James A. Floyd Sr. (1922–)

Palmer Square was owned by Princeton University, and they had their own separate corporation running it. . . . There was a move afoot to have the university under its profit entity, known as Palmer Square, incorporated,

A home at 82 Witherspoon Street, at the corner of Jackson and Witherspoon Streets, destroyed by the expansion of the commercial district

to declare the area blighted and go through an urban renewal program to acquire those lands and develop them, and simply squeeze out the African American population. And yet, there was no provision for where they were going to go, since they were constricted anyhow by realtors and by others. . . . It was a strategy. The area was nowhere near blighted. In fact, those homes, you can drive through there now, and those homes that are still owner-occupied are still homes that are in excellent shape. I heard comments like, "Your yards are too deep and it's not the best utilization of the land," and on and on. Well, you'd never hear that on the western side of town— that the yards are too deep and there's too much grass.

But anyhow, we thwarted that effort . . . *we*, because it was a lot of people. And even if they had been able to override the citizenry, they needed Mr. Griggs's restaurant. And he told them straight out he would fight them to the Supreme Court if necessary. And he did have to go to court, quite frankly. But we did organize. We got our congressman to come in. And we even enlisted the aid of some folks on the western side of town, for whom some of our members worked in a private family. We threw out the chap who was mayor at the time, even though he was of our same political persuasion, and we really voted for someone not of our political persuasion, but he was not about to demolish the area and declare it blighted and institute an urban renewal program. It was the neighborhood organization and the stance of Mr. Griggs that really thwarted that effort. That would have been catastrophic, because there was no place you could go. You couldn't build anyplace else. I mean, no one was going to provide for that. I've never seen urban renewal work.

That was really my first involvement in the community activity. We were able to do some things about the open housing and able to do some things about constructing some housing. In fact, when I ran for the Township Committee, I ran on a platform of open housing, additional housing, and low- and moderate-income housing. [Housing] has been my focus, because I feel that at the core of things, like integrated school systems or integrated schools, happens to be housing and location.

Kathleen Montgomery Edwards (1924–2000)

When I came back to Princeton in 1960, it was a brand-new Princeton. They were going through a HUD [Housing and Urban Development], a relocation of all blacks. This whole area, they were getting ready to wipe it out. They didn't care if we hadn't anyplace to go or not, because they wanted it, just like they want it now. I said to Brian [Van Zant Moore, an African American attorney in Princeton], "I can't understand you all just sitting here and not doing anything. I haven't been home ten days and I can see that things are not going right." I said, "You lazy people get up off it, because we are going to stop this thing dead in the water." I said, "Let's get up off it. Let's do it!"

But people were afraid. I said, "Well, look. I don't work for none of them chancellors. I don't owe any of you my job, okay. I will tell [the mayor] exactly how I feel about it." I said, "But I want you all, even if you don't talk, at least stand there behind me."

And we marched on City Hall. Certainly did. We made that march. That is just why there is a black woman sitting right here right now. Henry Patterson [the mayor] came in '63. I know that 'cause I went up there to see him and wanted to know how come they didn't have a black face up there working.

And he is the one that hired that one [pointing to Penney, her daughter, who was the first African American borough clerk in Princeton and the first in Mercer County]. He told me, "I hired her 'cause she had on that pink suit. She's so cute." I said, "What you telling me for, I know she's cute."

We did that march in 1960, just before we did the one for the schools. They wanted to turn around and integrate the schools. They wanted to take John Witherspoon School and make it a township school. We had just finished paying for that school. They were trying to regionalize the schools. Well, why should I turn around and pay your bill, when I've already paid mine? But if you don't like something bad enough, and you scream loud enough, they'll get up and do it because they want to shut you up.

The only thing that I don't like about Princeton is that the cost of property is just too high. I think a person should be able to live wherever they want to live without the undue hardship. I like living here now. Then I didn't. I wanted to see what was on the other side, and I couldn't go out there. I was too young. Otherwise, it's a pretty good place. We just want our children—and you are our children, too—we want you to be better than we were.

Donald Moore (1932–)

My grandmother sold a lot of property that was owned by the family because my grandfather went blind and diabetic and had to divest a lot of his businesses. He had a clothing store, a furniture store, and Spring Street is the first building on the corner, a white frame building, my father was born there. My grandfather built that building. The next building we own, the next building was my grandfather's furniture store, the next building was another building that he put up. They owned a lot of property. He owned property, I understand, in the western section. He couldn't live there, but they owned property. He was very involved in business. He sold Woodrow Wilson his first desk at the university. When he became governor [of New Jersey in 1911], he took the desk with him because it was enormous and a beautiful desk.

At the university my grandfather sold clothing. He would sell clothing to the students there and he would buy clothing. And in those days, they, students that were there, their families wouldn't give them money, but they'd give them credit. The male students would come, well there weren't female students back then. They would want to go to New York and they would go to I don't know, Harry Balsch, or whatever was there and buy a couple of suits. My grandfather would buy them for cash. They'd go to New York and have a great weekend and he'd have the clothes and he would sell them as used clothing.

The reason we [my wife and I] came back to Princeton is because we were looking for a house. I told Ruth it would be no problem because my uncle was a physician and well thought of in town. She called the realtor and he told her there were plenty of places. He couldn't wait to get down and show her. And he came to the door and started up the stairs and he saw her. And he said, "Oops. I can't show you any of the places I told you about." It was because she's black.

He took her up to Squibs, an area up there. If you breathed too deeply you might not make it through the night. Of course, we were shuttled into areas like this. We looked and we just couldn't find any. We went to Kendall Park and we were told that yes there were houses available. And you know, they really tried to be nice, they said, "Well, let's see. What do you have?" We said, "We have money in the car." He said, "Well, that's it. You can't buy a house here." I said, "We'll pay it off." So he finally squared up with us [and] he said, "Look, I can't sell you a house. We've got millions of dollars invested here." He said, "A black family coming in would just ruin it." I said, "We're going to try to do everything we can to get in." He said, "We're going to try to do everything we can to keep you out." So we decided, we spoke to the Urban League, and we decided, "Why should we put our children through this?"

Joyce Sinkler Robinson (1942–)

After my father fought in the war, he was in a battalion. It was a medical battalion and it was a small group of men, I guess maybe twenty. . . . And they were on the front picking up bodies and things like that. And so, he felt he had served his country. So, when he came back he thought he deserved what he deserved. He couldn't get any money from the bank. So, he would go to the lumberyard or some people who happened to be nice enough to give him some lumber and cement. Whatever he needed, and then he would pay them later. And that's how he built a house. The house is on Witherspoon Street. It's still there. It's 305 through 307. It looks like it's a double house. What it was is that my father built the first floor, my mother looked at it, and she put a blueprint on a piece of cardboard and said, "Go up, Robbie." So, he built a second floor. And then he needed some help with the roof. So it was, I think, September, when the college kids came back, so he got the football team, and they all came and nailed and put the roof on. We moved in in 1950 when I was two years old.

Estelle Johnson (1919–2011)

During World War II we moved from Princeton to Rahway, New Jersey, when my husband had a job at a war plant. Well, we lived up that way six years. Then we came back because our house had caught fire and we lost everything.

All we had was the stuff we had in a little bag. By that time, I had two little girls.

I came to Princeton to live with my mother on Birch Avenue until 1952. We stayed there in their three-room apartment, because my two brothers then were in the service so there was nobody home but her. My mother had allowed us to come there, and she slept on a little sunporch. There was the sunporch, then there was the kitchen, and the one bedroom that the four of us slept in, and the living room where she kept the couch so in case when my brothers came home from the service. So, we stayed there as long as we could, but they were going to tear this building down, see.

Like I said, they actually tore down everything under me and just fairly pushed me on out. I was upstairs. Downstairs was gone, and I was so scared. Somebody one night came up there and banged on the door, and I almost died.

In the meantime, they had put the water off, cut the gas off. And so one day, somebody called me on the telephone—they hadn't gotten to that yet—and they said, "Mrs. Johnson, do you want your telephone cut off?"

"No," I said.

"Well, your cousin called up and she said so, but we thought we ought to talk to you."

Paul Robeson and Christine Moore in front of Sport Moore's furniture and clothing store on Spring Street (about 1930)

I said, "I have no cousin who would do that. Please don't cut off my telephone," especially since I didn't owe them anything for that month.

So, she said, "All right." But that was all I had. So, the Italian family who lived next door, they came and brought me water and soup and everything until we had to move all the way out. Well, we didn't have anyplace to go, so I began to try to find someplace, because my husband had then begun to stray a little bit. Urban renewal really broke up whole communities, because Clay Street was gone. So was Jackson Street. The stable community was now gone. And families were broken up, because they had maybe two over here or staying with this family over there, just to stay here in Princeton. People moved out and some never came back.

It was just a lack of housing period for black people because they had torn out one whole street. The people off of that street had to find a place, and there was not that many available places anyway for blacks. If you got there and found a place, it would be a room in somebody's house or something like that. But people didn't want people in their house who had children. So, I had some people looking to try to find me a place. . . . It took me a long time to find someplace. I was certainly not the only one. Some people had to move all the way out of town.

The city showed me a house down on Alexander Street next to the coal yard. There was no electricity in that building. There was no water, except a pipe outside the back door. The toilet was down in the yard. I said, "No, I don't want this house," I said, "because here I'm getting ready to have another baby now. I won't have this. I don't want it." Well, my husband and I argued over it, so we split up. They said we didn't have to take anything worse than what we have. So I said, "I refuse this place." Well, he got mad with me, and so I said, "Well, go ahead. I will not do it."

He just went to pieces. He thought anything people offered you, you had to take. But I said, "No. I don't want to go backward." It was bad enough living in that apartment there all jammed up in one room.

Frances Broadway Craig (1943–)

My mother worked at Princeton University food services and my father did construction work in Princeton and surrounding areas. First of all, especially my mother, who didn't have as much education as my father, always instilled in all of us that we were to get a good education, and my father always read the newspaper [and he] would read to me every night. And we listened to the radio every night. So, I think as a result of this, this is why everyone in my family, my [six] brothers and [two] sisters, were always readers and we always thought about the importance of education. I read every biography, and I read all the Nancy Drew mysteries and the Hardy Boys. I think I read almost anything and everything that there was to read, and that's why when I went to kindergarten I didn't know that other kids couldn't read. 'Cause I guess I thought everybody could. Because when you come from a family that large, you just kinda know how to do everything.

Believe it or not, in that three-bedroom house, my uncle came to live with us. And, when I was *really* young, two of my father's cousins lived with us, husband and wife, because they had to live there until they could find a place. It's almost comparable to what's going on in town now; there are a lot of Latino families who have to live in a house with a zillion people, because you have to do what you have to do. It was cool. I was always inquisitive and talking to everybody, so it was okay. I mean, I didn't think it was a hardship. How do you know if you don't know anything else? . . . I think because we were intelligent, all of us, all of my brothers and sisters, we knew we were poor, but we also knew that we had the whereabouts to make it. We all knew that as long as we could do well educationally, we would be okay. And most of us did okay. I can only speak for me, but I think that's what got us through. I mean, like I said, we were poor, but it wasn't *that bad*. 'Cause, you know, we were a family.

Changes that have gone on in town, and whatever my living situations have been, for the most part I think they have been positive. I just think that even now, you know with the population of Hispanic kids . . . I always remind people, and I'm talking black people right now, that "don't forget, we had the same struggle they have." 'Cause a lot of people are saying, "Oh, the overcrowding of the houses in Princeton." You know, it's just that you have to do what you have to do! Everybody talks about Hispanic kids living in these houses—four and five families. You know how much they make? Some of these men are making like four dollars an hour. These people are exploited. They are paying rents, $1,400 and stuff. How can you make it unless you have so many people living in one house? You know, it was the same thing when I was growing up. Black families had to have ten people living in one house. It's that same cycle. It all turns out. People do things, whatever they can, to make it better for their children. And this [is] what my mother and father always did. They wanted us to have everything, and the best thing. Because they know they didn't have them, they gave us what they could and their values were high for us. We're appreciative of it, and I'm sure all my brothers and my sister would say the same thing—that we are happy that they gave us what they did.

Jacqui Swain (1944–)

I guess I didn't realize what a wicked place Princeton could be until I came back as a teenager and was venturing farther out of the neighborhood. By then, the housing projects were being built and it was very different. Many of my people fell for that when they sold their properties, because they really thought they were going to get this exceptional housing only to find out that they were just public housing. They really just bought the story that "we're going to help you people. We're going to tear down these old houses, these ramshackle houses, and you're going to have some nice new houses." And once they sold their houses, they didn't get enough money for them to buy houses on sale in Princeton.

Joan Hill (1942–)

As director of the Princeton Civil Rights Commission, I handled the daily complaints of the police and community relations, housing, and all of that, and we had a skills bank to help people find jobs. We were instrumental in starting or helping to continue things like the Witherspoon-Jackson Development Corporation. . . . We purchased homes and sold them at a reduced rate. We would also give the buyer a down payment loan. We also bought the houses because the developers of Palmer Square, Palmer Square Inc., wanted to come back down into the neighborhood a little more and take our properties, but because of Witherspoon-Jackson, we were able to stop that. We also ensured that a percentage of the profits of the Palmer Square businesses went toward moderate- and low-income housing. We came up with so many new ideas that the Princeton Borough and Township didn't even know about. Some of the things that we thought of in this community among our little group of people are now used by the state, such as using a consortium of banks to work with each mortgagee, with the only stipulation being that the home had to be sold back to Witherspoon-Jackson not for profit.

We had many people who would notify [us] of homes for sale. These homes were sold to Witherspoon-Jackson. We would buy the home and buy it at the rate they sold it at and if they put improvements, because we wanted to resell it to another minority and we didn't want to overprice. We had renovation loans incorporated in their mortgage and over thirty years because many of the properties needed a little renovation. It made the payment maybe ten dollars more, because it was over a thirty-year period.

It was really a good group and not only did it help the Princeton community, but it helped us mentally. It gave a lot of knowledge of different things that you could do. I was selected by the freeholders to be on a blue ribbon panel for New Jersey. And they were trying to think of ideas for low- and moderate-income housing. And many of their ideas came from Witherspoon-Jackson, believe it or not.

Hank Pannell (1939–)

A lot of hardworking Hispanic people have moved into this community over the last ten or twelve years looking to advance themselves. Some from Mexico, but mainly Guatemala. They have a right like anybody else to live here, but the problem is the rents are so high here that it takes more than one family. The price of housing has gotten so expensive in Princeton that this neighborhood has become a target for people at the university. They come to buy a house and stay one, two, three years, and it drives up the price of housing. That's put a burden on the community. There are a lot of older homeowners who have lived here for years and years. But their children can't afford to live here. My son has a beautiful, beautiful home in Atlanta, a big brick home. He paid less than $200,000 for it. The average small, little house in this town costs $180,000 to $200,000. You can't blame the younger people for moving out. A lot of housing has been bought up just as rental property.

The Hispanic people [who have come here] are working minimum wage jobs, and you can't blame people for wanting to have a good education and a safe environment for their families. They join together and the housing is overcrowded, but it's not their fault. The landlords have taken advantage and it's created some problems.

Penney Edwards-Carter (1947–)

I think a lot of young people move out of the community because it's very expensive, and they can't afford to live here. They can go to other places and buy the same $400,000 or $500,000 house at a price they can afford, as opposed to living in this neighborhood and then having to spend $100,000 to fix the house up or pay the high taxes that you have to pay in Princeton. Princeton has changed a lot. I don't think I would be as averse now to moving someplace else. But I am not a person to just pack up and move someplace where I didn't know anybody. I always had a sense that I had to deal with white people all day, every day, and it was nice to come home and see some black folks and relate. Now to use Hank [Pannell] as an example: I'm not in and out of his house. I don't have to talk to him every day. But I know he's there, and if I need him I can pick up the phone and call him or go look for him. Keith has said at various times, "Let's move someplace—like California." I don't mind going to visit, but I want to come home. To me, this neighborhood is like family.

Burnetta Griggs Peterson (1931–2013)

I have great hopes for the world. I hope that it would be a far more peaceful world. I hope that people will even in terms of their wages will have a better, you know, living wage. I hope that somewhere along the line that we will get some type of relief in terms of health because drugs are so high now. I think that with this housing situation, I just feel that many cannot afford the Princeton prices, and actually that we have to provide more affordable housing for people here. My husband and I were only too happy to let them have [my father's] land for affordable housing, and we sold it, of course, and that bears his name now, Griggs Farm. And I certainly hope that they would take into consideration our senior citizens who've lived here all along and are being taxed out of the community. I hope it will become better as time goes on, I really do, that the opportunities will be far more open and that it will be a more equitable world.

Jacqui Swain (1944–)

In 1963, I worked with the League of Women Voters to try to expose some of the racism in the housing policies here in Princeton. And that was quite an experience. In 1990, I worked through the affordable housing program in both the township and the borough, and that was quite an experience. And the realtor . . . hired for Griggs Farm—I went up for my interview—now this is March 1990—went up for my interview, and they had decided that I didn't fit within the criteria of those people who should be getting affordable housing, and my interview was called to a halt when the gentleman said, "Well, you don't fit in the criteria," and then closed his book. And I said, "Well, wait a minute. Who says I can't buy the house under the market rate?" He just didn't want to go any further with the transaction. So, I said, "You're going to interview me. I took off of work this morning. You will interview me." So, I'm saying all this to say that in 1990 things hadn't appreciated much from 1963.

7

Fighting for
Our Country
in Every War

Drum & Bugle Corps, World War I Charles W. Robinson
Post 218 of the American Legion (1922)

AFRICAN AMERICANS IN PRINCETON have always been extraordinarily patriotic. They've served their country in every major war, despite official state and governmental resistance to their participation. During the Revolutionary War and the Civil War, prejudice against them was so extreme that at the outbreak of each of these campaigns, their service was shunned. Only after a dire need for manpower showed itself did doors open to them as soldiers and sailors. And even then, they were assigned to segregated units and often relegated to mess halls and service jobs as valets, cooks, janitors, and dishwashers. Soldiers were sometimes given sticks instead of guns with which to practice. As blues musician and songwriter Josh White sang in "Uncle Sam Says," "Keep on your apron, son / You know I ain't going to let you shoot my big Navy gun."

When given a chance to prove themselves, however, black soldiers took up arms, fought bravely alongside white counterparts, and earned their respect. This pattern began during the Revolutionary War. New Jersey initially did not allow the formation of colored militia nor offer manumission in exchange for service. Nevertheless, some two dozen Negroes from Princeton—enslaved and free—traveled to join nearby state militias fighting for the Continental army. Several Princeton men enlisted as seamen and marine pilots along with some 2,000 Negroes who were part of the naval forces.[1] Altogether, some 5,000 black soldiers bore arms for the Revolutionary War and were praised as first-class soldiers who distinguished themselves again and again.[2]

What is little known is that the Battle of Princeton, considered a major turning point for Washington's troops, was fought in January 1777 throughout the village of Princeton and within the Witherspoon neighborhood itself.[3] This took place shortly after Washington's troops won a crucial victory in the Battle of Trenton.

Until then, the British had the upper hand. Since November 1776, in fact, the British and their hired Hessian soldiers had occupied Princeton and made Nassau Hall their headquarters.[4] Nevertheless, Washington's tired and bedraggled troops fought the Battle of Princeton throughout the tiny village—on the Hale Farm, a portion of the Golf Links, and within the black neighborhood along Nassau and Witherspoon Streets.[5]

The battle was so bloody that Dr. Benjamin Rush, tending the badly wounded men, observed that the ground was still wet with blood. "You would think it had been desolated with plague and an earthquake."[6] The majority of black troops who fought that day in Princeton were from the all-black Rhode Island Regiment.[7] Other black soldiers with the Second New Jersey Regiment included Princeton's own Oliver Cromwell, Henry Hill, an enslaved Negro named Prime, another man named Orange, and Cuffy Baird, a slave who was a fifer for the minutemen in the Battle of Princeton.[8] While many of the slaves who'd served in the Continental army were freed at the end of the war, some were not, despite having been promised freedom for their service.[9]

When Oliver Cromwell turned one hundred years old in the spring of 1852, he told a reporter about being with General Washington during the memorable crossing of the Delaware in December 1776 and the battles of the succeeding days. He said that in Princeton, Washington's army "knocked the British about lively."[10] Nineteen Hessian soldiers were killed on Witherspoon Street that day, and for years afterward, residents living in the Witherspoon neighborhood told ghost stories about one particular Hessian soldier killed during the battle who roamed the streets in eternal unrest.[11]

African Americans from Princeton also fought in the War of 1812 and in the American Civil War. When Abraham Lincoln issued the Emancipation Proclamation on January 1, 1863, and when in his Gettysburg Address, he linked the war to the nation's revolutionary origins, "conceived in liberty and dedicated to the proposition that all men are created equal," Princeton's black residents answered his call to fight for "a new birth of freedom."[12]

New Jersey State authorities, however, mimicking the US government, again initially forbid the formation of any black regimental army units, known as the United States Colored Troops (USCT) regiments, although they allowed naval enlistment. It wasn't until the second year of fighting, when Union troops desperately needed more manpower, that Lincoln reversed US policy. And so it was that twenty-two black Princeton men joined the US Navy's Union Fleet,[13] and eighty black men from Princeton traveled to Pennsylvania and New York to join up. The Union army paid white soldiers holding the rank of private thirteen dollars a month, with three and a half dollars for clothing, while black soldiers of the same rank were paid seven dollars a month with allocations of three dollars. In addition, blacks faced longer enlistments and less chance of promotion compared to their white peers.[14] Nevertheless, black soldiers showed themselves, as the secretary of war said in a letter to Lincoln, to be "among the bravest of the brave, performing deeds of daring and shedding their blood with a heroism unsurpassed by soldiers of any other race."[15]

Between the army and the navy, one-sixth of Princeton's small black population served in the Civil War. They joined with tens of thousands of other freed men as well as Southern slaves who ran away to reach Union lines. Eventually, former slaves made up three-quarters of the Negroes in the Union army. By the end of the Civil War, on April 9, 1865, some 180,000 black soldiers had served in the Union army, and 29,000 in the navy. More than 40,000 black soldiers had died. The war was won, but five days after it ended, President Lincoln was assassinated. The *Princeton Standard* reported: "With broken hearts and tearful eyes, the people assembled for prayer in the churches and in the seminary; and from their sad countenances as well as their dolorous words, there was no mistaking the deep and inconsolable grief which the cowardly murder of their President had produced."[16] According to Union records, a black regiment—the Twenty-Second Infantry Regiment, USCT—led the funeral procession for President Abraham Lincoln in Washington, DC. Eight of the soldiers serving in that regiment were from Princeton.[17]

World War I also got its share of Witherspoon soldiers. Although residents were outraged by US president Woodrow Wilson's executive order to segregate federal facilities and bar blacks from civil service jobs they had held for fifty years,[18] they listened when he asserted this war would "make the world safe for democracy." At home in Princeton, black men set up a home guard of fifty Witherspoon men to protect the community. Black women planted war gardens, sold flowers, and raised money to support the soldiers.[19] "World War I was really the first major opportunity since the Civil War when Blacks could demonstrate their patriotism and show they had as much stake in this country as anyone,"[20] says author Jack Washington, who has written about black activism and history in Trenton and Princeton in his books *The Quest for Equality* and *The Long Journey Home*.

However, once more at the start of World War I, blacks were not welcome. Policies from Woodrow Wilson's Oval Office discouraged Negroes from enlisting, echoing his policies as president of Princeton University, when he had turned away black students from applying for admission. As with previous wars, black men were only recruited for the final stages of the war, when most needed, and then they served in segregated units. The *Princeton Packet* noted: "Princeton's Honor Roll was greatly increased yesterday morning when twenty-one colored young men of Princeton left here for Camp Dix. This number includes all the local colored men in Class I. There were but 48 draftees left in the county, and 21 were from Princeton."[21]

At the close of the war in 1919, Princeton's returning soldiers were celebrated in a parade down Nassau Street, where "everybody turned out to pay homage to Princeton's own returned war heroes, both White and Colored."[22] The Witherspoon neighborhood was decorated with flags and flowers. Once again, it seemed a time of hope for black and white residents in Princeton. Black men had come home with confidence and carriage—standing tall in their own experiences. Throughout the country, however, an alarming rise of violence from mobs of whites drove black families from their homes and focused on black soldiers in uniform, whom they beat, shot, hung, and burned alive. White mobs throughout the country lynched seventy-six Negroes in 1919, the highest annual figure in eleven years.[23]

At the end of World War II, conditions were not much better for black soldiers than they had been following the First World War. In the military, blacks had faced different rules than whites. Blacks' entry into combat was delayed three years before they could begin training, while whites began training within months of being qualified. Blacks served in segregated units with white officers. Black soldiers, as they had in previous wars, did such outstanding work that they gained the respect of white officers and soldiers who had black platoons assigned to their companies.

Three of the men from this small Witherspoon community—Simeon Moss, Emanuel Rhodes, and Floyd Campbell—were given recognition for "heroic or meritorious achievement of service" during the Second World War. Simeon Moss, who was promoted to captain of his regiment, was awarded a Purple Heart after "a shell burst got me."[24] He was subsequently presented with the Silver Star Medal, the third-highest military decoration for valor awarded for "gallantry in action against an enemy of the United States," as

Thomas (Buddy) Phox in Italy (1943)

well as a Bronze Star. Emanuel Rhodes, an army sergeant, was awarded the Bronze Star Medal for "valor and heroic service in a combat zone." Rhodes's unit was under heavy fire and the Germans had severed their communication lines. Under fire, Rhodes ran out several hundred yards and spliced back the severed communication lines.

Floyd Campbell was also awarded the Bronze Star for valor and meritorious service after the invasion of Iwo Jima, where he and others had fought for days without sleep under enemy fire. That heroism did not put a stop to discrimination. After that battle, though white marines were returned to Hawaii, and some even allowed to go home to the states, Campbell's black company was detached from the marines, sent back to their regular army unit, and assigned the task of securing the island until February 1946.

"When Mr. Campbell finally was sent home to the states, he was subjected to more differential treatment and racism because of his skin color," wrote Catherine Hallahan, who interviewed Campbell. "The war won and finished, all he had sacrificed and done for his country seemed irrelevant. Being black, he was unworthy in the eyes of white America of a war hero's welcome."[25]

Many black American soldiers who came home to the United States from their service in World War II were not only snubbed, segregated, and offered penurious wages for work but were also arrested, terrorized, or murdered. Soldiers standing up to protect their families or themselves were often shot or lynched, and sometimes their wives were, too. In some cases, dozens of black people were killed or their homes set on fire because white supremacists deemed them "too uppity" and "wanting rights" after the war. Others were attacked and beaten, often by officers of the law, and then charged with assault, convicted, and sent to prison for defending themselves.

Following D-day, A. Philip Randolph and his colleague Grant Reynolds worked to end discrimination in the armed services. In 1947, they formed the Committee against Jim Crow in Military Service and Training.[26] In 1948, President Harry S. Truman signed Executive Order 9981 to abolish racial discrimination in the armed forces. This was followed by Executive Order 8802, which established equality of treatment and opportunity in the military "without regard to race, color, religion or national origin." These acts eventually led to full integration of the armed forces. The last of the all-black units in the US military was disbanded in September 1954 during the term of President Dwight D. Eisenhower.

Black soldiers, marines, and sailors from Princeton also served in the Korean War, the Vietnam War, the Gulf War, and in Afghanistan and Iraq. Unfortunately, black men and women still faced racism during these wars, and when they came home to the country whose ideals they fought for, they were still not granted full and equal access to the economic, educational, legal, and social opportunities of citizens.

When I was waiting for the invasion there was this radio personality called Tokyo Rose and she would ask all the black outfits over the air, "Why are you going to go and die for America? The white man doesn't want you." But America was my home. I was fighting for a safe place to live.

—FLOYD CAMPBELL

Susie Waxwood (1902–2006)

During the Second World War, the president of the United States said that any woman who was not working and who had children over the age of ten should volunteer to do something to help the war effort. My son Howard was ten years old, and I thought I wanted to work with the soldiers and their families. In order to do that, I had to be a member of the Red Cross. The Red Cross was a wonderful organization; it still is. But the thing that attracted me was that there was a group that went down to places like the McGuire Air Base and the hospital down there, and they served sandwiches and milk and chocolate to the soldiers and to families who had come. And I thought I'd like to do that.

Well, in order to do it, you had to take two courses that were given by the Red Cross, and when I went to register, they refused to let me register, but they went around [it] in a subtle way. [The interviewer] looked at me and said, "Oh, you can't be a volunteer because you have to have a college education." And I said quietly, "I do have a college education." And she said, "But you have to not be working," and I said, "No, I'm not working." And then she said another thing, I don't even remember what it was, but it suddenly dawned upon me that what she was telling me was that I was colored and that I wasn't welcome. And when that came across this stupid head, I became extremely angry, but I didn't say anything. I walked out and then tears came, because I was so humiliated.

In the South, they had told me, "You're colored, and you're not welcome," but here, they didn't say that. So I went home in tears. And my husband said, "What's wrong?" and I told him. And he said, "Go wash your face. Get back in the car, and I'm going to take you back to the Red Cross. I'm not going in with you, but you walk in there and simply ask one question, and that is the telephone number and address of the chairman of the American Red Cross. You get that information. Say nothing else. Just thank them." I saw the woman, and she gave it to me without batting an eye. When we walked in the door back home, the phone was ringing. I answered the phone, and the woman said, "Mrs. Waxwood, you are absolutely welcome to come in. The class begins tomorrow at the high school. We will expect you there." I thanked her very much, and I said, "I will be there."

And those were the kinds of things that I was constantly having to meet, and I was never bitter. I want everybody to know I might be angry, but I was always courteous, and I have never let it make me be bitter, because I guess that's not my nature. And it has not hurt me. It may have hurt others, but it didn't hurt me. I have been able to let it go. And you know, a good bit of this had to do with that Howard Waxwood, who was as strong as I was, and who gave me that kind of support. And, in turn, I gave him that kind of support.

I remember meeting with the hospital people and the American Red Cross, and somebody said that the American Red Cross was prejudiced. And one member said, "Oh, we can't be. Mrs. Waxwood is a part of the Red Cross. And she's there and she knows we are not prejudiced." I said, "Wait a minute. I am a member of the Red Cross, working as a volunteer. I am doing it because the Red Cross is the only organization that would give me the opportunity to do what I wanted to do, and so I'm a part of you. But you are prejudiced, and I know it."

I remember [one time at Fort Dix], I was standing up on a chair trying to pull something down from a cabinet, and I had my Red Cross outfit on, and here comes two black soldiers. And one pointed to me and said, "You see, there she is." And the other said, "Oh, she's got to be Indian." And I laughed. And I said, "No, he's right. I'm not Indian; I'm a Negro." And the other one said, "In the American Red Cross?" "That's right," I said, and, of course, the rest of us could laugh—the other part of the group, you know, we could all laugh together. So, I think that was a learning experience for both groups. They got to know that I was a real person, and I got to know that they were real people.

You know there's good in everything. I think it all has to do with your attitude and how you enter it. Life's been good. Princeton has been good for me. I am very happy to be leaving it and sorry that I'm leaving it. I'm going to miss all of this, but it's not my nature to sit and be quiet.

Simeon Moss (1920–2007)

I graduated from college in 1937. I went to Rutgers University, the State University. I was the only black in my class. There were two before me, and a number strung out, you know. Well, I went to Rutgers and it was 1941. And I was in ROTC but I wasn't accepted in the advanced course, because there was no one else. I would have had to train with the advanced course people from Howard University and that wasn't convenient with the military to do that. So they let me take the course but I didn't get wasaname [credit] for it. But as soon as I got out and graduated, they called me into the service in September of '41, just before the war. While I was in the service, the highest rank I obtained was captain, then I stayed in the reserves and came out of the reserves a colonel, full colonel, birds. I was awarded the Purple Heart and the Silver Star by that general there, Lieutenant General Truscott. You see what the date is, 1945.

And so that's my career in the military. Now here is something very few people know about. The Ninety-Second Division was a black division, all black except for above the rank of captain. The majors, the colonels, and the generals were all white.

The way the army operated, it had an area to operate in. In other words, the Ninety-Second Division had their own space. It was like you took a chart and blocked it off and you put the Ninety-Second Division here, the 442nd Infantry Division, which was the Japanese division, the Japanese guys whose families and parents were in the camps. They were next to us. And then there was an English division next to that. And then there was the ocean on the other side of us, so that they could push into the ocean when they wanted. What I'm trying to say is that they separated us. So when you went back into the rear, you ran into white soldiers. But most of the frontline people were Japanese, English, and black.

When the Japanese bombed Pearl Harbor, American blacks were just as patriotic as anybody else. And they always have been. I never had a guy say to me, "I am not going to fight because you segregated me." I never heard it the whole time I was in this division, and I am talking about a division with twenty-five thousand black men. They never said a word about "what am I fighting for?" And that is the truth, I'm not giving you any bunk. You can listen to other people. But everything I tell you, I did, I've done!

[I returned from the war in] 1947. Then I went back into a segregated situation. I couldn't get a job teaching school. So I got a degree at Princeton. I went back to Princeton. I went to Princeton University, to the graduate school, in Public and International Affairs. The Woodrow Wilson School was in its embryonic stages. It was small; I think there were only eight or twelve of us. But there were two white generals in my class; one of them became commander of NATO later, but that is beside the point.

I was over there for a couple of years. And it never bothered me. I never got any inkling that I was anything but a student at Princeton University from the students that I, uh, worked with. But I did get that inkling from some of the professors. There were a couple who doubted my ability, and I could see that all the time. This guy named Harold Sprout. His wife was a fine lady, but he was a [whispered] son of a bitch. He was. And, of course, I was very outspoken at the time, so sometimes it didn't stand me in good stead for some of the things I said to him. But some of them came back to me later and said, "You know, you did the right thing." But what good is it to do the right thing after the fact? You have to do it before the fact, that is what I tell people all the time. If we are going to fight for our rights, we fight for them every day.

Floyd Campbell (1924–2005)

After I graduated high school in 1942 I tried to enlist in the US Marine Corps. I had known some guys who had joined the marines and they were so muscled and well built that I wanted to emulate that. The advertisement was "We Need You," it didn't say white only, so I thought that meant me too. But they didn't have enough room for so many coloreds.

Four of my friends and I had tried to enlist in the navy and coast guard too, but we were given the same response—no more coloreds. We were five young black men trying to choose our service and not be drafted to work in dining halls and shining officers' shoes.

But I was drafted into the army in June of 1943. Less than one year after we had started training our outfit was attached to the Marine Corps outfit

Floyd Campbell (1943)

for the rest of my time in the service. I started off at Fort Dix in New Jersey and then went to New Orleans, Louisiana. From Louisiana we went to Pennsylvania and from there to Hawaii. From Hawaii we invaded Iwo Jima.

Being a young person [from Princeton], the army was the first time I was exposed to the world. You could exercise a freedom that you hadn't been used to. You were a big man. And you were in a different world now. The army had this truck called a DUKW. This vehicle could travel 60 miles an hour on land and go into the water at 70 knots an hour. We became part of a convoy that would pilot these DUKWs in the invasion. But we didn't know where we were going to invade.

While we were training and practicing for this invasion somewhere, one officer decided that the men should have something amusing to do. So he started asking for people who can do anything, anything at all, entertaining. If you could sing, he wanted you to sing. If you could act, he would ask you to act. I had an instrument.

I had been playing trumpet since the eighth grade, and I had picked up my instrument before I went to Hawaii. So I got together with three or four guys—at that time we didn't have a piano player yet, but we had a drummer, a saxophonist, and a bass player—and we started playing jazz for the men aboard the liberty ships. We called ourselves the DUKW Cutters. We put on a show almost every night.

Eventually, we set out for the invasion on January 1, 1945. We still didn't know [where] we were going to. Finally, we were shown a model of the landmass of Iwo Jima. On Iwo Jima there is only one small area where you can land these DUKWs and it is covered in volcanic ash. But the unique thing about this vehicle is I could increase or decrease the pressure in the tires from controls inside. So when I got on the soft, mushy black volcanic ash of Iwo Jima, I could deflate the tires to get better traction.

I landed on Iwo Jima at 2:00 p.m. My job was to drive the DUKWs from the ships onto the beach and provide ammunition. I couldn't go more than 500 yards on land, plus there were bodies floating around in the water. You're scared. You don't know what's going to happen and you're just praying that you're going to get through. We were never farther than 1,000 yards behind the front line.

When I left to go back to the states it was on an old C-47 headed back to Fort Dix. But we got caught in a storm over El Paso, Texas. The plane, the old C-47, just couldn't make it. So we landed there and we got out to eat. We were hungry and had been eating a lot of dry bread, salami, and cheese. We expected that, but we thought that here we would finally be able to get a sandwich and some hot soup. When we got out they stopped all us black guys and said, "You can't eat here." And we said, "But we're soldiers, we're with these guys." But they said, "We don't serve colored." So they brought us food. And what they brought out to us while we waited on the plane was plain white bread with mayonnaise and onions.

That was the first incident of hurt. You mean to tell me I went to war for my country and I can't eat with fellow soldiers? It brought tears to my eyes.

So the next day the colored place opened and we ate there.

Later, a few months after I had been back in the states, I was on a trolley car and sat down right behind the conductor. The conductor looked at me and said to a white man sitting near me, "Look what's sitting behind me." I was angry and I asked him, "What did you say?" But I had a friend and he told me to leave it alone because the law was on their side.

But I never wanted to leave America and go back abroad. America was my home. I was discharged on my birthday, February 27, and I came back to Princeton immediately. My mother almost fell down when she saw me. Her tears of joy were a pleasure to see. I had been away for three years. I was twenty-two years old.

I have five kids—Daffney, Sharon, Floyd Bruce, Lynette, and Mark—and they were all in the Princeton public school system. The school system was integrated but there were still problems. My wife felt they were ignored because they were black. So after school she taught them at home and we worked through PAHR [later evolved into the Princeton Community Housing Group] at changing things. All my children eventually went to college. Times changed. My son and grandson both were able to serve in the marines.

Bruce Wright (1917–2005)

My family used to always tell me I was too talkative. I was often told to keep my big mouth shut, and you'd go further in life. "You may as well be a lawyer," they'd say. And so I did. Went to two law schools. Went to Fordham with two other black kids, and then New York Law School. I started at Fordham and I had a racial dispute with one of the professors. The son of a bitch gave me a D, so I left that law school and went to New York Law School, from which I was graduated.

But I got drafted in 1943 during law school. And, of course, my big mouth got me into the infantry. I went in as a private and somehow ended up as a squad leader when I was discharged in '46. I certainly didn't volunteer for it. I'm a practicing coward. I hated the army. Are you ready for this? We called it Camp Motherfucker, Alabama, but it was Camp Rucker, Alabama. I was sent from Fort Dix.

I kept volunteering for something else to get out of there. I kept demanding transfer to an integrated unit. "This is America. You're talking about the four freedoms and all that sort of thing. And here you have me segregated. What kind of business is this?" I never had any faith in Christianity and, of course, my experiences in Alabama certainly certified the propriety of what I was thinking about white people in general. But then it was, "Oh, but your mother is white." Well, she was my mother.

And we had all-white officers. So they must've been penalized for something to be in command of a black quartermaster unit. Somehow my brother got in the artillery. That's where he served. And during the Battle of the Bulge, I ran into my brother when the Americans were retreating and I was then in the First Infantry Division, we were going out, a kind of rescue effort. My brother's a rather stalwart kind of a guy, and when I saw him, I yelled at him, and we shook hands. "Have you heard from Mom?" And he said, "Take care," and passed on into the night.

Donald Moore (1932–)

When you get older, you begin to understand better what's been going on and you probably resent it. In the army, I was in 969 Field Artillery. I was in combat. I didn't believe that they would put us in combat but they did. But we were a segregated troop. We had white officers and black enlisted people. They had drafted me. They dragged me out kicking and screaming and put me on a train and sent me away. I was nineteen and I had several birthdays in the army.

They used to say, they'd get into discussions in the barracks and say, "Yeah, this darn army." I'd try to get into the discussions and they'd say, "Oh, shut up. You volunteered." And that was like pushing a button. I jumped up in the air and was really ticked off. When I left the army they asked me if I'd like to join the enlisted reserves. I said, "No. All I want is a faint recollection of what happened here. Let me out." When I was in the service, I had some very bad things. We were fighting for this country.

When I was in the service, I was in Louisiana, a little town called Shreveport. This was a segregated town, legally segregated. I was coming out of the hospital, I had a couple days of furlough that Christmas. And I went into this station, and I bought a ticket. I came out and I sat for a while. I thought, "Jesus, I've got to get something to eat." There was a little diner just outside the station. To go to the colored section, I'd have to go about four miles across. And I wanted to stay as close to the station as possible so I went in.

I sat down at the counter and watched people walk back and forth. I'm in uniform now. And finally, this lady came up to me, she said, "I'm sorry, sir. We don't serve coloreds." And of course I know the act. And I said, "What do you mean?" She said, "Well, aren't you colored?" I said, "Of course not. I'm Spanish." She said, "Oh, my God, I'm so sorry." All of the sudden things started hitting and I'm sitting there chuckling to myself. But I'm scared.

She said, "What would you like?" I said, "Let me have a hamburger and a cup of coffee." The quickest thing I could get. Well, while I'm eating and drinking, here comes a black person out of the kitchen. He probably went back and said, "Oh no. He's black." So she came back out.

Now I'm still eating. I knew exactly what was going on. She said, "I really don't think you're one of us. My husband is sleeping upstairs. Do you mind if I bring him down so that he can take a look at you?" I felt like I was in the zoo. By that time I was nearly through with the hamburger and I was feeling a little bit better. I said, "That's it. I've been through this before, and you know, I resent it. Just give me my bill and I'll get out."

I had had something to eat and the train came in. I got on the train and sat on the train and it started filling up. And the conductor came in and he said, "Hey boy!" I was the only black soldier on the train. He was looking right at me. He said, "You can't ride on this train. We don't have accommodations."

He came back up to me [and] he said, "Would you mind riding in there?" The toilet. I said that this was my seat. So he yells out the window, he says, "Sam." He said, "Bring the curtain." They brought a curtain. Have you ever seen a shower curtain? There were plugs on this thing. You could plug it into the side of the car and they put it around two seats. That's the way I rode to Texarkana. Separate from the rest of the troops.

I got to Texarkana and I got off the train and there happened to be a black porter or station manager. He looked important. He had all these keys. So I said to him, "Excuse me. When's the next train coming in for St. Louis? I want to get on it." He said, "You can't get on that. All these white boys have to get on it." Well, of course I called him a few choice names. I said to him, "Look, I've been getting my backside kicked all the way up here. We're both the same race. All I want is to get on this train."

Well, this turned out to be something that worked out well for me. In those days they had what were called special troops. They had priority. And he didn't say that to me. The way it came out it sounded like he was pushing me aside. The train came in. There were a bunch of us standing there. Special troops got on and he was downstairs, like Penn station. You're upstairs, the train is downstairs. He said, "Is there a colored soldier up there?"

And I said, "Yeah." He said, "Come on down. Plenty of room." There was a Jim Crow coach. I was able to ride, the white troops were not allowed to get on this empty train to go to St. Louis. But that's the way I got in. As you came back, you'd have to ride like that until at one point you had to get out and get into a segregated car, when you got past a certain point down south.

These were things I certainly resented. But they are things I had no control over. I was a soldier about to be sent overseas to fight for the country. And doing that, coming back it was like, "Okay, we've done our job." A lot of people were dead. It was no better when we got back than it was when we left. People would pat you on the back and say, "Hey, it's good to see you." But that was about it. For the rest of your life, it's just going along. This is what we sort of live with.

Jimmy Mack (1935–)

I spent four years in the navy, and while I was there, I thought to myself, this is a good chance for me to take up a trade. Instead of being in here where they teach you how to kill people, I'd have something to do to serve the community.

We were in the port of Athens, Greece, and I was walking through a hallway and they had a sign on the tack board: Barber Wanted. I went to the barbershop and there were ten chairs. One was vacant because some white guy had gotten discharged. They didn't have any black barbers. The guy in the shop asked me if I'd cut hair before and I was yes! Now, you know that was a lie. I had never cut hair before. I was about eighteen years old. I didn't

James and Martha Phox Barbour (1944)

even know what pair of clippers to use. This marine needed his hair cut, so the haircuts people are getting now, that's what I gave that marine. He was mad and the guy in charge of the barbershop saw what was going on and came over to help me out. Then the nine other guys saw that I was just learning and they proceeded to help me.

I was on a big aircraft carrier over in the Mediterranean. Out of the 4,450 men [on my ship], there might have been 250 to 300 blacks. I was in France,

Greece, Turkey, North Africa, and Barcelona, Spain. When we came back from overseas, I was stationed in Portsmouth, Virginia. . . . On the way back from a movie, [another guy from the naval base] said, "Mack, let's go in there and get a sandwich." This was back in the days of segregation, so I said, "They're not going to serve you in there." He said, "Well, let's try."

When we walked in, everybody froze. We went to the counter and the waitress came and asked what we wanted. She threw our hamburgers in a bag and gave us two Styrofoam cups of coffee. We decided to stop at a booth and we sat down and started eating. So, she came from behind the counter and told us we couldn't eat there because it was against the law to serve colored people. She went to get the boss and he came out and said, "Look fellas, I'm sorry. It's not me, it's the state law that colored people cannot eat in here."

In the meantime, while he was talking to us, a cop was walking down the street and he looked in and saw us in there. In that Southern twang, he asked the boss, "Are these boys giving you any trouble in heah?" The boss told him he told us it was against the law for us to be there. The cop hit me [he points to his shoulder] with his nightstick and told us to get out. He turned around and hit the other guy. We had our navy uniforms on, but that didn't mean nothing. So he told us to get out and we left our food and everything on the table.

Thomas (Buddy) Phox (1920–2008)

I spent my twenty-first, twenty-second, twenty-third, and part of my twenty-fourth birthday in the army. That was quite a bit of years. It was very hard going back to school after the army. I had an athletic scholarship to Penn State. Three or four years makes a lot of difference when you're playing football. And there was a difference. I didn't have that same lust for the game that I'd had before I went in. When you're younger, you think, "Oh boy, I can move mountains, I can"—but after a while you start thinking.

I saw quite a bit of misery, a lot of pain, and a lot of death during the war. I was in the Fifth Army in Italy. I dream sometimes now—I think of one area, not too far from Pisa, right along the coast, in an inlet. The Germans had a position up in the hills, which we attacked. The air was so thick with shells that you couldn't tell the incoming from the outgoing artillery. There was a German tank that had taken a direct hit. Lying there on the ground were two kids, not more than seventeen or eighteen years old, with no visible wounds, dead. They were bleeding from their mouths. There have been a lot of times I choke about that. I would say on the average of at least two times a year, I still see those faces. And when it's all over you think, "What for?"

When I got wounded, the piece of shell that hit the helmet put a big dent in the side and it ricocheted off. I took a piece of shell that hit the arm, I got a piece in the back . . . I brought that helmet home.

I had another thing I brought home. . . . The Germans were surrendering so fast after the war. We were up near Turin, in northern Italy—at that time I was a military policeman, I was motorcycle patrol—and we got notice that there was a large contingent of Germans ready to surrender, and we had to find a place to hold them. We found this big sports stadium outside of Turin, and they were surrendering so fast the infantry didn't have time to disarm them all. I noticed a German captain walking along, and he still had his Luger at his side. So I went over to him, and I motioned to him, you know, "Give me your handgun." I took his gun belt off, and in the belt he had a little pouch with pictures in it. Pictures of his family. They were a whole family there. He started crying. I said, "I'm not interested in the pictures." I took the gun. He broke down like a baby. He thought I was gonna take those pictures. I used to dream once in a while I'd see that guy, too. You think of all the people that were involved in that war, all the families that were disrupted, and you know . . . they're all people.

I don't talk about my war experiences often; actually, I just started being able to talk about it within the last four or five years. I never did before. I wouldn't have done it at all, if it weren't for my grandchildren. They said, "You should do it." When I'm talking to people their age, people younger, I think, *you're the future.* Wars don't solve anything, no, they don't solve a thing. You take the cream of your country—your youth—and you expose them to something, because people can't get along. And there's no winner, you know, nobody's gonna win.

There was a family I met in Italy, the youngest was a boy, Andre, who was seven at the time. He came over to me and asked, "You got something to eat?" I said, "Yeah, how 'bout some chocolate?" and I gave him some chocolate bars. The next day, I was directing traffic, and there he was watching me. And invited me to his house and took me to meet his family. His father was a marble polisher in Coulon, and they actually were a very wealthy family. I established a friendship with him, and kept in touch after we moved north and headed up to Genoa. I used to come back down on a motorcycle and spend some time with his family.

After the war, the family contacted me. They said, "We would like very much to have you come back to Italy. You made such an impression on us, and were so nice to us." He called and said, "Don't worry about the money—you tell me when you can come and I'll send you the tickets." Believe it or not, that's what he did. My wife and I started going to Italy in the sixties, and we went fifteen consecutive years. It never cost us a nickel. As I said, he had a marble polishing plant, some of the best marble. They set up cruises for us in the Mediterranean, gave us the use of a car if we needed one, a stay in one of his houses. . . . The mother would spend so much time in the kitchen—Italians spend a lot of time cooking, it's just incredible. You take a lot of time sitting around an Italian meal, and every single course we sat there and savored it. They were a wonderful family. The boy, he's sixty some years old now.

Emanuel Rhodes (1921–)

My uncle Heziki, he came here after World War I. He came in 1918 or 1919 and my aunt, she came here before that. She owned a house right down Green Street and the house is still there. We came up later. My uncle Heziki, he was in the war in France and with the French army, because the Americans, General Pershing didn't want no black troops. So when he went overseas, they transferred my uncle and the other black soldiers to the French army.

The French said, "We'll take them and train them," and they took them and trained them. And when they were fighting the Germans, my uncle told me that the German said that the Frenchmen were getting so mad that they were turning black. You see, General Pershing, he was in command, didn't want no black troops. The Frenchmen were nice to them, treating them like they were really human beings. But it was the American general that didn't want them. And there was prejudice. They had them separated back in those days. Even when I was in the service it was segregated.

I went in the service November 19, 1942, and I came out December 11, 1945. I went overseas in '43 and came back in '45 from Italy. I was fighting with the Ninety-Second Division. We were called the Buffaloes and we fought in Italy until the war was over and then were shipped back home to Patrick Henry Camp, Patrick Henry, Virginia.

We had separate units. The Ninety-Second was all black. Soldiers was black but they had mixed officers: They had white officers and they had black officers, and we didn't have no problem with that. The only problem we had was when we were shipped down south to Fort McCloud, Alabama. That's when we couldn't go to places [to] sit down and eat. And certain places you weren't allowed to go to, it was off-limits to you. And it was even like that overseas. Some places they had set up for the white soldiers, but they said no black soldiers weren't allowed in, no colored wasn't allowed in there. But the Ninety-Second Division Buffaloes, our division, we would just go in there anyway 'cuz we figured we were just going in there fighting just as they were fighting. So we said that we were going to go on in there anyway. Sign's off-limits, but I told my men, I said, "Come on, if they can go in there, we can go in there too." So I said, "We just as soon gon' die here, came back for a rest from the front, as we go up there and the Germans kill us. We got to stick together." And that's what the Buffaloes did and that's why they didn't like us . . . 'cuz we stuck together.

It was just . . . it was just so prejudiced. The officers, the white officers, some of them from the North, my battalion commander, he was from, uh, Captain Hiner, he was from California. He wasn't prejudiced. He drank out of the same canteen I drank out [of], everything. But some of the other officers from down South, white officers, they were different, and they treated me different. But he told us just to ignore them 'cuz he was in command of headquarters. So he said, "Don't pay no attention to them. They say something to you, you don't like, just don't say anything 'cuz it's gonna get you court-martialed."

One black officer we had in the outfit, he was court-martialed. I was on CQ that night, I won't never forget it. I was in charge of quarters and this black lieutenant, he was Officer of the Day. They had what we called Officer of the Day. And he'd come into headquarters' barracks and told me, "Mr. Corporal, I'm going over to my barracks." And he said, "If you need me, call me." So, and I said, "Yes, sir," and so he went on back to the barracks.

Then this colonel, he was ol' redneck, sometimes redneck's what we called them, he comes into headquarters. . . . So he comes into headquarters and I salute, and he says, "Where is Lieutenant . . ." I can't think of the lieutenant's name now, but I knew he was black. But he said, "Where is the lieutenant at?"

And I said, "Sir, he's over at his quarters."

So he says to me, he says, "Are you sure?"

I said, "Yes, sir, that's where he's at." So he went over to check and came back. He says, "Corporal," he says, "He's not there. Are you sure he told you that's where he was going?"

And I said, "Yes, sir." So the next day, the same colonel comes back to headquarters and Captain Hiner, he was there, our battalion commander, so he had him [the lieutenant and me] in his office. So Captain Hiner asks me, he was talking to me, he said, "What happened?" I said, "Well, the lieutenant told me he was going over to his quarters." I said, "I must have made a mistake and he told me that he was going to see his wife and he'd be back at such and such time."

So he says, "What did he tell you?"

And so the lieutenant says, "Yes, sir, I told him that I was going over to visit my wife. He misunderstood me when he thought I said I was going to my barracks." So the colonel says, "That calls for you being court-martialed." And I said, "Court-martialed? What did I do to get that?" He said, "Because you made a mistake. See, you don't make mistakes like that in the army." He said, "Now, if you make mistakes, you can get a lot of people killed." And I tell him, I said, "Yes, sir, I realize that. It was my fault."

Well, anyway, they court-martialed me and they took all my stripes and made me a private. [But] when the court-martial was over, I still got the same pay 'cuz Captain Hiner called me into the office and said, "Corporal, don't even take your stripes off." He says, "That little redneck cracker," that's what Captain Hiner said. And he's white. He said, "Redneck come and cause trouble 'cuz he don't like the colored soldiers." We said colored instead of black. He said, "You'll still get your same pay as a corporal." So, I still got the same pay and everything turned out all right.

So the lieutenant, the black lieutenant, he came over to congratulate me and Captain Hiner was in the office, and he said, "The lieutenant wants to

Military Wives' Tea at the YW-YMCA (1944)

congratulate you for what you did." He said, "'Cuz you got busted and he didn't." And I said, "Well, it was better for me 'cuz I'm a two striper and to lose two stripes, than him, who was a lieutenant, to lose all his grade as a lieutenant. And he was a first lieutenant." So he said, "That was a brave thing you did." And I never forgot that. And then after that, I don't know what happened to the lieutenant or to the colonel. I've never seen them again. No, that incident didn't affect me. I just had the idea that we were going overseas to make a record for ourselves. 'Cuz nobody wanted us to go overseas 'cuz they said black soldiers are cowards. They won't fight. That's what the general was saying about the black troops.

So, anyway, we went over there and made a record for ourselves. And I ended up getting a citation for bravery. And I got a Bronze Star for that. It was right outside of Pisa and there was a crossroad, where two roads cross one another. And the Germans had zeroed in on that crossing. And that's where we had all our lines lead. The whites had a line too, but we had to service our lines, and my men and I had to service the powered lines to get to the infantry and artillery. So we had to go to the front to the infantry and then to the artillery and get communications so they could locate the Germans. But what happened, the Germans, they knocked the lines out and they weren't getting no communications.

So I told my men, I said, "You guys, get the hell out." And I said, "I'll stay here and service the lines." He said, "Corporal, you better come and get out of here. You see the shells flying right by." I said, "They trained us when the shell hit here, no shell will hit in the same spot." So if you go to the spot where the first shell hit, you're safe and then you can repair the line that's knocked out. And that's what I did from one where the shell hit to the other and repaired the lines until they got communications. Headquarters and the OP, they called it Observation Post, where they could see the Germans . . . when I got OP and then I got headquarters, I said, "Is this Corporal [unclear]?" He said, "Yes."

I said, "OP, can you hear me?" He said, "Yes." I said, "We can see the German guns, Corporal." He said, "Just hold tight. Don't move and just stay where you are." He said, "We'll spot the guns and we'll knock them out." So about ten or fifteen minutes they had knocked all the German guns out.

It was all clear and I got up and when I went to move that time, I couldn't hardly move from the shell. I guess it must have knocked me in the head. It must have fractured my back or something. So I went on the ground and sit there for a while until I could get up. When I got up, I took the telephone and put it over my back and I had to walk about a mile to get back to headquarters because my men had come left. They left me there 'cuz I wasn't going. I told them to let me stay. I said, "But you guys get out." I had six other men under me. I said, "Makes no sense in all of us getting killed." I said, "I'd rather just one person and I'll stay here." I stayed.

When I walked that mile and got back to headquarters, at headquarters when they saw me walking they started running and hollering and yelling. They said, "It's Corporal Rhodes!" And Captain Hiner come up and said, "It's unbelievable!" And then he started asking me questions, "How did you survive?" And I told him, I said, "It just wasn't my time. God was on my side." I said, "I'm just lucky, that's all." And I still look at it that way. When your time comes, you gonna go. And I'm like General Patton: Ain't nothing I hate more worse than them cowards. If I had to go over there and I had some men that didn't want to follow behind me, if I go first and they don't follow me, I don't want them. 'Cuz that's what you go over there for, to fight a war. You either live or you die. And this was the same for the white and black soldiers. They may never come home. [The] Ninety-Second lost a lot of black soldiers. [The] Eightieth, they lost a lot of white soldiers.

But we all figured it was for a good cause. 'Cuz the way Hitler was going and the way he was killing the Jewish people in these concentration camps and gas chambers and things he was putting them in, and we said, "Well, that's not right." We figured we was treated bad enough in the South when they was hanging black men for different things. Sometimes the black men didn't do it, but they'd hang them anyway, 'cuz they was black. Or they'd try to run away, they'd catch them, in slavery, they'd catch them and hang them. They did all kinds of things to them, and that stuck in our minds. That's what made us stick together.

And after the war was over, they came, they took pictures out that showed us how the Germans had treated the Jewish people, putting them into concentration camps and how they [were] burning them and all that. And we were standing there with tears in our eyes. We couldn't believe it. Standing there with tears running in my eyes. I couldn't believe that they did Jewish people like that. We knew that they was white, but they were human beings. So how can you do a human being like that? You don't even do an animal like that. And we said right there, if we would've known that, we would have just took them German prisoners and would have killed every damn one of them. When they wave the flag up, we would have killed them. But we didn't know it. That's why they didn't tell us 'cuz we would have been wrong doing that. But that's the way we felt about it, knowing that we were treated the way that we were treated. And when you think about it, it's a hurting thing. It's still in the back of my head now. I still can't believe that those Germans did the Jewish people like that. Just because they were Jewish. We can't help what race we are, or what color we are. We're all human beings and we should be treated as human beings. And that's mostly what's wrong with this country now.

I still don't have hate in my heart. I'm seventy-eight years old and I don't hate nobody. I love everybody, white or black. And I never do nothing to break nobody. I used to hear my grandmother say and my father say, "There some good white people and there some bad white people. There's some good black people and there some bad black people." So what they do, they crucify you 'cuz you black, saying all are the same. And they're not. Until they start changing, now it's getting better, but it's still not like it should be. I would say, it's getting much better.

8

Racism
Poisons Our
Whole Nation

"Segregation is not humiliating but a benefit,
and ought to be so regarded by you gentlemen."

—*Woodrow Wilson*

Woodrow Wilson at his desk in the Oval Office (about 1913)

WITHERSPOON'S AFRICAN AMERICAN RESIDENTS have, over centuries, lived as a peaceful, law-abiding community and shown themselves to be alert and responsive to the world around them. As a people originally born of slavery, they've witnessed the single-minded efforts of some whites to exclude, exploit, and vilify them, block their paths to full justice, and violently punish them for their success and victories.

Black residents who have lived with racism all of their lives keenly feel the impact of national, state, and local policies designed to thwart them. They readily recall a famous Princetonian who not only denigrated them but also worked to push them backward. "When you think of Princeton's racism and segregation, Woodrow Wilson just jumps out at you," Hank Pannell said one afternoon when he, Penney Edwards-Carter, and I were talking. "To me," Penney added, "Woodrow Wilson is the face of racism."

When he was president of Princeton University, from 1902 to 1910, Woodrow Wilson's intense loyalty to segregation and the exclusion of black students contributed to the cultural solidification of Princeton as a Jim Crow town. When Wilson got to the White House in 1913, the federal government and civil service had been integrated since after Reconstruction. Wilson turned that around. He mandated the segregation of all federal facilities, created separate and inferior restrooms for "coloreds," and even put up screens between blacks and whites who had been working together peacefully in the same offices for more than fifty years.

African Americans, who'd voted in large numbers for Wilson because of his pre-election promises, protested. One of the delegations that visited the White House and urged the president to undo these policies was led by a Boston newspaper editor, Monroe Trotter, a Phi Beta Kappa graduate of Harvard. "Trotter stated to Wilson that the segregation was unmerited and far-reaching in its injurious effects."[1] Wilson's response was dismissive:

> It will take one hundred years to eradicate this prejudice [against colored people], and we must deal with it as practical men. Segregation is not humiliating, but a benefit, and ought to be so regarded by you gentlemen. If your organization goes out and tells the colored people of the planet that it is a humiliation, they will so regard it, but if you do not tell them so, and regard it rather as a benefit, they will regard

it the same. The only harm that will come will be if you cause them to think it is a humiliation.[2]

In 1915, cinematographer D. W. Griffith produced a silent film, *The Birth of a Nation*, based on the novel *The Clansman* by Thomas Dixon Jr., who was a close friend of Woodrow Wilson. The silent film presented the Ku Klux Klan as saviors of the white race and used quotations from Wilson's scholarly writings (regretting the outcome of the Civil War) in its subtitles. Actors in blackface depicted African Americans as grotesque rapists and criminals. When the NAACP publicly denounced the film, Woodrow Wilson held a private screening of it at the White House for his cabinet and their families. "It's like writing history with lightning," Wilson said, "and my only regret is that it is also terribly true."[3]

———

Throughout their history, Witherspoon residents heard about atrocities against African Americans, especially those killed by white mobs, from travelers passing through, and by word of mouth and mail from friends and families. In 1734, Princeton's small black population no doubt heard about the "slave rebellion" in nearby Somerville, only fifteen miles from Princeton, where a Negro told a white man named Reynolds that he, the Negro, was as good a man as Reynolds and that in a little time Reynolds should be convinced of it. This caused Reynolds to suspect a Negro plot.[4] "It was not clear if there really was such a plot," writes historian Howard Green. "[B]ut evidently one man was hanged in retaliation, several had their ears cut off, and others were whipped."[5] Likewise, Princeton's residents would have heard about the enslaved men who were convicted and burned alive for setting fire to seven barns in Hackensack, New Jersey, in 1741.

In the many decades since then, African Americans in Princeton have struggled against the harsh realities of racist violence and inequities that, with rare exception, touch every aspect of their lives. From their beginnings in this country and still today, African Americans have enduringly created a range of strategies to take care of themselves and one another.

Earlier generations sent money south in order to buy freedom for more of their family and friends, and then helped them adjust to new circumstances when they arrived in Princeton. In the 1830s, the neighborhood's commitment to freedom was evidenced by its being an important "station" on the Bordentown route of the Underground Railroad, passengers traveling north to freedom.[6]

The Underground Railroad generally operated on dark nights, when fugitives hid in covered wagons, often under loads of hay or produce. "Conductors" drove them to the next station. The danger was increased by violent proslavery forces, slave-catchers, and harsh laws against anyone helping runaway slaves or hindering their arrest.

In Princeton, black freedmen and enslaved African Americans were at the forefront of efforts to provide care for the "passengers."[7] They were aided by white abolitionists, many of whom were Quakers. When a runaway got to Princeton, local people provided a change of horses essential for the continuing journey. "Agents" and "station masters" fed and hid the escapees in private homes, barns, outbuildings, cellars, and garrets, as well as in churches, hotels, and stores.[8]

The Mount Pisgah African Methodist Episcopal Church became the principal place in Princeton for hiding and transporting escaped slaves. For at least three decades, this assistance was an integral part of the AME churches' service, which provided a foundational structure for the Underground Railroad throughout New Jersey.[9] Some members of the Witherspoon Street Presbyterian Church, the other black church in Princeton at that time, most likely assisted the Freedom Train, but no historical record of its involvement has been found.

The full extent of Princeton's contributions to the Underground Railroad aren't known since its survival depended on secrecy. What is known, however, is that Blacks and Whites in Princeton were among some 3,000 conductors and agents on the Underground Railroad. Its networks traversed 14 northern states, as well as Kansas and Nebraska, and helped at least 75,000 to 100,000 fugitive slaves escape to freedom.[10]

The Witherspoon neighbors also collectively dealt with racial tensions and faced down threats of violence directed against them. In a protest against the Civil War in July 1863, for instance, a number of armed Irish laborers walked off their railroad jobs and roamed the streets of Princeton, making threats against Republicans and blacks. Heavy rains limited their activities at night during the protest. On the third day, an African American resident told the Irish that if any black family or house was harmed, local blacks were prepared to burn down every Irish house in Princeton. The threat had its desired effect. The local Catholic priest intervened and the Irish protesters returned to work the following day.[11]

Shortly after the Civil War's conclusion, Princeton's African Americans responded with joy when in 1865 Congress passed the Thirteenth Amendment to the Constitution, which legally abolished slavery and involuntary servitude, except as a punishment for crime. Three years later, in July 1868, they celebrated the passage of the Fourteenth Amendment, which granted equal rights and citizenship to all male persons born or naturalized in the United States. And when the controversial Fifteenth Amendment in 1870 granted that the "right of citizens of the United States to vote shall not be denied or abridged by the United States or by any state on account of race, color, or previous condition of servitude," the Witherspoon community came out in full force to celebrate. What jubilation! The *law of the land* had affirmed the right of Negro men to vote! Families paraded up Nassau Street with banners, songs, and speeches that expressed deep relief and optimism.[12] At last, it seemed, black people had a voice in their own destiny in this country. Finally, they were headed for citizenship and equality.

———

For many generations since then, residents of the Witherspoon neighborhood have continued their efforts to create equality for the entire human family. The threat of violence, ever present for black Americans, meant that they often owned guns as a matter of necessity. Hank Pannell recalls that as a child, he never knew his grandmother carried a weapon until he was at the First Baptist Church of Princeton when he was six years old and about to be baptized. His grandmother had made his baptismal gown. "We got to the church, and she tried this gown on me, and it was rolling up at the ends where she had hemmed it. So she went down in her garter and pulled out her pistol and put bullets around the bottom of the hem to hold it down.

So I wasn't scared about being baptized or going in the water or anything. I was terrified of those bullets going off. Before that, I never knew she carried a pistol. But she was a really no-nonsense lady."[13]

In the 1920s, as the Ku Klux Klan grew to approximately five million members throughout the country, ten thousand of New Jersey's Klansmen marched in Mercerville and Yardville. The Klan held public rallies in nearby Hamilton, Pennington, and Trenton. At a rally in Princeton, the *Princeton Packet* reported hundreds of people were gathered "at the foot of Witherspoon Street . . . [when] without previous warning, the flaming cross of the Ku Klux Klan blazed forth on the hill a few hundred yards away."[14] University professors and city fathers saw the Klan as unenlightened, without merit, and socially harmless, but this view was not shared by the Witherspoon residents, who knew that the Klan could be deadly.[15]

As their stories show, Princeton's black residents struggled against racism in ways big and small. When it came to the chronic racist "pranks" and attacks on their homes from drunken college boys, neighbors imposed a strict curfew on their children so that they were home before dark. They put out the word that they would not tolerate destruction of property in their community.

"Blacks did not let [threats or] barriers dictate their lives nor the color of their skin dictate their rights," student Lou Arrindell concluded. "While many others might have been content to ignore the hostilities the world posed against them, the residents of the John Witherspoon neighborhood were not. . . . In the face of opposition, they came together and devised appropriate solutions."[16]

Generations of Witherspoon residents advocated for change through their membership in Princeton's influential chapter of the NAACP. In the late 1930s, a small number of progressive white Princetonians joined black Witherspoon residents in actively working for equal rights. They applauded President Franklin Roosevelt's New Deal, designed to mitigate the Great Depression and then, after FDR's 1945 death, President Truman's Fair Deal.[17]

In the 1950s and 1960s, Princeton residents were inspired by the political activism of the Montgomery Bus Boycott and the civil rights movement to continue confronting segregation in their town. In 1954, Witherspoon men initiated a meeting between the men's groups of three Presbyterian churches in Princeton. "This was quite a historic decision . . . because these churches had not really had official communication with each other for over 110 years, particularly the black and white churches," according to Leonard F. Newton, an early leader in the fair housing movement in Princeton.

> The point was to take up the way Blacks were being treated in our community. . . . Princeton's Blacks and Whites were living in separate and unequal communities. The Blacks were not welcome to participate in the traditional civic roles in the community, in government roles, in being heads of any major community activities. If they wanted to do that, they had to do it in their own groups. . . . And good jobs were really not open to blacks, irrespective of their qualifications. . . . [Eventually] there was a call for action. A handful of people . . . began to plot how to change the intolerable situation. . . . This quickly evolved into a focus on housing. This focus led to establishing the Princeton Housing Group, a civic organization that later grew to include several hundred people working to make housing affordable and available to all its citizens.[18]

Witherspoon activists participated in sit-ins at Woolworth's on Nassau Street and at white-owned barbershops and other businesses that refused service to African Americans. Many residents, young and old, traveled to join national marches. As mentioned previously, residents created the Princeton Association for Human Rights. This interracial organization mobilized several buses to carry black and white Princetonians to the 1963 March on Washington. Princetonians worked for voter registration in the South in 1964 and traveled to Selma, Alabama, to march with Martin Luther King Jr. People from the Witherspoon community and the university joined the Poor People's March on Washington, participated in the Freedom School boycotts, and protested the Vietnam War.

Also in the 1960s, Witherspoon church members actively worked with the League of Women Voters, the Princeton Human Rights Commission, and the NAACP to force access to equal housing and jobs. The Joint Commission on Civil Rights was established in Princeton Borough and Township in 1968 as a forum for the community—and also as a place to handle

The Joe Lewis and Jackie Robinson teams for YMCA
membership drive (1948)

cases of discrimination in housing, education, public accommodation, and police-community relations. The spirit of the Harlem Renaissance and the Black Power movement of the 1960s and '70s traveled through the Witherspoon neighborhood in the music of John Coltrane, Miles Davis, and Aretha Franklin; the poetry of Amiri Baraka, Nikki Giovanni, and Gwendolyn Brooks; and the writings of Langston Hughes, Richard Wright, James Baldwin, and Zora Neale Hurston, among many others.

In 1970, James A. Floyd Sr., one of the founding members of the Princeton Association for Human Rights, which later became the Princeton Housing Group, was elected mayor of Princeton Township. He was the first African American to hold the office. "If I were to recall the positives regarding civil rights," says Jim Floyd, "there were few to none as it related to the government of Princeton Township and Princeton Borough. Quite the contrary, unfortunately, our governing bodies did not become concerned for the civil rights of all until [community groups and individuals] prodded, pushed, organized, and had your voices heard. Unfortunately . . . there is still a void on the part of our government as it relates to the equal and civil rights of our citizens in this community."[19]

In the 1970s, '80s, and '90s, African Americans in Princeton continued to discuss black liberation and address ways to end racism and police abuses, which included frequent stops of blacks driving cars (known as "Driving While Black") and walking ("Walking While Black"). Men in their sixties and seventies have lost count of how many times they were stopped by police when they drove across Route 1 to Quakerbridge Mall.

The problem continues. Even black professors who live in the township are stopped for "suspicion" because they're driving "too slowly" in their own neighborhoods. African American students report that they're not surprised when police stop and frisk them, even when they haven't broken any laws.[20] A seminar held on racism by the YMCA in Princeton underlined the reality that the police focus disproportionate attention on the black community on the false assumption that African Americans are more likely to commit crimes than whites. If African Americans are arrested, judges set higher bail for them and detain them for a longer time than whites—a pattern that remains prevalent throughout the United States today.

In 1991, when many white people assumed that racism had been ended by the civil rights movement, the Ku Klux Klan ignited a seven-by-four-foot cross at the corner of Route 206 and Princeton Pike. Of course, for Witherspoon residents, the event was chillingly reminiscent of the 1920s cross-burning, as well as another more recent one in 1971 at the triangular intersection of Nassau, Stockton, and Mercer Streets. The Klan dismissed the cross-burning as merely part of a recruitment drive—an explanation that seemed to calm some Princetonians, but not those in the Witherspoon neighborhood.

Many Witherspoon residents are still active members of organizations that deal with the pernicious effects of racism, including the Princeton Association of Human Rights, the Joint Commission on Civil Rights, and the Women's International League for Peace and Freedom.[21] African Americans in Princeton who hold high-paying jobs, live in all parts of town, and work in almost all fields still experience the legacy of slavery from white people conditioned to equate dark skin with dangerousness.

As Lois Craig said, "Down here in the John Witherspoon neighborhood, things are getting better. But uptown, on Nassau Street and in Palmer Square, they are not different. Race relations have been improved slightly, but racism is still here."[22]

> Even as Du Bois was predicting that the problem of the twentieth century would be the problem of the color line, new, effective if inane arguments advanced by journalists, politicians, even educators, insisted that the Negro was a beast, a threat to civilization, a drain on the economy and even a scourge on the body politic. In the wake of these allegations, new patterns of racial segregation and discrimination emerged, along with new forms of racial ostracism and humiliation, and new practices of economic and political degradation.
>
> —JOHN HOPE FRANKLIN

Bessie Parago (1907–2007)

When I first came, I'll tell you one thing. I will never get over when I hit this town and it was June 1930 and I went on Nassau Street. What first struck me, I went in what was then the Balt, I believe, and they said, "Oh, Bessie, you can't go in there and sit down and eat." I said, "You've got to be kidding, in this dirty little old place! Oh, no." I can't get over it. It was terrible. When I came here, I said to Wilson, "Let's go to the movies." So we're going down to the movie and I'm goin' on down there. "Bessie, Bess, Bess," he's all, "you can't go down there."

"What do you mean I can't go down there?"

"You have to go over here." You know, you weren't too young, but you had to sit down in a certain side of the theater. I said, "I don't believe this."

Robert Rivers (1931–)

The first time I knew that there was a race problem was how I reacted to it. There was a carnival and they had this black guy in big overalls sitting in a cage. You throw a baseball at a lever, and then watch him fall and splash in the water, and everybody laughs. How in the world could somebody put up with that? Then, the thing that really got me all spun around, [I] was thinking, "Maybe that's why they don't like us. For whatever they did to us in slavery, we're trying to rip them down. Maybe they don't like us for that reason." As a youngster, I couldn't understand why people could be so friendly one minute and be so unfriendly the next minute. I couldn't understand why I couldn't go swimming in the pool or why my family couldn't go eat in a restaurant around here. We could fix their food in the kitchen, but we couldn't go eat in a restaurant in Princeton. A lot of people don't realize this, but in the forties, Renwicks and Lahiere's were places you couldn't go eat.

So I couldn't resolve this whole business of segregation and discrimination in my mind. I couldn't figure out what the problem was. How could I pull all that together with the fact that we fought World War II because some klutz over in Germany thought he was superior to everybody else? But the upshot was I wasn't going to be second class to anybody. I was going to do whatever I could do, and I was going to reach as far as I could reach. And that was just our feeling about how to deal with it. You gotta live your own life.

Joe Moore (1941–)

The first time I was ever called a nigger in my life was by the police chief—for playing basketball on a basketball court behind the YMCA. You had this innate fear of cops, just because you were black. It was like they were putting the fear of God in us for no reason at all. You could be walking up the street, and they'd slow the car, stop the car, and harass you. So that was a major concern with at least the group that I was a part of—"Here comes the law." Even though we did nothing wrong, we would run because we knew what was coming.

If we walked one block over from where the YMCA is now to pick apples, because they had apple trees over there, five minutes later, here comes the cop. We were literally told a hundred times, "You do not belong in this neighborhood." So, you knew your place, and there was nothing subtle about that. It was very obvious. And then they were talking about something called integration of schools? So the only time we were really allowed, with any degree of freedom, to move about was when we went to school.

Boys' Boxing Club at YMCA (about 1920)

Harriett Calloway (1906–2005)

You know, growing up, I didn't think about race. I knew there were certain places on Nassau Street we couldn't go. I mean you could go in and pick up and come out, but I mean like now you can go in and sit down and eat. But it's always been prejudice and I guess it always will. It had been that way around here and I had lived in this area so long it didn't bother me. If I knew I couldn't go, I didn't go. I wasn't going to fight to get somewhere where's nobody wants me. If they don't want me, I don't want them, so why raise a fuss?

Floyd Campbell (1924–2005)

When I got older I started to wonder why I had to walk way uptown to go to school. And, eventually racism began to rear its ugly head. I played trumpet in a high school band that had both white and black students. But there wasn't any fraternizing between students of different races. Since we were separated in elementary school, we hadn't built relationships with each other. There was an indifference toward people of other races. You would get bitter about it sometimes when you thought about it, but that was just the way things were.

There were those who thought the colored boys were somebody you didn't play with and they would make disparaging remarks. I would go to the university during the football games to sell newspapers and I would have proctors telling me, "Alright, it's time to get off the steps and get on back downtown, you know." The game would be over around five thirty or six and you would walk around to see if you could carry someone's bag and make a quarter and you would be told to leave. We weren't allowed to stay on the campus after dark.

Clyde (Buster) Thomas (1934–2004)

I used to hear as early as 1945 about how Paul Robeson was blacklisted. He never admitted to being a communist, but they certainly labeled him as that. Now, Paul was really just like Malcolm X. He was a spokesperson for his people. He really didn't care so much about how he was being treated or how he would be benefited. To me and some of the others, they were the true leaders of African American people. Today, many of our so-called leaders don't really speak out on the real issues or problems that black people have, and they go along with the flow because it's in some ways beneficial to them money-wise or position-wise. Later on in life, you find out what happens to the people who are a real threat to the power structure. We lost a lot of people who were really involved in the political struggle, and we don't really know how they died.

I have found out that once you get exposed, you sort of limit your effectiveness. Even today, I don't really speak out, but I do a lot of things behind the scenes with people. Even with the jobs that I've had, discrimination is still very blatant, like in the unions. There has been a lot of legislation, a lot of changes, but you can't legislate individual prejudices. I was in business school at Penn State—my minor was labor relations and my major was business administration. Upon graduating Penn State, I went for some advanced studies at Cornell in labor relations. Then beginning in 1961 I worked for the Labor Department. I worked for Unemployment Compensation for about three or four years, and then I was involved in a statewide program where they tried to increase the number of minorities—African Americans, Latinos—in the building trades. That was a real eye-opener.

Right after the riots of '65 in Trenton and Newark, the building of the new medical college in Newark was the first project that I was involved in. The issue really was to get more minority students into the medical college, more professors and certain job opportunities, both procurement contract opportunities, and my area again was to try to get more minorities into the building trades. Traditionally, as you know, there are very few laws that really control the unions. They have ways of weeding out minorities. There is a long list of ways they do that. Today they're still very successful at it. We had to go to court to get a lot of the unions to take minorities into their apprenticeship programs, which are like four- to five-year programs; that's for twenty-two building trades. And we still had a lot of dropouts, because of the harassment and intimidation that a lot of the students faced during their apprenticeship program.

It's being brought to light now with all these police unions in New York City, but that's no different than any other town. You may find one or two that are very progressive, but on the whole, they're pretty much the same. It may take another fifty or one hundred years before it is where it should be today. That's the slow progress.

And I think we fail to realize, when you look at the history of this country, you figure almost 250 years of slavery when you have gotten free fruits and labors from people. Then you tack on another 100 years of segregation, lynching, and discrimination. That's 350 years of damage that's done to the psyches of both sides. You're not going to wipe that out in 15 or 20 years. People don't realize the damage that's being done, and how long it's going to take to undo a lot of that damage on both sides of the fence.

There's no way to really measure the damage of racism and sexism and so forth. It goes deep. It certainly is affecting a lot of people psychologically. It's going to affect them physically, as well. We don't really talk about the medical problems, the stress that it causes. I've seen firsthand, cases on the job, how it actually affects people, and this just makes me that much more angry about the situation.

So, it's just discouraging when you deal with it now. You look at certain businesses that minority people are not in, and it's because of what was accomplished during the period of slavery and the accumulation of wealth, property, and all kinds of assets. People don't give up their privileges easily, and they want to hold on to their privilege of being able to allow their friends and relatives into their union, so we're still fighting among ourselves for whatever crumbs that are left. I don't care what kind of job you have, the contractors have contracts with the unions to supply all the labor. So, if the minorities aren't in the union labor, they don't get referred out to the job.

As I said, I was involved with trying to get more minorities involved in apprenticeship programs and the unions. I did that until 1974, and then I went to the New Jersey Sports Authority, which operates the Brendan Byrne. They call it the Continental Arena now—there's a racetrack and a giant football stadium where the Knicks and the Giants play. Primarily I went there to write and develop the affirmative action plan for doing the construction phase. Again, it was to get minority contractors and businesses involved in the construction and in the operation phases because traditionally throughout the country minorities were not into running arenas and the sports industry.

Well, I'll tell you, we had a lot of opposition in that job. People are talking about leveling the playing field. Well, you can't do that unless you know where you are or how it is topically, and I've designed reports that would give them that information. They don't want that information. They didn't even want to know what you thought about it, because they knew they'd have to address it. I thought I had the authority to do something about the situation, and I found out I didn't.

Emma Epps (1902–1989)

Who was the man who wrote, "Now if you want to keep the Negroes down, keep them from a book?" If you can't read and write, you can't do much. And that's the attitude, I'm afraid, of a lot of people here. After the March to Washington, the Martin Luther King march, one of the professors at the Woodrow Wilson School asked me to speak on how I felt and my whole attitude toward the march. And I spoke that night. I spoke before this big

Members of the Friendship Club who raised scholarship funds, fed the poor and elderly, and supported black education and the NAACP (about 1940)

audience. Afterward he came up to me and said, "I had no idea that you could speak like that." The idea was I wasn't a professional. And to me, I don't think I can ever explain how it hurt me.

It's just the idea of not having the chance, you know. I remember my sister's daughter in high school and she said, "You know, I don't like that Miss Jean Wright." And my sister looked at me and I looked at her funny because we knew our mother at one time did laundry for her father, Dr. Wright. Her daughter said, "She calls me into the office and asks, 'Why are you taking this type of course, an academic course, and all these extra languages? Why are you doing this?'" I answered, "Because I'm a Negro and the job may open up sometime, and then I'd be ready." So it went on and on. When I later saw Ms. Wright, she said, "Oh, I had no idea your mother was any relation to you." I said to her, "Miss Wright, the fact that my mother was a laundress in your house was not the fact that she didn't have a brain but that she didn't have a chance."

Penney Edwards-Carter (1947–)

I maintain that African Americans are not seen. I don't mean that they don't notice a person necessarily, but they don't see, really see, the person. All they see is a black face. I have been in situations where people don't speak, and they know clearly who you are. I mean, they see you every day. But I maintain they don't really see us. All they do see is a black presence, and they react to that.

I can remember one time I went to pick [my daughter] up from school. She had either missed the bus or she stayed after school for something, and she was sitting in the window at Stuart, but when I pulled up, this white woman walked up to her. And when she got in the car, I said to her, "What did that lady want?" She said to me, "She asked me if I was waiting for the bus." And I said to her, "What bus?" And she said, "Well, the City of Trenton sends a bus back for all those kids that participate in sports activities, so that they have a way home." So I said to Katryna, "Not all of us live in Trenton. There are African Americans that live in Princeton and that woman shouldn't have assumed that just because you were black, you lived in Trenton."

Burnetta Griggs Peterson (1931–2013)

My parents told me not to go into any facility, any place of business that did not choose to serve me. I'll tell you about the Betty Right shop. That was on Nassau Street, and I went to buy a bra, and shortly thereafter I'm greeting her, she handed me a piece of tissue paper to use when I tried on the bra, and I handed it back to her, walked out, and I never went back to patronize her. When the Playhouse opened, my mother told me not to let the ushers lead me over to the right side of the theater because that is where they were seating African Americans, and I *never* sat on that right side.

Albert Hinds (1902–2006)

The difference between the South and the situation here, you see, one thing about the South, you don't have to wonder. Up here, to me I've always considered the North, like quinine pills. Of course, we don't have anything like quinine pills anymore. What I'm sayin', what I'm talkin' about here, is the outside is sweet, but when you suck it, it gets bitter. And to me that's up here. Down south you *know*: I can't go here, I can't go there, I can't do that, I can't do this. Here it's more difficult, you don't know whether you can or not. So I consider it like that quinine pill, I feel more comfortable going to a white store in Atlanta, Georgia, than I do in a white store up here! . . . You go into a store up here, some white person is lookin' at you.

My daughter's been in Atlanta. But ya see, you better stay in Atlanta, you know, you better stay in Atlanta. There are other areas in the South that aren't too good. . . . But now in the South, I mean we were living in Atlanta, and my wife was teaching, and this is within the past ten years, outside of Atlanta. She was from New York—and some things that she wanted to do, progressive school, and all that bag, and the white people didn't like it, and they were going to run her out of town, and all that. Outside Atlanta. It's still in Georgia, so as I was saying, all cities aren't the same. We moved back up here but I like the South, I like the South.

Burnett Griggs (1888–1977)

I guess I'm rather a peculiar sort of person. I never go places where I'm not wanted and I'll get along without things if I've got to be segregated. So, I've never experienced too much of that because I was always very careful where I went. I remember I went in a drugstore with a man here some years ago. It's been a long time now. I think he was getting a prescription filled or something for his wife. They had a soda fountain in there, and he said, "Come on and have a soda." And I said, "No," because I knew that they didn't cater to Negroes. So he insisted, and the man who ran it said, "Come on, Griggs, and have whatever you want." I said, "No, I didn't want anything." And this thing sorta caught this man and he wouldn't take anything then either. He got the prescription, and then we came out. He said to me, "What happened?" I told him. I said, "Now look, I happen to know that they don't serve Negroes in there. Now I don't know whether the man would've served me because I was with you or because he knew me as Griggs. But, I said, 'how 'bout that Negro he don't know? If he don't want to serve him, I don't want him to serve me." And I never went places that wanted to wrap something up for me and take it out, not me.

I remember I was going home to see my mother, and I got down . . . I think it was Richmond, and I was hungry. I had to change trains there. And I said to one of the porters there, I said, "Is there a place around here where I can get something to eat—a colored restaurant?" And he said, "No, all those places around here is closed." He said, "I can go over in the other part and get you something and bring it over." I said, "No thank you; I'm not hungry." Never let anybody bring me something; I'd go hungry first; I've been that way.

Jacqui Swain (1944–)

I came back to Princeton when I was eighteen to go to Rider College, so I remember the marches in front of Woolworth's here on Nassau Street in the '60s. I remember the Bull Connor demonstration when he was here on campus. A student group or somebody invited him to speak on the steps of Nassau Hall. We just demonstrated and carried on to voice our opposition to the philosophy that he espoused.

I guess I started becoming aware of Princeton [attitudes] at Rider College. I had some experiences that you would just not believe. I had a very dear friend by the name of Doris Cooper. Her family had a big name here in town, and we were very good friends, and we wanted to room together at Rider College. But the administration kept throwing all sorts of roadblocks in our way. When I confronted the administration, basically they said we could not live together because one of us was white and one of us was black and our cultures were too different.

We both decided we weren't going to live on campus so we commuted. She was a very, very good friend to me, because there were probably ten African Americans in my whole graduating class, but Doris never forsaked me. She wanted to join a sorority; they told her she could join if she got rid of me. She wouldn't. We would go bowling together, and they would make snide remarks toward her, because she would bowl with me rather than with them.

She had a good friend, Rae Raeder, she tried to be liberal. She took me to her house one day and her father was home. He had a natural fit that there was a black woman standing in his living room that didn't have an apron on, pushing the vacuum cleaner. If you're African American in a place like Princeton, it's one thing after another, especially if you don't stay in that box that they want to keep you in. Those were my first inklings that Princeton wasn't all that it [was] cracked up to be, Princeton and its surrounds. I was going to school and learning a little something about the world and seeing some things that were so narrow in the protectiveness of the community in which I lived. I've seen just wonderful intellect wasted because of the protection and the, what do you call it, the insulation that that community gives. I often think, though, sometimes a kid has to suffer some of that pain in order to learn.

My grandmother ran a pantry over at the Commons at the university. So she would often bring the young [white] boys home to feed them at our house. We did everything we could to keep them comfortable and not make them feel that they were so far away from home. [One time] the guys were talking about the meal that was so good. They were saying, "Isn't she a nice woman?" and "She made good fried chicken." One of the boys said, "Yeah but she's black." Like she doesn't really count. I just couldn't believe it.

I love living in Princeton, and I love my childhood days that I spent in Princeton, and I have fond and wonderful memories of all the people that I know and have met in Princeton. But Princeton means you have to stand up for what's right and stand up when you see wrong being done. Princeton is still a place where when you come out in the morning, you're ready to do battle if it should present itself.

Sophie Hall Hinds (1875–1974)

I went to school in the country, two places. I used to walk from out there to come to Sunday school here in Princeton. It wouldn't take long driving a horse and carriage, you know. But sometimes we had to walk it, and we could walk it.

The white boys got behind us while I was goin' home from school and kick all the dust so you couldn't see. Clouds between myself and my sisters. They thought it was fun, I suppose, but it wasn't much fun for us. One time my mother got after the kids and they was scared to death. She used to walk sometimes down to the school building with us and they wouldn't bother us there. 'Cause she wouldn't take tea for feed, my mother wouldn't. She's different from me. Now I'll take anything almost from anybody and I never hardly fight back. If they think they're right, I just let them go on and think they're right. Never a whole lot of arguing or doin' like that. God brought me this far and He's going to still keep me.

[At the country school] when it come to recess time, we never played with the white kids much. Some of them, some of the girls was sort of nice, and some wasn't so nice. Of course, I personally never bothered nobody. Made no difference how everybody treated me or would treat me—I never bothered them. I just paid attention to my own business. And I know I had some tough times.

When April came along they gave you a certain period of time that kids went on home and worked for their father or whose ever farm it was. Just like a vacation I guess it was. Except it was hard work when they got home. Nothing ever seemed too hard for me. If I had something to do, I just went on and done it. That's all there was to it. There was no foolishness. I never did from the time I was a child. We had different classes, you know. We used to go by A, B, C, and all like that practice. But we didn't have but one teacher. That's all we needed, I guess. You had to learn from yourself in those days and times. Nobody cared what happened to the next person. If you get your lesson, you got it. If you didn't, that was your fault.

Joan Hill (1942–)

When I was in school, I never went on any of the sit-ins. I'm glad I didn't because I wasn't the type just to sit and let people beat on me. I would have been killed. As a youngster, we went to Virginia every summer to visit my mother's relatives. I can remember one time going into Richmond to get ice cream or something and the blacks just had to wait until the white ones were waited on. I said, "I'm not waiting. My money is just as good as theirs." So I went up to the front of the line. Surprisingly, the man served me because he could tell by the way I talked that I wasn't from Virginia.

My little cousins said, "Oh, you weren't supposed to do that!" I think the Lord knew that I wasn't supposed to go on any of those sit-ins, because we had busloads that left from Central and went down south. I never went on any of them, and it was because I don't have the temperament to keep my mouth shut. I have to voice my opinion, and when I disagree, I verbally disagree.

Arthur Lewis (1931–2013)

One thing that stands out in my mind is that when you went to high school and you would be in class with these white kids during the day, and you would come down Franklin Avenue and out from school and they went on out of Moore Street toward Nassau, and the same kids that you were sitting in class with about a half an hour before, they didn't even speak to you. And they would be going to Veet's or the Balt or Renwick's and we couldn't go with them. You felt really inadequate, inasmuch as the same people who wanted to copy off your paper in class now don't even want to talk to you. And I remember going to the Witherspoon School, which was the black school, and seeing the books were sent down from the Nassau Street School, because I could see the names of the kids who had had books before we got them. Here I could play with some of these same kids in the afternoon and have to use their hand-me-down books at school.

I can remember that we were the better basketball players, but yet still, when it came to choosing the team, I was the fourteenth person they gave a uniform to, and that was on the JV [Junior Varsity] team. There was a fellow by the name of Joe Friel, and he came to Princeton High School as a teacher, and they had a game where he was filling in for the coach. He started them and he said he didn't care about what they were, he started them. So for a couple of games, I played.

The older people in the family used to tell us that you had to study, you had to do this, you had to be twice as smart as the white man to get anywhere in life. They said, "Don't fight. Just walk away from it." But I can remember vividly, coming from a football game, and the University of Virginia played Princeton University. We were coming home and the traffic was going down the street and these young Virginia students were hollering out of their cars and whatnot. They didn't realize they were coming along Nassau Street, that they were in our territory. And the cars got stopped because of the traffic. I can remember going to the cars and punching them and hitting them and trying to get them out of the car.

In [my] senior year of high school, we used to have a senior trip to Washington and we protested. We didn't want to go because the black kids would not be allowed to stay with the white kids. So myself and some others, we protested. There were probably about a half dozen select kids who did go, but they stayed at Howard University. They'd meet up with their classmates. I didn't want that kind of trip, didn't want to be part of it.

Bruce Wright (1917–2005)

I'm not too keen about Christians—the great slave-owning populace of this country. I didn't go to places like churches when I was young. I was sensible. I was sane. I played hooky when I was sent off to church from the time I was really little. My parents never made any protests, not to me. They heard too many of my speeches about white Christians in America. Even when I was young, I knew the stories about slavery. I was never a little kid. I was an avid reader.

And before I became an avid reader, I heard about slavery in conversations with teachers, like Miss Carolyn P. Gates. She said slavery was a cruel hoax for people especially who called themselves Christians. But some of the preachers, she said, were nice and decent people, just deluded. She gave me a whole list of black heroes, and I became interested in blacks' participation in history, although the mention of them is mostly suppressed. Miss Gates was one of my favorite teachers. And she used to tell me what prospects existed if you were smart, stayed in school, and did well, and went on to college. I mean, I'll never forget her. She wanted me to get out of Princeton and, of course, so did I.

She was at the Witherspoon School where I went through eighth grade, with Miss Cousins as my principal. They had made a very timid approach at integration in Princeton by allowing certain black kids to go to the public schools on Nassau Street, which were all white, except for these small instances of integration. My sister went to school under that system. For one year I went to high school in Princeton and I was on the high school hockey team. We were playing the Princeton freshmen and we went over to the Hobey Baker Rink, and my teammates all went in, and I was stopped at the door. I never spoke to one of those bastards ever again. You gotta be black to have these great experiences in life. This country, I hated this country. Alleged Christians, which is supposed to suggest some kind of moral value, and I couldn't get in the goddamn rink.

Jay Craig (1930–)

Ronald Reagan made some very cowardly remarks about people of color, not only in this country but abroad when he referred to the African National Congress freedom fighters as "agitators." People—natives in their own land, their own nation—who could not vote and had to be off the streets at 10:00 at night, and he referred to them as agitators. He also referred to Russia as "the Evil Empire." When my mother and father were born in the first decade of the last century—my father was born in 1885 so the century before that—they were born in the Evil Empire, this one. Any white American male who can refer to another nation as an evil empire without reflecting on how evil this empire once was, has got to be a jackass.

Leonard Rivers (1934–)

We were very, very fortunate. You see, Princeton's had some interesting things happen. A little, old Jewish man probably had more influence on the Princeton black community than anybody else. A guy named Irwin Weiss. Irwin Weiss was our gym teacher. This was back before integration was popular, but I mean, he personally took a lot of kids by the hand and said, "C'mon, let's go, let's do it." Irwin Weiss was, at that time, one of two white teachers in Witherspoon School. And he went over and got Pete Wilson and brought him over the Witherspoon School to talk to gym classes because I know he thought at that time, it was important to bring a black role model into the school. Now, I'm talking about the '40s, I'm not talking about the '70s. You see, but he went out and did that, and Pete Wilson, as the black captain of basketball at Princeton, spent a lot of time with us and people got to know him, and it was through Irwin Weiss.

Leonard Rivers, Princeton University's baseball coach
from 1976 to 1980

Irwin Weiss has touched a lot of people. He touched me. Probably one of the reasons why I took a career in athletics was because of him. I can remember going to the Penn Relays with him [in his] old DeSoto. Me and a kid named George Mudd. I mean, that's the kind of guy he was. My brother ran the hurdles. So Irwin Weiss went out and built a hurdle. My brother used to practice in the driveway all summer long. Track shoes, he got track shoes for people, and he never asked for anything in return. He was a class, class, class individual, and I'm talking about back in . . . the '40s and '50s.

I don't know if you know the name Bruce Wright. They called him "Turn 'em loose, Bruce." He was a judge in New York. Well, Bruce Wright was born and raised here in Princeton, and Irwin Weiss tried to get him into Princeton when Princeton was an all-white institution. Had him file [an] application, and when he filed [the] application, Mr. Weiss told him, "Don't put race in there. Don't fill it out." And then the application went over, and they called Bruce Wright over for a personal interview, over on campus in the admissions office. And Irwin Weiss went with him. And they threw him and Bruce Wright out of the office. And Mr. Weiss didn't go back on that campus for ten or fifteen years. You see, that's the kind of white role model we had in our community and in our school. And when he passed away, it was a heartfelt sorrow that fell over the John Witherspoon area because everybody had Irwin Weiss stories.

Jay Craig (1930–)

I got along fairly well with the white kids in high school. I can't recall any instances of name-calling, as far as race is concerned. But I could see on the teachers' faces. For instance, there was a teacher named Ms. Steiner—and I could see how the other elitist teachers treated her like, oh no, you're not part of us. You don't eat over here. There were a couple of teachers that I really cared for. There was one who excused us from grammar because we were so up on it, and she seemed to be a really fair teacher. Ms. Steiner also was an excellent teacher. She was a science teacher, always helpful, always with a smile on her face.

Miss Haight was a teacher that rubbed me the wrong way, particularly when it came to African Americans. She taught history, and we were labeled communists. If you speak up, you're a communist. I mean, this was her big thing. She was definitely against Paul Robeson. He was a communist. In other words, he wasn't *appreciative*.

We had to write an essay about a current event, and I chose to write about a photo editorial from *Ebony* magazine, called "A Time to Count Our Blessings," about how as African Americans, we should be *appreciative* of where we are and what we've done, or what white Americans have done for us, something to that effect. I wrote it and she took it around and she showed it to every history teacher. I think she gave me a double A+ on that.

But it wasn't what I felt. I was bright enough at that age to know how I was going to get good marks, maybe a B+ or an A or a double A—she always used that double A. I wrote exactly what she wanted to hear. If I had written my real feelings deep down inside, she may have kicked me out of the class. I would have been ostracized.

My real thoughts were just the opposite.

When I first became aware of racism, it wasn't through the school system. It was through newspapers and personal experience. I was educated reading the *New York Times*, because I deeply loved the editorials, whether I agreed or disagreed. Once in a while, I would buy the *Daily News*, but I would always read the editorials in high school. That's where I was educated—not in Princeton High School. From the newspapers I could get some insight into what was happening in the world, but particularly in politics, and what was happening to us as African Americans. It wasn't covered, but if you were bright enough, you could tell exactly what was going on.

I've spoken to my own kids more about racism than my parents spoke to me. But I could *see* racism in Princeton. We would go into Princeton University on the campus. I can remember the occasion of being asked what I was doing there. I will never forget these words: "You have a place." It was one of those cracker proctors at Princeton University who said, "You have a place to play downtown," while my white contemporaries were playing right next to me on the lawn with a ball.

When I was fifteen or maybe sixteen, I was in areas in this town, particularly in the western section, Cleveland Lane, Hodge Road, where I was stopped by Princeton Borough police, saying, "Well, what are you doing over here?" Whereas that would never be asked of a white contemporary of mine who was walking on the street in that area. What I was doing there, I really don't remember, but we walked all over town when we were young; we just walked.

Joe Moore (1941–)

My civil consciousness really emerged as a freshman in college, as opposed to my involvement as a high school student in Princeton. I went to an all-black college in Ohio, to a place called Central State University. It was an all-black experience. It was fantastic, because you were now in a community of all black folks and the culture was just alive. And you were meeting people from all over the country. And the community is vibrant. And it's an intellectual community. And you no longer had to be fearful of the man. You no longer had to be told by white teachers, "You don't know what you're doing," or "You're not smart enough to understand a compound sentence." So Central State provided for me the impetus for my intellectual growth. It also provided me the opportunity to challenge the system, as it were.

It was a land-grant school, which meant that an ROTC program was mandatory for your freshman and sophomore year. And it was also the Vietnam War era. So everybody wore these green monkey suits, and you'd have to get up at 7:00 in the morning on Thursday mornings. I didn't like it, but I had to do it. My first term sophomore year, Captain Smith got up and talked about national security, why we should defend this country. And he went on and on and on and on and on. So, when he finished, I stood up, with all my friends in this class. I say, "Can someone give an opposing view?" And he said, "Yes, sir. Cadet Moore, come on up." I went to the front of the class, saluted him, and I turned around, and I told the class about thirty different reasons why they shouldn't support the Vietnam War.

The next day, the FBI was there, the military brass came from Washington—and I was thrown into this room and kept there for forty-eight hours, just because I opposed the war. I was given a battery of tests by a group of psychiatrists from the military. I knew they had profiled me to death. I was thrown out of ROTC for that semester, knowing full well that you could not graduate from this land-grant school unless you completed two years of ROTC.

But there's a caveat with that. The following year, I had to repeat this course in order to graduate. So one Friday evening, I was in the local pub and the ROTC brass was in there. And Captain Smith was at the bar. He called me and he said, "Moore, I want to talk to you." I said, "Oh, god." So I went over—but I knew that we were on neutral ground at this point, because we were both bar drinking—in the same place. So he says, "Moore, have you ever considered becoming a commissioned officer of the US Army? You have so much potential." Well—you know, this is the same guy who had me thrown out. And I couldn't believe it. Well, anyway, I called him so many names. I went up one side of him and down the other side, and I said, "You're out of your mind."

Another story from that time. . . . Students from Antioch College in Yellow Springs, Ohio—it's about six miles away—would come to campus every

The Witherspoon YMCA Phantom Baseball Team,
City-wide Softball Champions, A-League (1947)

Saturday to try to recruit students from Little Forks, another black college adjacent to ours, and Central State, to come over to Yellow Springs and protest against this white barber who refused to cut blacks' hair. So, finally, after about a month of them coming over, I went—got on the bus and next thing I know we were over in Yellow Springs. We got there, and there were police, fire trucks, state troopers—the whole nine yards. Little did I know that when I got out of the bus, I was now in front of the line. And next thing I know, the water hoses came and I was dragged into a paddy wagon. Next thing I know, I was in Green County Jail. The irony of that story—there were 110 of us. Ninety percent were white students from Antioch. So that night, they have a special court. All the white kids from Antioch were putting up their money—whatever the fine was—and they were gone back to Yellow Springs. So the judge—when my turn comes, he says, "How do you plead?" And I say, "I plead not guilty." He says, "The fine is . . ." So I say, "I'm financially incapacitated." He says, "Three days in jail."

I wasn't financially incapacitated. I mean, the fine wasn't that much. I could have gotten some friends to put it up or whatever. But the principle of the matter was that there were only about eight of us who spent those three days in jail, who followed it from A to Z. It was three days. I ate the bologna sandwiches and glass of water three times a day. So that to me it was an awakening of the degree to which whites took civil rights seriously. I mean, what were they doing? Using us to come and protest and then—you know—hey, we're out of there. So, that stuck with me.

Arthur Lewis (1931–2013)

The Trenton Police Department didn't allow its black officers to ride in the cars. We broke that in '62. I came back from the March on Washington and Mayor Howard, he was the mayor of Trenton, put me on his Civil Rights Commission. Two weeks later, I put a picket line around City Hall to allow the black officers to ride in cars. I guess we'd been there three hours, and this police car, speeding down the street, stopped, and Bob Neale—the black police officer—jumped out. And I was on the mayor's Biracial Committee and so I was always shooting my mouth off at the meetings and whatnot. Soon they had the first black detectives, Herb Fitzgerald and Leon Smith. In Princeton, we had one black policeman when I was a kid, Sergeant Phil Diggs. But it was still the status quo over here.

I do remember those early years where people like Joe Moore were hired over at Princeton. I remember Walter Harris on the police force. He was killed in the line of duty. They always wanted to have a black face on the police force. The next one was Tom Moore, and he stayed for about a year. He didn't see himself a police officer, so he came off. For a couple of years or so, we didn't have any black policemen on the force. But the next thing I knew, the lily-white police force hired Fred Porter.

I was busy raising a family, but I was still doing other things. I think every major demonstration that's been in Washington, DC, from 1963 on, I was there. When Reagan fired the control tower operators I was there. I went down when King had the Tent City in Washington. One thing that sticks out is when I brought my oldest daughter down there.

One person stands out in my mind. He was right in the midst of it, shirt-sleeves rolled up. It was US senator Clifford Case. Jersey had the best two senators in the country at that time, Harris[on] Williams was a Democrat and Clifford Case was a Republican. They were there. They stood tall, both of those guys.

9

Standing Strong

and

Moving Through

The 1903 Chauffeur and Butler Club Formal

AN EXTRAORDINARY DETERMINATION AND grace seem to belong to these Witherspoon residents who not only survived but have also lived full lives. Dignity and fairness are hallmarks of the journeys they and their ancestors have made. But how do they manage to face such overwhelming negativity toward them and still remain positive?

Seventy-year-old Jay Craig spoke earlier of his dignified father, Peyton Craig, who worked as a butler and houseman at the Cap and Gown eating club on Prospect Avenue. One day, while he was laying a fire in the living room, several white students came up behind him and laughed as they rubbed their hands into his hair for "good luck." Had Peyton Craig responded with the rage he felt when that happened, he most likely would have been fired or possibly jailed. If he quit, how would he support his wife and eleven children? Instead, those constant humiliations ate at him. "[He'd] come home from the club and count out his tips on the table, slapping down the money and saying, 'Goddamn crackers, Goddamn crackers.'"

To deal with such personal assaults being delivered with startling regularity, Witherspoon residents call on the power of the human spirit and friendships with others to keep on standing strong. Stories help, too. Especially ones about parents and ancestors recovering from life-altering shocks or forging victories over adversity: Frederick Douglass, who escaped slavery and became one of the country's most persuasive abolitionists and authors; Harriet Tubman, who kept traveling back down south to lead more than three hundred enslaved people to freedom; Joe Lewis, who beat Max Schmeling for the World Heavyweight Championship in boxing; Jackie Robinson, who integrated professional baseball and set world records; and Wilma Rudolph, who had polio as a child and was told she'd never walk again, yet went on to become the first American woman to win three Olympic gold medals in track and field. Closer to home, young people only had to look up to see the heroes who paraded through their lives on a daily basis—their fathers, mothers, grandparents, aunts, uncles, friends, teachers, and neighbors.

A favorite local story is about a young man named James C. (Jimmy) Johnson, who changed his last name when he escaped from slavery in Baltimore in 1839. He'd run out of money before he got to Princeton, but the day after his arrival, he got a job at the college as a bootblack and stayed on doing a variety of service jobs. After four years of freedom in Princeton, he was walking down Nassau Street when a college student, who was a previous neighbor of Johnson's former master, recognized him. Without alerting Johnson to the fact he'd been recognized, the student promptly reported him as a runaway slave. Princeton's sheriff arrested Johnson, and according to "Stories of New Jersey," collected by the WPA Federal Writers' Project,

> [t]he case was tried at the city hotel, amidst great excitement, caused especially by the southern students, who feared that opposition to the Fugitive Slave law would be so great as to defeat the claim of the owner. They also apprehended that an effort would be made by the colored men of the town to rescue the slave if he should be remanded to the owner. Marshal Jeffries of Baltimore was on the ground to take possession of the slave in case the claim of the master should be established.[1]

The all-white jury, which included Quakers, but did not, of course, include blacks, decided in favor of the slave owner, to whom Johnson was to be remanded the following day. Since the deliberations had gone into the evening, the sheriff kept Johnson under heavily armed guards overnight. The next day, before Johnson was to be delivered back to his owner, Miss Theodosia Prevost, a former Southerner and direct descendant of President Witherspoon, paid the plantation owner his price of $550 and then set James Johnson free.[2] Immediately, Johnson set to work to pay back his whole debt, which he did within four years. Among other jobs, he sold peanuts, apples, and juice from his neat wooden cart, which he pushed to locations on campus and in town. At his death, university students collected funds for his burial in the Princeton Cemetery. His headstone reads:

James Johnson
The Students' Friend
Died 1902
Erected by graduates of Princeton University

Another enduring inspiration to black Princetonians is Betsey Stockton, a community matriarch and "one of the most widely traveled, highly educated, and socially useful beings of her time."[3] In her lifetime, Betsey Stockton's roles included, "[s]lave, hired domestic servant, seamstress, pastry cook, schoolteacher, medical nurse, missionary journal writer, surrogate mother, common school and Sabbath school founder and principal."[4] She was born around 1798 to an enslaved mother, in the Robert Stockton II household. At six she was given by Stockton to his daughter, Betsy, and her husband Ashbel Green, the eighth president of the university. They had three sons, one of whom first taught Betsy to read and write. Ashbel Green allowed "Bet," along with his other children, to use his personal library. ("Green's household was in love with Christ and the written and spoken word: language was used for praising God, for healing, for consolation after children's deaths, for treatment of the mentally ill. Letters, sermons, essays, hymns, books, chapbooks, magazines and newspapers infused every aspect of daily life.")[5]

Betsey worked hard at her domestic chores, and Green, observing her inquisitive mind, became a spiritual and academic mentor who discussed literature and religious philosophy with her.[6] When Betsey was twenty, Green freed her and began paying her wages for working in his household. She had joined the First Presbyterian Church of Princeton and belonged to a Bible society for young scholars. When Betsey was twenty-one, Green wrote a letter recommending her for missionary service to the Sandwich Islands, which are now Hawaii: "At the age of twenty, as near as I can judge, I gave her her freedom; and have since paid her wages. . . . I think her well qualified for higher employment in a mission, than domestick [sic] drudgery. She reads extremely well; and few of her age and sex have read more books on religion than she; or can give a better account of them."[7]

Betsey Stockton more than proved herself as the first unmarried woman in the United States known to have become a missionary. On her five-month voyage to Hawaii, she also proved herself to be an extraordinary writer. Her descriptions of life aboard a whaler were so vivid that Herman Melville used her narrative as primary source material for *Moby Dick* and, later, James Michener did the same for his novel *Hawaii*.[8] In her journal, Stockton wrote:

I was much interested in witnessing the harpooning of a large shark. It was taken at the stern of the ship, about 6 yards from the cabin window, from which I had a clear view of it. It was struck by two harpoons at the same time. The fish (if we may call it one, for it has very little the appearance of a fish) was so angry that he endeavoured to bite the men after he was on deck. His jaw bone was taken out and preserved by one of the missionaries. We see a great number of them and take them often. . . .

The colour of the water near land, is of a greenish hue; a little farther out it is of a bluish tint; and in the middle of the ocean it is of dark blue, and very clear. I never saw a more beautiful green than the colour of the water off Cape Blanco, where we were nearly driven by an unfavourable wind. From this we steered S.W. by S. between the African coast and the Cape De Verd islands; and then directed our course S.S.W. to the coast of Brazil. If it were in my power I would like to describe the Phosphorescence of the sea. But to do this would require the pen of a Milton: and he, I think, would fail, were he to attempt it. I never saw any display of Fire-works that equalled it for beauty. As far as we could see the ocean, in the wake of the ship, it appeared one sheet of fire, and exhibited figures of which you can form no idea.

We have bathed during this month frequently, and find the water very refreshing. Yesterday, at 8 in the morning, the thermometer stood at 80°. The missionaries all went in to bathe, with their pantaloons: Mr B. wore his shirt also, and dived three times from the ship; the last time he staid too long in the water, so that the strength of his arms was exhausted, and he was not able to get into the ship alone. Mr. Lane, the second mate, dived from the bowsprit, with a rope, and tied it round him. At the same time another was thrown from the side of the vessel. We felt alarmed for a few moments, but there was no real danger. . . . I must finish this year by saying with the Psalmist, "When I consider the works of thy hands, Lord[,] what is man that thou art mindful of him!"[9]

In her own view, Stockton's most important contribution was starting and running a school for nonroyal Hawaiians, mainly farmers, who previously had not been educated.[10] While in Hawaii, Stockton, a natural linguist, learned and spoke the Hawaiian language—and because of her efforts, some six thousand children became educated within just a few years after having established the school. Of course, for the Witherspoon residents, the most important thing she did was to return to Princeton in the 1830s and establish the first educational system for Princeton's black commoners, which brought a new richness of life to many thousands of children and adults from 1835 to 1865 and beyond.

In her gifted teaching of small children and adults, both through the Witherspoon Street Presbyterian Church, the common schools, and the district schools, the elegant, charismatic Stockton, whose carriage spoke of royalty, had brought literacy and broad thinking to people who had been denied any formal education. "Among the older people, her influence was supreme . . . her judgment always thoughtfully given and with great dignity, was regarded with the greatest respect."[11]

Another legendary Princetonian of this era, William Drew Robeson, had traversed the minefields of slavery, cast off its chains, and taken a breathtaking ascent into the life of the mind and spirit. Born a plantation slave in 1845 to Benjamin and Sabra Robeson, who were enslaved on the Robeson plantation in Martin County, near Raleigh, North Carolina, William Drew Robeson escaped when he was fifteen. He traveled north to Pennsylvania around 1860 via the Underground Railroad, and served in the army as a laborer. When the Civil War ended, he made his way to Lincoln University, in Oxford, Pennsylvania, outside Philadelphia, where he studied theology, the classics, Greek, Latin, and Hebrew, and graduated as one of the top seven scholars in his class. While he was earning two additional degrees in theology from Lincoln's Divinity School, Rev. Robeson met Maria Louisa Bustill, a schoolteacher of mixed African, Lenape Native American, and Anglo-Quaker descent, who was also attending the historical black university.[12] Louisa's father and mother, Charles Hicks Bustill and Emily Robinson Bustill, were prominent black Quakers and abolitionists. Louisa and William married in 1878 in spite of her parents feeling she was "marrying down" in choosing a dark-skinned man who'd been born into slavery.[13]

In 1879, the newlyweds moved to Princeton, where Louisa taught school and worked as a tutor and a force for good in the community. Rev. Robeson became the beloved pastor of the Witherspoon Street Presbyterian Church and a powerful voice for human rights and social justice for the next two

Family with hats, banjo, and accordion (about 1880)

decades. His eloquent sermons inspired congregants, as did a stained-glass window inscribed, "In loving memory of Sabra Robeson," Rev. Robeson's enslaved mother. Rev. Robeson and Louisa had seven children. Two died as infants and five lived to be adults—William, Reeve, Benjamin, and the only girl, Marian. Their sixth living child, the youngest of the surviving children, was Paul Leroy Robeson, who later wrote of his father, "Though my father was a man of ordinary height . . . his physical bearing reflected the rock-like strength and dignity of his character. He had the greatest speaking voice I have ever heard. It was a deep, sonorous basso, richly melodic and refined, vibrant with the love and compassion which filled him. How proudly, as a boy, I walked at his side, my hand in his, as he moved among the people!"[14]

Rev. Robeson's leadership caused the Witherspoon Street Presbyterian Church to flourish. With his presence at the helm, the church became an important center for the black community—a place for worship as well as a forum where congregants could voice their concerns. One of the most urgent of these in the 1890s was the widespread murders of black Americans by mobs of white men who held public lynchings they referred to as "picnics," sometimes with thousands of attendees, including women and children. Lynching was by no means confined to the South. It occurred all over the country—from Oklahoma and Nebraska to Pennsylvania, New Jersey, and New York. On April 9, 1898, the day Rev. and Louisa Robeson's youngest son Paul was born, Ida B. Wells, a black female journalist active in the antilynching campaign, brought a delegation to the White House to protest the situation. Wells informed President William Mc-Kinley that nearly ten thousand black Americans had been lynched in the previous twenty years—between 1878 and 1898. She said, "Nowhere in the civilized world save the United States of America do men, possessing all civil and political power, go out in bands of 50 to 5,000 to hunt down, shoot, hang or burn to death a single individual, unarmed and absolutely powerless."[15]

In November 1898, a black person was lynched nearly every four days. Antilynching bills had been submitted to Congress, but none had passed. Rev. Robeson and his close friend since their student days at Lincoln University, Abraham P. Denny, who was superintendent of the Witherspoon School for Colored Children, scheduled a meeting at the Witherspoon Street Presbyterian Church. The pastors of the Baptist and AME churches joined them to discuss the best ways to speak out against the "race riots" throughout the nation.

At the meeting, the attendees worked out a written resolution urging President McKinley and Congress to pass laws to stop these widespread murders. The *Princeton Press* wrote about Rev. Robeson and others who spoke at the event: "[Their] addresses were carefully prepared and eloquently delivered. . . . They advocated no violence, no retaliation; they opposed violence in every form. They thought there should be Christian sentiment enough to prevent such disgraceful outrages. They thought it possible to enact laws to enable the general government to protect all its citizens."[16]

Despite this newspaper report, the white power structure in Princeton considered this gathering alarming. They deemed it unacceptable that Robeson and Denny had spearheaded resolutions appealing to President McKinley and the Congress to enact laws to stop the widespread slaughter of African Americans. Princeton's white school board fired Denny from his job as school superintendent, and not much later, the white presbytery forced Rev. Robeson from his job as well. After this tremendous blow, Rev. Robeson moved his family from the parsonage to a small house around the corner, on Green Street, where

> he changed his garb from the traditional black frock coat of the minister to the blue denim overalls worn by laborers like his brothers, Ben and John. Rev. Robeson—the title would remain as much a part of him as his patriarchal manner—was now in his fifty-sixth year. Fortunately for his wife and children, his strength of body (he was broad of shoulders and powerfully built) was equal to his strength of spirit, when like Adam, he was in effect commanded: *In the sweat of thy face shalt thou eat bread.*[17]

With what savings he had, Rev. Robeson bought a mare and a wagon and began to support his family by hauling coal ashes from houses and driving college students in his horse-drawn wagon. His son Paul was only three at the time. As the beloved pastor of a large Negro congregation, Rev. Robeson had served his followers in many ways—"seeking work for the jobless, money for the needy, mercy from the Law," and this work did not end when he became an ash man.[18] His son would later write:

> That a so-called lowly station in life was no bar to a man's assertion of his full human dignity was heroically demonstrated by my father in the face of a grievous blow that came to him when I was still a baby. . . . A gentle scholar and teacher all of his adult life, my father, then past middle age, was forced to begin life anew. He got a horse and a wagon, and began to earn his living hauling ashes for the townsfolk. This was his work at the time I remember him and I recall the growing mound of dusty ashes dumped in our backyard at 13 Green Street. A fond memory remains of our horse, a mare named Bess, whom I grew to love and who loved me. My father also went into the hack business, and as a coachman drove the gay young students around town and on trips to the seashore.[19]

But even more tragedy came for Rev. Robeson and his children. In 1904, his beloved wife, Maria Louisa, who had been his helpmate and closest confidante, died in a tragic fire in the Green Street house when an ember from the coal stove ignited her clothes and burned more than 80 percent of her body. Paul Robeson was six at the time.

Not once did I hear him complain of the poverty and misfortune of those years. . . . Not one word of bitterness ever came from him. Serene, undaunted, he struggled to earn a livelihood and see to our education.[20]

Eventually, Rev. Robeson moved to the African Methodist Episcopal denomination and led the Saint Thomas AME Zion Church in Somerville, New Jersey. Rev. Robeson's youngest child adapted to life with his father once more in the pulpit, giving rousing sermons, urging integrity and Shakespeare's admonishment, "To thine own self be true."

Paul Robeson absorbed his father's lessons—especially that of measuring himself by his own potential rather than by the yardstick of another. He excelled in high school and broke more barriers at Rutgers University as one of two black students in the class of 1919. A champion orator, he lettered in four sports, was twice named All-American in football, and graduated as valedictorian of his class.

He also earned a law degree from Columbia University, but made his mark onstage, rather than in the courtroom. His powerful voice filled the Metropolitan Opera House, Broadway theaters, and concert halls throughout the United States, Europe, and Russia, in a variety of languages, including Spanish, French, Yiddish, Czech, German, Hebrew, Chinese, and Gaelic. In 1925, he gave a concert in New York "devoted exclusively to African American spirituals and secular music. The impact was electric . . . 'All those who listened last night to the first concert in this country made entirely of Negro music . . . may have been present at a turning point [in musical history].'"[21]

Paul Robeson's commitment to the "oneness of mankind" inspired people around the world. At every opportunity, he spoke out against racism and oppression. He sang for coal miners and striking workers, and protested

Four women friends (about 1900)

against fascism. "In Spain, he sang for the international volunteers fighting Franco. . . . He went to Africa and lent his voice to the struggle against colonialism. In Salt Lake City, where Joe Hill had been executed in 1915, Robeson defied the copper barons by giving the first public performance of 'Joe Hill' in Utah."[22] In the Witherspoon neighborhood, as in Harlem, Paul

Robeson was "The tallest tree in the forest." To millions of African Americans, he was "a champion who devoted himself not only to the struggle of equal rights, but to an ongoing celebration of the dignity of his people and their culture."[23]

Fifty years after the meeting that his father had held in the Witherspoon Street Presbyterian Church, Paul Robeson founded the new American Crusade to End Lynching. His friend Albert Einstein joined forces with him and cochaired the organization. In 1946, Paul Robeson led a delegation to the White House to make an appeal to President Truman to support antilynching legislation.

During this time, the CIA, FBI, and the US State Department had Robeson under intense surveillance. They concluded he was one of the most dangerous men in the world. In the 1950s, the US State Department confiscated his passport, branded him a communist and a traitor, shut down his access to perform abroad or in public venues in this country, and called him before the House Un-American Activities Committee (HUAC). At his hearing, Robeson said, "Anything I have to say or stand for, I've said in public, all over the world, and that is why I am here today. You want to shut up every colored person who wants to fight for the rights of his people."[24] When a committee member asked why he didn't move to Russia, Robeson said, "Because my father was a slave, and my people died to build this country, and I'm going to stay right here and have a part of it, just like you."[25]

For eight years before the Supreme Court returned his passport to him, Paul Robeson kept performing in black churches and open spaces, despite threats on his life and public smearing of his name. He even gave concerts over the telephone to audiences in other countries, and, banned from Canada, gave a concert on the Canadian border that was attended by tens of thousands of people from both countries.

Despite the assaults Robeson experienced, he advised, in keeping with the spirit of his father and the Witherspoon community, "Have faith in the whole people, the emergence into full bloom of the last estate, the vision of no high and no low, no superior and no inferior—but equals, assigned to different tasks in the building of a new and richer human society."[26]

See, our leaders were the stewards at the clubs, the restaurant owners, the guys who pushed the brooms in the schools, the janitors. They were the leaders. They produced kids who became leaders.

—SIMEON MOSS

Helen Ball Hoagland (1920–2009)

My father came here because there was nothing in Annapolis for him to do. From what I know most of all about my father was that he had a chance to work over at Princeton University at the Canon Club and he, like the rest of them, just served and did what the students wanted done. Until one day he was going past and some students were on the floor playing cards or something and one of the guys said, "I'm gonna rub Bob's head. Bob come here and let me rub your head, and maybe I'll have some luck." And my father said he had a stack of wood, he was getting ready to fill the fireplace in there. He had the stack of wood and then he put the wood in there and walked out. That was the end of his employment over to Canon Club.

'Course, after that he was very much in need of a job, and he got a truck and he used to paint and he used to cart things around town, moving, helping people like that. And then he was a very good painter, doing a lot of painting all around and then he said, "There must be something better I can do."

Well, right around the corner, there is a small driveway and he took that driveway and built a children's store. It was a community store. Ball's Fountain Service had both black and white customers. Ice cream, it was hip, you know to buy, and the store stayed open until eleven o'clock almost every night, and he had all the black papers, all the black newspapers, such as the *Amsterdam News*, the *Chicago Tribune*, the *Afro-American*, and the *Pittsburgh Courier*, which I foolishly did not keep. Oh, there was a local paper, too, that told all the scandal that was in Princeton. Ah, it was just a real Mom and Pop store.

While he was doing that, my mother got into baking, and she would bake for Dean Witts over at Princeton University, a wonderful man, and he would come down and pick up the bread. He entertained the boys in the university, some section of them weekly, and he would pick up this home-made bread. And then my mother started putting bread out in the store to sell that she had made, and she also took in laundry work, and she was never away from home. She was never away from home.

Alice Satterfield (1922–2010)

Right in this area, we had the best time of our lives—and among ourselves, we got along beautifully. . . . It was there—growing up in that time, we had prejudice. There were stores uptown where you couldn't go. . . . But I didn't miss that. . . . We had our own. Griggs' Restaurant was the best restaurant in the town, food-wise and in cleanliness. . . . Mr. Griggs served *everybody*, and he had friends and he served the best food at reasonable prices in town, and a lot of people preferred to go to his place.

When I used to go with my mother occasionally, when I was younger, when she used to go to the homes and clean, I remember so well my mother being on her knees scrubbing floors, and that is what hurt me. And then the woman would sit in her chair and say, "Oh Annie, you didn't get in the corner." And I said to my mother one day, rather I burst out and said, "Now Mom, why does she call you Annie, and you have to say *Missus* to her?" And that thing, that bothered me for many years, and I never got over it. They didn't have respect for my mother, yet she had to have respect for them, and that I did not appreciate, nor do I today.

She was a wonderful, loving, caring, Christian woman. In fact, to me, my mother was an angel. She cared about us, she cared about people regardless of whether you were white, black, or whatever. She loved and cared for everybody, and they loved my mother, white, black, and all.

Susie Waxwood (1902–2006)

As a principal when they were trying to desegregate the schools, [my husband] had a lot of things happen. There were some white parents who were certainly not happy about it [desegregation]. And I think there were some black parents who were concerned about how their children were going to be accepted and treated. And I think they were absolutely right to have concerns about what would happen to their children. My husband played a big part in talking to those students and telling them, "Don't give up. Keep going and fight for what you want." So I never missed a class at the Red Cross. And then I took the second class and got high marks both times. When I got the certificate from the National American Red Cross and joined a group, I was never late. When it was my turn to be what we called the "Officer of the Day," I did everything that I was responsible for. Nobody could say that I did not live up to what I said I would do.

Fannie Floyd (1924–2008)

I think Princeton is a community like most places: you have to keep on your toes. You can't go to sleep. Even a lot of people of goodwill don't realize what they are saying that might affect your feelings or they just don't think. As situations arise, if you see a need, you have to let people know that you are not accepting of the way things are.

Doris Burrell (1919–2015)

The fireworks started when it was time for our first child, Sondra, to start school in September of 1946. My husband went to segregated schools here [in Princeton], but I didn't. So we talked it over, and I said, "No. This is ridiculous. . . . What right do they have that they can ask us to send our tax money up there? We live in Princeton, we're paying taxes for our child's education, and they're supposed to educate her." We decided she wasn't going to school up on Quarry Street. I had nothing against the principal there or against blacks. It wasn't that. It was just morally wrong. That's all. So, we decided we were going to enroll our child at Valley Road School, where she was supposed to go. And that's what we did. I went down, and . . . the principal was wonderful. It was almost like she was glad to see us. I thought that she was going to give us trouble, but she didn't. She registered our daughter and made sure I had everything right. She had a little smile on her face like she was happy. And, so that was all done.

My daughter went around with about five girls and they were all going to start school. So, I went to their parents and told them to register their children there. None of them . . . were happy or pleased about it at all. One of them asked me why I wanted her to go there, and I said, "Because she's supposed to go there." . . . So I talked to them about segregation . . . I said, "It's not that I don't want our children to be with blacks. I'm not ashamed of being a black person by means. But it's not right. They are forcing us to do something whether we want to do it or not."

Then the phone started ringing. People were calling—blacks, whites, all of them—calling and calling me. Calling me all sorts of names. "Who do you think you are? You think you're better than everybody else?" That was from the black ladies. And the white ladies would say, "You think you're going to integrate with us, but you're not."

There was a black woman who came to see me who worked as a maid at this very, very wealthy white woman's house—one of the wealthiest white families in town. So she came and said, "Doris, I want to tell you . . . I think you're making a mistake in sending your child down here to school. Because the woman I work for, she had a dinner party last night and they talked about this situation. [They said,] 'Who does she think she is sending her child down to the Valley Road School? She thinks her daughter is going to go there, but she's not.' And she told her maid, because she knew she came to my hair salon, to tell me the same thing. So her maid said, 'I don't think you better let your child go to that school because you really don't know what they'll do to you.'"

I said, "You just go back and you tell them that I said, 'Come hell or high water, our child is going to that school. I don't care what it costs. We will take them to court for the rest of my life.'" . . . Everybody was upset . . . I began to wonder about our human race. God makes birds of all kinds and animals and they all live their lives together.

So we took her down there the first day. At first the children and teachers treated her pretty bad. Later on, she told me, "Mom, I didn't tell you all the things they did because I didn't want to upset you." The children would stone her. That's what bothered me the most. I was trying to set up my appointments so I could get down there and bring her home. . . . The principal told me, "Why don't you join the PTA?" So I joined the PTA and became [a] secretary. I really did a lot, all kinds of things in the schools. . . . We all learned a lot. There were prejudices in the school . . . but this woman who threatened me, she didn't do anything. I didn't care. I was ready. I said, "I'm sick of this foolishness."

Sondra stayed at Valley Road, and when it was time for my younger daughter, Fredericka, to go to school, she went there, too. By that time, the schools were integrated, but we had to take the time to stick with our girls and run up there [when] a teacher was prejudiced. . . . When Sondra was a senior, she came home and said this teacher was going to fail her so she couldn't graduate from high school. So, we had a roundtable discussion with that teacher, other teachers, and my husband and I. It was really pitiful. [Her teacher] blurted out, "She told me she wants to be a teacher. What does she want to be a teacher for? Who's she gonna teach? Is she gonna teach black children? There's no sense in teaching black children 'cause they can't learn!" He said it right there in front of us and the other teachers, who all just looked at each other. Then he said, "What difference does it make whether I pass her or not? She's just gonna be cleaning houses or something like that." So I knew he was sick right there. I felt really sorry for him. Since then, he's done some other horrible things. Just about five years ago, they expelled him. He was still there all that time. Now, can you imagine how much damage he must have done?

Shirley Satterfield (1940–)

When I lived in Murray Hill, New Jersey, my older daughter came home one day and said, "Ma, am I black?" So, I had to sit her down and talk to her. And then my younger daughter came home one day and said that a little boy in her kindergarten class called her a name and hit her. So, I said, "Dawn, there's three things you can do. You can ask him why, and if that doesn't work, then you tell the teacher, and if that doesn't work, then you have to defend yourself." So, a parent came to me and said, "Your daughter hit a boy over the head with her lunch box." And I said, "Not my daughter." So I asked Dawn three times, and she said, "Mom, I didn't do that." So I said, "Dawn, you're the only little black girl in kindergarten, and they say they saw you do it." So, finally she told me. She said, "You told me to do three things. He called me a nigger. I asked him why. He didn't say anything. I told the teacher. She didn't do anything. So, I hit him over the head with my lunch box." I said, "Well done, Girl!"

Joe Moore (1941–)

In 1969 I was asked to run for city council in Princeton. Since I had a policy-making position at the university, I thought I might be able to get the university to respond to the community in ways that they had not responded before, and make some serious interaction between the university and the black community. Also, the white people came to me and said, "Hey, you need to run for borough council. You need to think about being a councilman to effect the policy in the community." So I accepted that. And I won, by the largest majority ever in the history of Princeton. I think a lot of it was the white guilt vote, but I still won.

So here I am now, sitting on city council—this little poor kid off of Jackson Street—now he's making decisions for the university and the community. And that period was very difficult for me, because, on one hand, people were saying, "Well, who does he really represent? He works for the university. He wears two hats." I remember the time that it was suspected that I was more loyal to the university than I was to the community. Then there were other times where I was suspected to be more loyal to the community than I was to the university.

The first year, they made me fire commissioner. It was like being Malcolm X in charge of the Ku Klux Klan. That was a trip. What happened is in the beginning of the year, the mayor would come by and say, "All right, what do you want to do?" And everybody would say, "Well, I want the budget committee," "I want public safety," or "I want sanitation," or whatever. And a lot of these liaisons are very critical. Some are not very critical. So, the first year I wanted to be police commissioner, and they said I was too new and too militant. So the first year, the mayor said, "Well, you be the fire commissioner." I said, "You're out of your mind." Because the fire department is like a social club. It's an Aryan social club, everybody knows that. They may have a few token blacks on it, but—you know—give me a break.

That first year, I was concerned about the disparity between what whites and blacks got paid in municipal government. The disparity was that wide and so obvious. So at the next budget go around for the borough, when we put the budget together, I made sure that all the minorities and the

Princeton family at the beach (1925)

low-paying white folks were put into parity, you know, made sure that they got the kinds of wages and increments that were due them. There was no way else of adjusting to that issue.

Then the second year, I said again, "I'd like to be police commissioner." He said, "Oh, no. We'd never make you police commissioner." He said, "Well, that only goes to seasoned council members." I said, "What are you talking about, seasoned?" I said, "Everybody's elected." I said, "The guy who was the police commissioner last year, it was his first year on [the] council." So after about three months of protesting, he appoint[ed] me police commissioner. My very first act was to fire the police chief who called me a nigger. Fired. And you have to remember that, as a kid, you'd see this towering guy and he'd make no bones about calling you a nigger and makes no bones about making sure the other white officers called you a nigger. And I reminded him of that in that meeting, where we asked for his early retirement paper. I said, "You remember me playing basketball? You went in and told Mr. What's-His-Name—you said, 'Don't ever do anything for these niggers in this town, because they never appreciate it.' So where'd that come from? Came from your racist background. Get your early retirement. Get a *Mad* magazine and lollipop and hit the door."

But on a serious note, that was a major shift, in terms of the police department's response to this community. You're familiar with profiling. You're familiar with all the issues that go on. This is a real issue. Just because of the nature of your skin, you are perceived to be a criminal. It's not peculiar to Princeton. It's national. But, in any event, that broke some ice, in terms of the council's saying, "Okay, you can do that," and restructuring of the police department.

What's critical is a respect for authority. Other colleagues had a difficult time respecting our authority as council members. White citizens had a difficult time respecting our authority. Some black citizens had a difficult time respecting our authority. One of the things that would happen in city council is that they would make decisions without you being there. They would get on the phone and they'd call everybody but me. So they already knew when they got to [the] city council what they were going to do. Unless they really needed my vote. And on the school board it was worse. They'd have private meetings at their houses. That's illegal. That's why you have the Sunshine Law. The Sunshine Law says everything has to be public except for certain personnel issues. I told them, "You're crazy. I'm elected just like you're elected—and not only that, but I got more votes than anybody when I ran. So why are you doing this?" I can go on and on. Hank and I were kidding when we were getting out of the car, because we grew up together. We're now senior citizens. I'm fifty-nine years old. I know he's sixty-one. What is the sense of his contribution to this community? What is the sense of my contribution to this community? All this list of the people that you see [to be interviewed], they all have something that has contributed to the vitality and the survival of this neighborhood. The essence of our existence is the ability to penetrate racism and say that we can make contributions—that we have made contributions. And nobody says that more eloquently than Maya Angelou and James Baldwin and Cornel West. I don't mean to preach, but you got me off on that tangent. So how legitimate was I? How legitimate was my serving eight years on city council?

When you're at that level, when you're isolated like that—the only black on city council and the only black in the Dean of Students Office—you know, all of a sudden, you're a domino in the sea. So, in a way, it's like—going back to that question that you asked me before, "Is there a certain amount of anger because of that experience, is there a certain amount of anger because you can't cross Nassau Street?"—No. The issue is, there is a certain amount of anger because you're black, wherever you might be and whatever you might do. That's what it boils down to. I haven't got time to be angry. I just know that it's ever present—ever present. You hope that racism in the year 2000 is decimated.

Penney Edwards-Carter (1947–)

I've always had a great affinity for Princeton—the borough of Princeton, I should say. The mayor here, Barbara Sigmund, genuinely cared about the community. She didn't know the word stranger. She was just amazing, and her presence is still missed by a lot of people in this community. . . . We have not had the same kind of care from public officials as Barbara. She visited the people here; she was friends with people in this neighborhood.

Jay Craig (1930–)

I wish I had been active in politics on the local or national level, but I never have been. I'm very active where I drink coffee at the Carousel Restaurant in Princeton, the greatest, greatest restaurant in New Jersey. I sit in there and get in political conversation from 6:30 a.m. until about 8:00 a.m. every Saturday and Sunday without fail. Many times I've sat in the Carousel and had coffee with millionaires, with very, very wealthy people at the same table in conversation with them, and you would never know it. They wear their money well. That's probably why they go there, because of the kind of people they are. I can learn something from them and they can learn something from me. The Carousel looks like just four walls with some tables in it, but it's the people, the characters in the place that make the Carousel . . . and the food; the breakfast food is fantastic.

President Shapiro and his wife are there, not probably on a weekly basis, but every other week. There's no telling who you'll see come in those doors of prominence. My friends and I have coffee every morning together in there. I've been going to the Carousel thirty-five years. Yeah, I remember the old

Kathleen Montgomery Edwards as a young bride (1947)

counter, when the counter was there, and I was going in there twenty years prior to that.

Helen Ball Hoagland (1920–2009)

One group that I was in, the Elizabeth Taylor Byrd Fund, was taking place in the sixties, and we became, what's the word when you're officially, go through the law and all, incorporated. We were incorporated at my house here, Nineteen Quarry Street, I have the papers and all on that. But anyway a very, very sweet woman died and a group of her friends, including me, decided that we would get together and have an organization to help kids and it was a successful thing. It was so good and you know, I don't know if it's still going on now today or not. I think it's inactive, but I couldn't swear to it, but we started that back in 1960–64, something like that. We started working in '63 right after this woman's death, because she was a prominent person and loved kids, and believe me, we did an excellent job in that group. We had a lot of men and women working in there; of course, we were all young then and we started giving annual dinner dances up to the club up here in Palmer Square, what's that called? The Nassau Inn. And we had people from all races attend that. People speaking with prominent black people from all over, and it was a very good thing, because the whole community rallied around us and supported us and then every year we would give scholarships to black students. I know we started at $500 the first year, and then we'd follow the kids through their college and see if they had enough money to continue and that kind of thing.

If the kids didn't make college and were doing things elsewhere, we would help with their books. Now that is the one thing that students over in the university could do for black students. I think that something like that would be good to be involved in and working closely right from the school system. Now, I suppose you should start at the nursery school, but definitely down in the lower grades where kids are trying to make it and find themselves in the world before they get all twisted up by this terrible place we live in at times. But we followed those kids, we gave all kinds of concerts for them, and I'm gonna tell you, we introduced black and white to black people who were successful all over. I guess, I was in there about seventeen years.

Hank Pannell (1939–)

A couple of years ago, I was at a meeting with Gloria Hernandez and Frances Bliko. They run MCHA, the Mercer County Hispanic Association. We just started talking about this community and its changing complexity and the need to bring everyone together. And we formed an alliance. The Neighborhood Alliance we call it. We have meetings and address a lot of problems in the community. We're bringing everybody all together—white, black, Hispanic—and there's a lot of things we have accomplished.

I think it's going a long way to sit down and talk to your neighbors. On July 22, we're holding a Wellness Day Clinic at the playground, where we're having not only doctors come into the community, but bankers and different caregivers. We had a kickoff potluck with all kinds of ethnic foods. People from the community came to the Learning Center and brought dishes. It was really a wonderful experience. That's the first step. People have to talk. They have to know that we're all here trying to survive. Just to get to speak to each other is important. Walk up the street and say hello, and people feel comfortable enough to say hello back.

Some Sunday mornings, I drive the church bus for the First Baptist Church. My wife, Eileen—I can never thank her enough for putting up with me being involved in community things and her support of me doing this. Without her, I couldn't be doing what I do, so, I just thank her for all her wonderful support. When my mother passed away when I was sixteen years old, this community rallied and helped me and my family exist. I owe this community something—and I'll never finish paying them back.

Clyde (Buster) Thomas (1934–2004)

I felt growing up that we were essentially happy people—everyone was close and came from wholesome families—and we had good times within this confined area, but I kept hearing things at home and seeing things. We had books that came from other schools. I learned that probably in third grade, because we could see names, and I would ask somebody, "Who is this person?" and someone would say, "That's nobody that goes to school here. They're from another school."

"Well, why are we getting books from another school?" And they would say, "We get what they're finished with." These kinds of things started popping up, and you would get bits and pieces, like the one doctor that we had in town. I remember him, because I had some kind of problem with my ankle, and I would go to Dr. Anthony, who was right on Witherspoon Street. What concerned me was that he wasn't permitted to practice at the Princeton Hospital, and I could never really understand that. And we didn't go into a lot of places on Nassau Street to get food. I think there were one or two places you could go. We used to go on Saturdays to the Garden Theatre,

Clyde (Buster) Thomas, football captain at Princeton High School (1952)

and occasionally we would go to the Playhouse Theater, and I noticed probably in fourth or fifth grade that black people or Indians were never in prominent roles in the movies.

I would hear people talking at home about people being lynched and how they were being treated and so forth. And at the same time, everybody was affiliated with one of the three or four churches that we had. Everybody in the town went to church. Then I was getting confused about Christianity. How could it tolerate this? I never really discussed this because I was embarrassed. I kept feeling that this was something I wasn't supposed to discuss with anybody. I just felt that if there was a God, if there was Jesus Christ, then why would all these things happen just to black people? And so, I became a very bitter kind of person at an early age.

When I got older and started reading about what was really happening on an international and national level, I got more confused about a whole lot of different things. I could see the difference in the practice and the treatment of people, and I guess that made me feel a lot of bitterness in a real sense. So I used to engulf myself in playing sports to try to get away from some of the things that I was internalizing. From around fourth grade on, I spent all my days involved in soccer, football, tag football in the fall, basketball in the winter, and track and baseball in the summer months.

When I went to high school, the only jobs I had were during the summer as a counselor at Princeton Summer Camp, which is in Blairstown, and then I used to clean offices on Nassau Street. The dentist I was going to at the time gave me the job, and then there was another doctor that he convinced to give me a job. I also had a job at the McCarter Theatre. It was fortunate that because I played sports, there were a few people who sort of took a liking to me and offered me employment. And also because of sports, I became sort of proficient at an amateur level as an athlete, and then finally I got a scholarship to prep school and went to college. That's how I managed to go to Penn State—it was basically track and football.

Joan Hill (1942–)

I was also involved with a newspaper called the *Black Word*. This paper was initially started to give the community a chance to voice their opinions and to discuss with the rest of the community things that they wanted to bring to the forefront. It was a free paper. I remember we used to go to the Youth Center on Saturdays, and Hank [Pannell] would have the printing presses working. He had volunteers that would staple and paste and do all kinds of things. It was interesting to have a black newspaper to read aside from the regular news of the world. We had recipes and health tips, and we also discussed civil rights issues. It was a way, besides of giving information, of us getting together and communicating with each other. We were young and we were radical and we would let people know what was going on as far as black issues. Not that they were, things were, that bad in this community, but we knew we had to bring our community into the limelight about issues that were just being discussed in civil rights. When we first started it, it was almost like eight by ten pieces of paper stapled together, and when we finished it was actually a newspaper.

I was asked to leave as the director of the Civil Rights Commission because I was too radical. I was one of the ones who [was outspoken]. They also said that I brought bad press to Princeton. One night I was stopped for drunk driving, when all I had was one drink. [They said I had] a .20 blood alcohol level, I had an expert witness from Rutgers come in and they said that I would have to drink two quarts of alcohol to reach a .20 level. They just lied to get me out of that position because I was not one of their "Yes sir, yes ma'am" people. It was their loss. They said it wasn't racial and it wasn't sexist. I received nothing after they terminated me after twenty years, but life goes on. It hasn't stopped me from doing things.

Joe Moore (1941–)

My mother died when I was in the seventh grade. Howard Waxwood was the principal of the Quarry Street School, which was an integrated school at this point, and I was determined, because of my own experience in my household, that I was going to go to college. But I also was going through a period in my life where sometimes my emotional response was greater than my targeted response. So I signed up for the academic program at Princeton High, leaving Quarry Street School in the eighth grade, going over to the high school at the ninth grade level. And I was discouraged from doing that. I was told, "No, he's not academic material," and "He's going to fail," and "You can't do that." Well, Mr. Waxwood, who was the principal at Quarry Street School, fought on my behalf and made sure that I got put into the academic program when I went over to Princeton High.

He really had to fight, I don't think just for me, but I remember the fight on my behalf. I think there were other kids who also wanted to get into the academic program. Essentially the way I read it was that the high school was saying—you know—these kids, based on their prior performance, can't be in the academic track. A lot of the students, black students before me, were not being allowed to get into the academic track at the high school.

We knew that it was racist, but—you know—it was not where we were running around saying, "Well, yeah, the white teachers and administration at the high school or even the white board of education are not allowing this to happen." We to ourselves knew it was really wrong, but we didn't articulate it. I think it was articulated by other adults in the community who would try to correct the situation. But as far as students were concerned—no, I didn't go around saying, "This is a racist school system."

There were occasions where I did challenge the teachers—you know—"I'm no dummy" or "You're going to teach me," or, you know, "I'm going to college in spite of you." So there were occasions where those kinds of barriers, those kinds of prohibitions were challenged. But it was a constant thing. Part of growing up in Princeton was indeed crossing Nassau Street to be challenged or going over to Library Place and picking apples and pears.

My high school experience was a bomb. I mean, I had a lot of leadership skills and everybody knew that, but I was also an emotional disaster, because I was in puberty and my mother had died. So I wasn't focused. And because I wasn't focused, it was really hard for teachers to get me to be focused. They knew I had potential—I could get anybody do to anything, except myself. I didn't have the security that I could succeed, and that wasn't given to me. They interpreted leadership as nonacademic. My freshman year, I did fail. I had to repeat my freshman year. Eventually I began to settle down more emotionally and intellectually, began to concentrate, because I really knew I wanted to go to college.

And I began to get help outside of the school system. The Witherspoon Street Presbyterian Church, for example, with Rev. Benjamin Anderson and David McAlpern, began to identify the fact that not only did I have leadership talent, but I was very intelligent. So I got support from that venue, if you will.

There was also a lady on my street named Helen Palmer, who was in her late eighties, early nineties, and she sort of adopted me after my mom died. She was blind and would call me every day between 6:00 and 6:30. I would have to go down and read the newspaper to her. I'd read one end of the newspaper to the other end to her, and hence, my love of reading. But that was not given to me at the high school at that level. My love of reading and my love of books and my self-confidence came from outside of that environment—it came from Mrs. Palmer and the Witherspoon Presbyterian Church and other people in the neighborhood that had given me that kind of encouragement.

When I was a senior, I was offered a full scholarship to the University of Boston, where Martin Luther King was, to study theology. So I was on a roll. This was a way of fulfilling my mother's dream—she always wanted me to become a minister. I didn't want to become a minister, but I liked the idea of theology and philosophy, and so I had decided to do this. I was trying to fulfill two dreams. One was social work—the care of the community, the care for the quality of life issues. And the other was a religious, spiritual need that I had in terms of what my mother's wishes were.

Actually, when I graduated from Central State, I went to work for the Job Corps. I recognized it was a time that I had really seriously made my own decision—I couldn't continue to live my mother's dream. That was Lyndon Johnson's Great Society Program. And we were taking kids from all over the country. It was in Edison, New Jersey, in the old Camp Kilmer. It was a military base that was built for returning GIs coming home from the Second World War, which they turned into a Job Corps center, where they gave kids vocational training experiences, all kinds of stuff—carpentry, plumbing, electrical stuff, construction, engineering types of things—as a way to put them back in the workforce and make them, I guess, dues-paying members of society. I was a group leader. I had sixty kids from all over the country. So, anyway, I did that for about a year and a half. From there, I went to Central High in Trenton and was recruited to create a school within a school using Outward Bound techniques.

Essentially what I did was create a program that went seven days a week, twenty-four-seven. We were not only in class seven days a week, but we were out every weekend, whether it be mountain climbing, canoeing, hiking, spelunking—you name it—all the kinds of stuff that Outward Bound was created for. It was an attempt to urbanize the Outward Bound concept. And so, I brought that concept to Trenton High. I had a staff of teachers who taught, and it also required the teachers to go out on weekends with us. And basically it was designed as another alternative to traditional education that was being offered in the urban setting.

We got raving reviews for our work and the program. We had kids who went on to college. I was pretty adamant about the fact that it wasn't going to become a generalist program. If you climb a mountain, it doesn't mean that you're going to be successful in urban life. But it does mean that it may give you enough character and enough strength to make some things not happen that would ordinarily happen.

At the same time, Central High broke out in a series of race riots. I was asked by the superintendent of schools to take these youngsters and educate them. So I created another school for the white and black leaders of the race riots at Trenton High in 1967. I created the school in the basement of the faculty building. I didn't base it on Outward Bound. I based it on the fact that these kids were all leaders that could be educated. This was another form of protest, because some people wanted to throw them out of school.

That was probably the best experience of our lives, even outside of the Outward Bound experience, because these kids—both white and blacks who, two months prior to that, were fighting each other—came together in a basement to learn. I hired a teacher—I called her my Jewish mom—out of Lawrenceville, and she taught them English. A guy at Lawrenceville Prep, who was teaching history, quit Lawrenceville and came over to teach these kids history. There was another guy who had a science background, so he taught science. And the school psychologist, he had a background in another one of those arts, so he taught that.

But those kids came every day—never missed a day. There was no conflict, no tension. There were kids from the regular school begging to get into this school. So, it was a very powerful experience, because the kids responded to it so well, and the interaction between the faculty and the staff was just overwhelming. What happened at the end was that the faculty at the high school did not want to acknowledge the seniors in this class—who were part of this group—in the school. So I went to bat to make sure that these kids completed the requirements successfully. But the faculty still didn't want them to march with the regular class. So I went to bat for the students, and the Department of Education made it possible for those kids to receive their diplomas at the same time. It was a very powerful experience.

Mildred Trotman (1941–)

I got involved with the Civil Rights Commission, where I served for a number of years, probably eight to ten. During that tenure, I was a member, chairman, secretary, treasurer, held every office. That was during the seventies and I was a member until the first year I ran for [the Princeton] Borough Council in 1984. [The] council makes all decisions governing the borough. I was sworn in January 1, 1985, and have been on [the] council ever since. That's a long time. I'm completing my sixteenth year. The reason

I got involved was because I thought, "What does one do if one wants to change things?"

Of course, I wasn't that adamant about the council until Barbara Sigmund, who was the mayor (who died ten years ago), came to me. I had been a very, very vociferous member of the Civil Rights Commission and some other things in town. She came to me and asked me if I would be interested in running and I immediately said, "No." I am not a campaigner and I sure didn't relish the idea of going door-to-door campaigning and shaking hands. I didn't have the time. I had two kids, a job, and wasn't sure that I could win in this society. There were two attorneys running and I thought they would just overwhelm me.

A dare actually convinced me to do it. People saying, "You could never win anyway." That, coupled with my own feelings about going against two attorneys, who were very well known, and a real estate person, who was certainly well known at the time. I thought, "Nobody knows me. They know the John Witherspoon area, but . . ." The John Witherspoon [area] was certainly in my mind. It wasn't that the neighborhood had been underrepresented because I succeeded a black male, Joseph Moore, who had served on the council for nine years. Actually, my ex-husband was also on [the] council. But I certainly thought that some representation needed to be continued. But I will say that Barbara Sigmund was probably the most driving force. And then, of course, I did run and was successful. Jane Terpstra, my very, very good, dear friend, who is an attorney; Marvin Reed, the current mayor; and I ran together on the same ticket for the first time between sixteen and seventeen years ago. We must have walked every inch of Princeton Borough's 1.76 miles. We had to shake so many hands. And, as it turned out, I enjoyed it. I really did. I saw places that I never knew were in Princeton— houses that sit back, little coves, little dens. I don't think "surprised" can even come near to describing how I felt when I walked into headquarters the first time I ran and found I won. "Mildred, you won!" "How can you find out so quick?" "All the districts are in and we won! We won!" I was so surprised.

The reason I ran the second time is because so many people said it was a fluke the first time and I had to prove them wrong. I mean, the first few years I was on [the] council, people didn't know I was a councilwoman. They just saw another face—white people did anyway. And I could go in a store, and Princeton isn't that big, and would overhear things. I constantly experienced other not-so-overt, although not verbal, acts that were clearly discriminatory. I remember once in Borough Hall, we were talking about the affordable housing program. I was, and still am, the liaison to the affordable housing program. We were meeting this morning with a group of bankers because we were trying to get a consortium of bankers so that when people applied for affordable housing, we would have some banking institutions to tell them to go to. This consortium was in the conference room in Borough Hall this morning, and I walked in and said, "Good morning." People were talking to each other and continued talking to whomever they were talking to, and I sat down. Barbara Sigmund was her trademark late, so I went in her office across the hall. She got off the phone and we walked back into the conference room together, just the two of us. As she walked in the door, every man stood. What was I when I walked in fifteen minutes earlier? A piece of chalk? Of course, when she introduced me, it was, "Oh, good morning, Councilwoman Trotman." Well, I was that same councilwoman who had entered the room fifteen minutes earlier and who had gotten not more than a nod and go on back talking. It's these kinds of things blacks experience. I guess if I had walked in with someone else, they might not even have noticed.

I really ran the second time with a vengeance. Really. And I'm being honest. I did a great job the first three years I was on [the] council and I enjoyed what I was doing. It was gratifying. And I do think I made a difference. But I don't think I would've run if I didn't just need to prove something to myself. But I haven't felt that way since the second time. Didn't feel that way the first time, because I didn't know what it was all about. Everything was just overwhelming. When I ran after the first and second times, I felt I really was making a difference. My voice was really being heard and I was doing some good.

James A. Floyd Sr. (1922–)

In the 1960s, they were busy going about the business of planning exclusionary zoning—zoning that manifests itself in large-acre building plots at a cost that no one less than close to a millionaire could afford—planning that would result in a single-class community. What opportunities did the governing body have then? The governing bodies were those who decided on a master plan, and the zoning ordinances that implemented. They had every opportunity to make this a whole and total community rather than one that resulted in the denial of equal opportunity for all. . . . There was then and there continues to be a need for an active and aggressive Civil Rights Commission. Call it what you may, it is still needed.

10

Yesterday, Today, and Tomorrow

Black and white friends (about 1930)

WHILE THIS BOOK WAS approaching its completion in the spring of 2016, in a song of synchronicity, the Princeton Municipal Council voted 5–0 in favor of an ordinance to create the Witherspoon-Jackson Historic Preservation District. Following earlier designations for Princeton Basin, Delaware and Raritan Canal, and Princeton Battlefield–Stony Brook, the neighborhood became Princeton's twentieth historic district.[1]

Under the auspices of the Princeton Historic Preservation Commission, Wise Preservation Planning LLC had conducted a thorough survey and evaluation of the Witherspoon-Jackson neighborhood, which was defined as "a mostly rectangular area just north of Nassau Street, Paul Robeson Place, Bayard Lane, and Birch Avenue."[2] The Wise Report underlines the Witherspoon-Jackson neighborhood's "historical, architectural and cultural significance to the Princeton community" as "a cohesive and intact expression of Princeton's largest African American community that resulted from years of social, economic and education disparity brought by discrimination and segregation."[3]

It notes that African Americans were joined in the twentieth century by Italian and Irish immigrants who stayed in the community for various periods before moving on. More recently, Hispanic and other minorities have settled into the neighborhood. The ordinance describes the "distinct characteristics of streetscape, vernacular architecture theme, proportions of small scale structures on modest properties, and a high ratio of contributing resources" necessary for historic designation and significance on a national, state, and local level.[4] In its introduction, the Wise Report states:

> In addition to the University campus, the town boasts a number of diverse communities, among the earliest the Witherspoon-Jackson neighborhood. This largely residential section has served as cradle to several emerging ethnic groups, including the Italian and Hispanic communities. But its dominant character was created and remains that of the African American community. Unfortunately this distinct history was in no small part forged by discrimination and segregation.
>
> African Americans made up a sizable part of Princeton's population, and they have been here since its beginnings. It was a very visible population and one that interacted, mainly through vocation, with both Princeton's permanent and student population, who were pre-

dominately white. For most of that time, Princeton's African American population (which included slaves and former slaves) faced racism in many aspects of life. Quite simply, the result was Witherspoon-Jackson, a neighborhood as it was, and as it is today. This history of discrimination impacted most all aspects of Princeton's African American life. It created social-economic disparity which resulted in Witherspoon-Jackson: its people, history, architecture and streetscape. It was and remains significantly distinct from the rest of Princeton.

What happened at Witherspoon-Jackson is an amazing and deeply significant story, even more so that it occurred in Princeton, New Jersey. Discrimination based on race created a dichotomy between the white and black communities that only in the last few decades has thankfully started to become undone. But it is also a story of incredible perseverance on the part of Princeton's African American community. Indeed the community certainly survived and ultimately thrived. Today the neighborhood is attracting people who just a few years ago may not have given it a thought. Witherspoon-Jackson's newfound popularity is coming at a cost however; demolition of its resources and new construction can and are rapidly altering the neighborhood's historic fabric.

The municipality now has an opportunity to preserve at least the physical fabric of this remarkable community. In this way, when the people who experienced this discrimination and continue to tell the story are long since passed [sic], at the very least its built environment will continue to show that something happened here to make this neighborhood truly different. Without that tangible fact, this incredible story may once again be overlooked and forgotten.[5]

The Wise Report includes a letter from a "long-time resident of Witherspoon-Jackson, who wished to remain anonymous." She/he writes:

The people who had lived there were big souls—dignified, glowing, hardworking, ambitious and passionate, social and community minded. Yet they were stopped, stymied, blocked by society, by the town, by realtors and bankers using red lines, by restaurants who didn't serve them, by schools that were separate. By the very neighborhood itself, set by the highway and lying perpendicular and in mocking contrast to the mansioned Hodge Road. I have heard derisive comments and seen smirks on real estate agents' faces when talking about my street and my house—sometimes not knowing I was an owner there, other times knowing but not caring.

It is only in the past few years that I have understood how lethal it is for one's life plans to be denied access—to restaurants, cafés, clubs, political societies or schools—since I have been in business and have met clients here and there and have had no limit to whom and where I could meet. I know now that if I could not meet most of my clients at most of our meeting places I would not have a chance at success on any level.

My own life in the house is not important—an ordinary life in ordinary circumstances—but their lives were important and significant precisely because of their ordinariness—because the community and society at the time kept them below where they naturally would have risen—devalued and downgraded their trajectory and life destinations.[6]

As I write these last words of my own, million-dollar structures are rising around the borders of the neighborhood, and some within it. I marvel at all the stories the Witherspoon residents have to share and think of all the thousands of people who have lived and raised families here, surrounded and impacted by the racism that Albert Einstein called "America's worst disease." Gentrification continues to encroach on the neighborhood. A high-rise building is under construction on the site Princeton Hospital occupied, and condominium apartments in Palmer Square are selling for millions of dollars. Taxes are climbing, and developers and homeowners are investing heavily at the expense of the integrity of this powerful African American community. So far, no real estate tax accommodations for Witherspoon residents have been proposed or approved, and without these, many of the older people who live on fixed incomes and social security, which reflect the low incomes they were paid, will have a difficult time keeping and maintaining their homes.

Residents are keenly aware that the majority of their children are choosing to live elsewhere in the country where they can find meaningful work and live comfortably in a variety of communities, especially in the South and West. The parents, grandparents, and great-grandparents who remain in the community feel the loss of the remarkable intimacy they've shared across generations throughout their lifetimes.

The historical landmark designation, which became a reality after more than a year of public hearings, discussions, and debates, will, at the least, support the physical integrity of the neighborhood and may slow its transformation. On the night of the vote in favor of the new historical district, Princeton's mayor Liz Lempert thanked the Witherspoon residents for making the yearlong deliberations so meaningful: "It's been a long process. It's wonderful that the neighborhood turned out. It's been wonderful to feel the love for each other and for the neighborhood."[7]

After Rev. William Drew Robeson was forced by the all-white governing body of the local Presbyterians to resign from the post he had held for twenty-one years, he preached a farewell service. On that occasion in 1901, "Every seat in the pews and gallery of his church was occupied, chairs and benches were placed in the aisles, and many people had to stand in the rear" of the beautiful Witherspoon Presbyterian Church. In his remarks, Rev. Robeson made no mention of the presbytery's action. He thanked his own congregants and those from other black congregations who were there that day. "In concluding, he enjoined his hearers—as he must have been telling his own heavy heart, 'Do not be discouraged, do not think your past work is in vain. . . . Gird on your armor and with renewed courage strive to do well the work the Master has assigned to you, daring ever to do right, to be true; remember you each have a work to do that no other can do, and doing it so kindly, so truly, so well, angels will hasten the story to tell.'"[8]

The spirit of that injunction was with Rev. Robeson's son, Paul, half a century later when he, too, was effectively deposed by the federal government's campaign against him,[9] and I believe that Rev. Robeson's spirit is with the Witherspoon residents who are still standing strong and true today—more than a century later. If you listen, you can hear the deep, full, and sonorous voices singing from the trees and streets and homes of this neighborhood. May the beauty and truth of the lives lived here forever guide us into a better future.

Your country? How came it yours? Before the Pilgrims landed we were here. Here we have brought our three gifts and mingled them with yours: a gift of story and song—soft, stirring melody in an ill-harmonized and unmelodious land; the gift of sweat and brawn to beat back the wilderness, conquer the soil, lay the foundations of the vast economic empire two hundred years before your weak hands could have done it; the third a gift of the spirit. . . . Our song, our toil, our cheer. . . . Would America have been America without her Negro people?

—W.E.B. DU BOIS, *THE SOULS OF BLACK FOLK* (1903)

Joan Hill (1942–)

I think that if by some miracle Martin Luther King just happened to come back to life, he would be very, very saddened by the current state of affairs. I think it is a sin and a shame the things that they have done to our black men because one race is afraid of them. I think trying to stop Affirmative Action is terrible. I don't mean giving anyone things that they don't deserve. We work for it. I think that it is unfortunate that black people, people of color, still have to work extra hard to get ahead in today's society. When we were coming up, we helped one another. Now it's the haves and the have-nots, and the haves don't care about the have-nots. I see a lot of adults not liking what the kids do.

The kids do the same things that we did and we have to appreciate what the kids do, but guide them also. Don't stop them from having vision and the ideas that they all have. Each era has their likes and dislikes, and we need to work more together to help each other. We really do.

Joe Moore (1941–)

I think for every black person—whether they shovel the snow or whether they're a professor laureate or Toni Morrison—the question is whether or not you can make a legitimate contribution to your society and for that contribution to be accepted as a legitimate bona fide contribution. I can read anybody who's black and the same question emerges—"How do you penetrate the white psyche to say that we can make a contribution to the society which we are a part of?" The whole essence of being human is to pass through this life contributing. We have to have the ability to penetrate racism and say that we can make contributions, we have made contributions. And that's all I was about on a little parochial, provincial level, in a little, small town called Princeton.

Florence Twyman (1916–2001)

My aunt rented rooms in our home out to people because there wasn't anyplace for blacks to stay in town. Big people, like Dorothy Maynor from the NAACP and Oscar De Priest, who was a congressman, stayed with us. And you know, when bands would travel south, the blacks in the band had to find places "across the tracks" to stay, and that's why we had people in our home, because Princeton's really a Southern town. The eating clubs at the university would have house parties, and they'd invite big bands to come, like Cab Calloway, and the black members would have to find different places to stay. They'd set up tents around and we would stand outside, out of the way, and listen. We worked at the clubs to earn extra money, and for the house parties we'd have to press these elaborate dresses for the women, you know back then they really dressed. Sometimes they'd tip you, especially if they started drinking. One night, when I was older, it really stormed, and I couldn't get home to my kids. You never knew when you were gonna get home working over there. But that's nothing new, we've always had to work two or three jobs, do anything to make ends meet.

My first husband, Walter Harris, we married in 1936, and we moved to John Street. He was a policeman, but to supplement his income he also worked at the [eating] clubs as a houseman. He was the first black policeman killed on duty. He joined in the 1940s, and was killed in 1946. He wasn't on that long, and was treated pretty well, but then he had grown up here, and it made a difference in those days. It was a different time then, they knew that blacks would stay in their place. But now, after civil rights, they're worried because blacks are getting—I'll use it—uppity. Now we have racial profiling and all, but it's nothing new, it always stayed in the closet. You know nothing just starts; it's always been there.

It's hard to describe. Most black kids didn't even know what it was to go up on Nassau Street because they weren't welcome there. The police would call up white families if their kids were bad, but blacks they'd just lock up. You know you should punish people the same way, but that isn't life, that isn't real life. Things were just very prejudiced in Princeton then. And now, whites are moving in but they don't stay, they're just waiting to move up to the white neighborhoods. Older families are moving out, and the young ones don't want to stay because they can't buy a house because they're all too expensive, and they still can't get good jobs. Unless you fight, nobody does anything.

Nothing really changes—it just looks different. The schools are almost segregated again now because the whites move out, you know the Community Park School is a controversy. You hate to go around thinking you have to keep your guard up, fists up. Do you sit there and defy them or what, it's hard to know.

Shirley Satterfield (1940–)

My family, church, and community were my support. They were just always there. My family told me to be proud—I mean, they were just proud people, and I don't know how to explain it. We were poor but we were proud, and that's where the healing came. People should take care of each other. My neighbor is the kind of neighbor I remember, who will take care of the house when we go away. There's not a lot of people who'll do that now. I think it's important to have solidarity within the community no matter what color you are. But it's not like that anymore, because people are more selfish. There's not that togetherness, and I don't know how we'll get it back.

Romus Broadway (1939–)

I don't see collective attitudes about race changing. Maybe individuals are changing, but not collective attitudes. In fact, I don't see racism lessening— only increasing. All the fighting and tension around the globe is a matter of race. White against black is a worldwide problem. In this community there is division with the Hispanics that results from a lack of desire to understand and comprehend cultural differences. It's the same way whites could not understand the cultural differences between them and us. Neither group is aware of the other's culture. I don't see that the black community feels close to the white community. But I don't see that it feels close to the Hispanic community either.

Many blacks don't approach the Hispanics because they see them as being white. I know this to be a fact. I have heard the young kids and older people in the black community talk about the Hispanics this way.

It's a daily process of teaching that you have got to respect other people. You have to understand the differences. I can specifically remember my father just telling us to try to understand people. If you like them, fine, if not, then don't bother.

Growing up, I expected exactly what my children are experiencing now. But they don't face the same fear that I did, so they don't know that it is there. Just because you can't see a snake in the dark doesn't mean that it isn't there. We would never reach in the dark; we knew something dangerous was there. The teachers at the Witherspoon School constantly reminded us of the dangers of white society. Today, kids are not getting these frank lessons until it is often too late.

I can give you a good example. A big problem in the community right now is drugs. And there is a great difference in the proportional sentences that black youth receive when compared to white youth. When we see black kids hanging around white kids, and there are drugs involved, black parents tell their kids, "Listen, do not hang around the white kids if they're doing drugs. Because if you get caught, you're going to jail, and they're going free or they're going to some rehab program." Some black kids think that if they hang around with white kids, they won't face a stiff penalty. They face a stiffer one though. But they find that out too late.

We currently have an African American chief of police and many black officers. The borough had a token black for years. One. About sometime in the '50s the township hired their first black officer, who eventually became the chief. Most people here, especially the young people, have a suspicion of the police, because you can get arrested by the police. And the police have their suspicions of us.

I only know two young black residents that aspired to be policemen. One did, but the other never got in. In the 1950s, one of the members of the black community came out of the military and passed all the courses to become a state trooper, but they still wouldn't hire him. It wasn't until about 1962 that the first black state trooper was hired.

My hopes and dreams, as a child, all became a reality. I wanted to join the military, which I did. I wanted to own a motorcycle, which I did. And I wanted to travel, which I did. And I wanted to go to college, which I also did. So the dreams of my boyhood youth, I have captured.

Penney Edwards-Carter (1947–)

Kids now would never not date someone because of their ethnicity, whereas, I would never have dated a white person. And it wasn't that my mother or anybody else said to me, "You can't date a white person." My mind just wouldn't have gone there.

Joe Moore (1941–)

I would like to be optimistic for my daughter and son and my grandkids—and for Hank's [Pannell] grandkids and his son. But I'm not totally optimistic. I don't know how to put this, but you wake up, and the difference between you being born white and me being born black, it's evolution, you know? It's a quirk that is going to make our experiences dramatically different. We're made of the same particles, except for the color of the skin. And then having to live a life of penalization for that?

I certainly haven't spent my life twiddling my fingers. There were times I was very optimistic. There were certain indexes along the way that you could see on a national level and say, "Oh, this may change." At the end of the Vietnam War, when the war was over, there was a sense that things were going to be different—more opportunities, more advancements. But there was backsliding with the Reagan era, in terms of denial, in terms of not making things possible on a national level . . . a conservative element. I want for my grandkids not to worry because of the color of their skin. And I have a problem with the fact that I'm not so sure that will happen. And I don't want to appear fatalistic, but I'm not that optimistic. The struggle is not over. It's not over.

Johnnie Dennis (1903–2007)

I never wished I was in the world better than anybody else. You know, so many people think they better than you are—they want to change you. But you can't change if God made you. You're not just sitting in a corner like a cat. You don't sit around in one little place. You see them people walking on Nassau Street, passing each other, use the same table, drink the same water, just enjoy the same sunshine, the same life. And if they respecting each other, they happy.

Burnett Griggs (1888–1977)

I wanted an education, and I don't like to talk about it because I fill up [he cries]. But even now when I see what's going on in the world and so little that I can do and I feel that had I been able to finish my training, I might be able to lend a hand. We live in troubled times. To me, it's very sad. I see these kids today with the opportunities that they have—that I never had.

I guess I'm rather critical about some things. When I came to Princeton, they had a section over here in the graveyard where they used to bury all the Negroes; they called it "the Colored Section." Well, we have a segregated graveyard in Virginia, in my hometown—Farmville. And I made up my mind I wasn't going to be buried in anyone's graveyard. I have it in my will. I want to be cremated. I go fishing; I love it. I love it out on the water. You just forget your troubles and everything else. . . . I want to be cremated and my ashes turned over to my captain. Take 'em out and sprinkle 'em on Barnegat Bridge.

Buster Thomas (1934–2004)

We have to get involved with the school system here and find out what new initiatives can help many of our students, because we find that most of the new initiatives are starting at the kindergarten level to try to avert the problem of dropouts.

One of the things that I really enjoyed most was that I used to mentor some young boys from first to fourth grade. They were from Lawrence, and they were referred to me by teachers at Ben Franklin School because they didn't have males in the home and they were experiencing problems. We used to do cultural things every Saturday. This was when my son was still at home. We would take trips. I was at the Sports Authority at the time. We would go up when they had the circus and the games. I would get tickets for them. We would go to the Science Center in Jersey City, and we went to the Franklin Institute in Philadelphia. We would go to the museum in Trenton, particularly during black history month, and I would make a point of giving them comic books that had life stories of a lot of African Americans. . . . There were seven or eight of them, but half the group was on Ritalin, and they were very hyper.

It was a real fun time for me. We used to go up to the Haunted House at the Arts Council, and it was nice for them to be exposed to cultural things, but they had academic problems. They really needed tutors. That's the thing I got really upset with because what they really needed, I couldn't provide for them. I only spent a small time with them on Saturdays, and they would go back to their home environment and that would just turn everything that you were trying to do upside down. . . . A couple of the kids, even at their age, saw someone get murdered. It was a real tragic experience.

For a while, I thought I was doing some good. There were two African American men who did therapy and handled young people in Lawrence, and I was able to take a couple of them there. They worked with them with no charge. And that went well for a couple of years, but then some of these kids, their problems couldn't get resolved. They felt that the mothers of some of these youngsters needed therapy worse than the sons, and the whole program just got out of whack. I mean, it was eye-opening to me how vast the problem is with some of the youngsters that really need help. And these were kids that were considered not to be the worst.

You can almost see the pattern. When they get to fourth and fifth grade, they just really go right out the front door with their problems. . . . It was unmanageable because I think the need was a one-to-one basis and more often than once a week. I still hear from them every once in a while. I was able to get several of them up to Princeton Summer Camp, which I felt good about.

I wish that I could have kept with them, you know, because it was something like what I was searching for when I was their age. My attitude was bad from like fourth grade on and it was so bad, even in sports, that they

YMCA Men's Meeting (about 1947)

would not allow me to take Phys. Ed. for a whole half year. That kept me off the honor roll. As I said, I wasn't getting answers on something I really wanted to know, and that made me a real problem—speaking out of turn, saying the wrong kind of things, trying to encourage other students to do something other than what they should be doing. But I had a lot of people that were working with me for whatever reason. . . .

I think of Mr. Holmes, who spent a lot of time with me. He was very interested in young people. He took me to my first Harlem Globetrotters game. He and his wife had like a young people's group, and he had a Y team. So I had a lot of guidance. I mean, there was a genuine interest. You felt that because somebody was chastising you, that they loved you, they cared for you and they were hoping that you would do better. Everybody had a stake or interest in you growing up to be a nice young man or woman, and they saw that as part of their responsibility and maybe even duty. I really feel sorry for youngsters today, because they are out there dealing with things that they don't know how to deal with.

It's funny, but I'm always sort of yearning for those old days. The friends that I grew up with, we talk about things we did, and whenever I can be around a lot of the old friends, I try to be there. We make a lot of telephone calls and write to one another. We all go back to the same conversation that we'd go back to when we were in sixth, seventh, and eighth grade and laugh about the different things that happened. We just made our own fun, and there was a lot of interaction between us. We didn't have television, but we had our broken bats and balls. We used to put stuff together, play hopscotch, boys and girls, pick-up sticks, and all that kind of stuff. I think in a sense we had everything we needed. Not everything we wanted, but everything we needed. I wish a lot more kids could experience that.

Jay Craig (1930–)

I tell young people today that an education beyond high school is of primary importance, beyond the college level to a master's degree or a doctorate. If I were growing up now, I would have gone to college without even thinking of anything else. I would have done something with government, something where I might have ended up in the State Department, or in the Congress of the United States or, who knows, maybe president. I'm not stopping there, you know. I'm sure that is applicable to many blacks in this town and every other town. We would have gone to college, but we couldn't. I mean, me and my sister Lois, we never even thought of it. We had very little resources, very little money.

Romus Broadway (1939–)

Compared to my own children, I grew up in an era with a lot of segregation, which kept me on my toes. Because my children are not exposed to segregation, there are hidden dangers that they cannot see, and there are a lot of things that they take for granted. But by and large, I haven't seen much change in the world. People have been changing their focus, but not their attitudes.

I would say racism has for a long time been cultivated at home as a difference between black and white. I don't find whites altruistically accepting of blacks in the same way that they accept themselves or their family members and friends. The persons who are responsible for this racism must change. They know what the golden rule is—it's not difficult. I cannot change a person's heart. They have got to change.

Hank Pannell (1939–)

I've been at the Housing Authority as chief of maintenance for twenty-eight years. One of the things that I could do through the Housing Authority was to employ a lot of kids in the summers and after school. That's one of the things I'm really proud of because I think I had a lot to do with a lot of kids learning about life, certainly learning how to keep a job. Kids still come back and tell me that I taught them about being on time and other job skills. Most of the kids who worked for me went on to college and just about all of them are successful in life now. I'm proud of that.

A group of us men got together six years ago and formed a club, "Save Our Kids," to work with young kids and teenagers. We took them to camp and ball games and met with them one on one, to help in any way we could. Ms. Toni Morrison wanted to get university students involved through her Atelier program in doing a twelve-minute film on "Save Our Kids" and another one about the Princeton Nursery School. Louis Messiah, he's a noted filmmaker, he talked me into working with him on it—he didn't have much talking to do. I really got involved.

We built a computer room up here [at the Clay Street Learning Center]. A couple of years ago, I went to Marjorie Young at Community House, and the university donated four computers. I advertised in the papers and begged and borrowed and got more computers. Then we got a young man and my son, Henry, to teach computer classes. On Saturdays, we had a morning computer class for kids and an afternoon computer class for grown-ups. And everybody who completed the course—we got them a computer. I have grandmothers who are online now. I'm quite proud of that. We've put a lot of computers into the community, and it's still going on. I have a shop full of [used] computers that I need to find time to work on because I've got a lot of kids that want one.

I got an award, the Vivian Hood Community Service Award, which gave a grant of a couple thousand dollars, and I used that to buy modems and other computer parts and software, to fix up these computers. We've got computer classes up here on a regular basis, every Wednesday. I think it's really important—that's the future.

Eva Redding (1922–1997)

Princeton is home. Parents, grandparents, to me it's home. The challenge to me is to see it get back to the way we grew up. When we were growing up, we were all very active in doing so much and doing things to change the community and we did. We made a lot of inroads. But now I find that there is more prejudice and more bitterness among people than I have ever seen before in this area. I was used to speaking to everybody, knowing everybody, working with everybody and find it quite different now. When we were growing up, we were limited, but we were allowed to move in areas and open up jobs that were never opened before. I resent, and I tell them this, people who sit on the board at management where I live who feel like they, as senior citizens, need to be taken care of. I tell them to their faces, "I resent that." We have lived a life where we have gotten a certain amount of wisdom and understanding. The older women should help to train the younger women to show them what to do instead of them trying to rule and change us.

Frances Broadway Craig (1943–)

The only thing my mother and father said to us was: you treat people the same way you want to be treated. Period. The end. And I'm not saying that we didn't know there was a difference [between black and white]. You know, Stevie Wonder could see that. But, honestly, that was what was always instilled in us: always treat people the way you want to be treated.

There are so many values that are not taught to children [today]. And I see it. Manners definitely are out. And I don't care what socioeconomic level they come from. Most kids do not come here with manners, and that's one of the things they *do* have to have in this room. From there we go right on to how we treat each other, respecting our classmates, *and* our teachers. And I think it makes a better learning environment.

The only prejudice that I can truly say that I've felt [was that] I always had to prove myself to parents [of my students]. . . . But I wasn't really judged for intelligence at first. And I know it sounds so crazy but it's true. Because I wear high heels or I wear jewelry or whatever. I think at first many of them thought, "Wait a minute. Can she teach? Will she be able to teach my children?" So, once I prove that: wait a minute, there's a brain here, and I can teach your kids. . . . I've never had a complaint from parents but it was always just that initial thing of proving myself. But I felt it. I don't even know if they knew they were doing it. But it was always there.

I do know now that I feel that more minority teachers should be hired in our district. And it seems like that's slowed down. When I got hired, like I said, it was 1969, that was the big "push year." That year and the year after, I think. I have never really seen a big push on minority teachers since then. There are just as few now, as I guess have been for the past ten years, and I think that needs to be reemphasized. And when I say minority, I mean of all races. They did just hire two [or] three Hispanic teachers in my school. Other than that I haven't seen any new blacks coming in for about the past ten years.

Leonard Rivers (1934–)

In some ways racism is worse today. Back in the movement, when we were in Mississippi, someone said, "How'd you survive that?" You survived because you knew what you could do. The line was drawn. People would call you "nigger" to your face, and then you knew how to deal with it. They told you, "I don't like you; I'll help you." Today that line is not there anymore. You got to guess. You wonder what they're thinking. Some of the people, you think they're supporting you, but when you walk away, they're calling you names and taking away opportunities—and that's tougher to deal with. But racism is alive and well. Don't let anybody tell you racism is gone. It is a little harder to distinguish sometimes, but it's still there.

My father taught me, and we were all taught in the John Witherspoon area, that you take a negative and you make it a positive. You could take that negative and say, "Ah, crap, what's the use?" But you got to take that negative and say, "Well, hell, if that's what you think, stop me if you can. I'll go work a little harder. I'll go do what I got to do."

When my father passed away, you know, he was my man, and when he passed away, I started a scholarship fund in his name. And I spend a lot of time with tutorial programs and mentorship and all that type of thing now, in my father's name. My mother is still alive. She has been very active in, I call them, the Gray Panthers, she's very active in the Senior Citizens groups now, and in the Baptist Church [which] has always been big.

I think that the black community now, we have got to go to the polls, we've got to start voting, we've got to start participating, we've got to start reaching down, pulling other people up. For a long time, we used to hear an expression: "I made it, you got to help yourself. I am beyond that and I never look back." Well, as black folks, we've got to look back. We've got to look back and grab somebody and pull them up.

I was fortunate, I had a mother and father that worked their selves almost to the grave, by making sure my brother and I got the opportunities we got. And I can remember my father telling me, maybe a year or so before he died, "Just do it for somebody else." And you know he's right, he's right. Because there are a lot of people out there who need somebody to grab them and pick them up and say, "Hey, let's go do it." You know, we as a race have got to become more active in terms of helping each other, in terms of not turning your back on your brother, but saying, "Hey, what do you need? Let's see if we can get it for you."

Donald Moore (1932–)

There are so many stories you can tell about people. How do you feel being black? Let's supposed you lived here, and you're white. And you go pick up your paper in the morning. Both your neighbors came out too and they are both black. You got in your car and headed for the office and as you looked around driving, most of the other people were black. And then a policeman pulled you over, and he happened to be black. And you gave him some guff. He handcuffed you and took you to the jail. Most of the people there were black. They take you to court and the judge was black. This is what we live with. So living in this society, you have to say, "Hey, let's see how we can sort of get past this." Life tends to go on. You don't want it to get worse, you want it to get better.

Robert Rivers (1931–)

My oldest son Michael came to Princeton University in '77 and graduated in 1981. He was as prepared as any kid coming in from anywhere. Yet, he and three of his friends thought they were going to flunk out. Three of them are doctors now and one of them is a tenured professor. They just felt that they did not belong here. A lot of minorities, no matter what their background was, they just never felt comfortable here. I had another friend whose brother came here in the '70s, and he ended up committing suicide. It wasn't that these youngsters were not qualified, it was just really difficult coping here.

A lot of what has to do with Princeton has to do with the past. Princeton, mid-1900s, was considered by some folks as a Northern community with the niceties of [a] Southern [one]. It has a Southern mentality, there was no getting around it. You really can't talk about the university or the town without talking about the black community and the black supports they had; you really can't do it.

As my father got along in age, he joined the crowd that get up in the morning and walk up to Nassau Street, and they'd stand up there and talk and reminisce and do all these things. It's amazing all the good things and the bad things, the bumps and the bruises, and you still end up with the bottom line. He knew he had a son who went to the university and one who coached baseball there. And my mother—she's still alive—can you imagine the satisfaction she has, having four grandchildren who have gone to Princeton University?

Times have changed, but you have to be careful, because sometimes they haven't. Every once in a while, you can see this stuff coming back. There's an old Princeton still floating around out there—but on the other hand, what's happened to Princeton in the last fifty years, I never would have believed. We've come so far. I never would have predicted that all these wonderful things that have happened would have happened. I have to say, Princeton has defined my life—for better or for worse—it has defined my life.

Sophie Hall Hinds (1875–1974)

In the [Great] Blizzard of '88 [1888] I was working on the corner of Chestnut and Nassau, and my father was working at the grocery store, delivering groceries. And he had to take a wheelbarrow and push his groceries down to where everything would go. There were a couple of boardinghouses and the owner had to have food for her boarders. So he took a wheelbarrow and went down there. He couldn't get anywhere else, and couldn't take the horses out of the stable. And where I was living, the snow was so high where the house stood next door to us. It was much higher than this room and that was almost covered.

I remember when the lake was constructed, but I was too busy working to watch when the trees were coming down for it. And I remember the day President Garfield was killed. People put pennies down on the railroad track for when his train come by.

I was married fifty years when my husband died. He was from South America. He worked for different places before he came to Princeton. The college was closed in the summertime and the fellas had to go look for some other jobs. That's the biggest thing they had to depend on then, was the university and boardinghouses.

I was married a block or so down on Witherspoon Street, where you come to Clay. There was no party afterward. Pardon me, but my father was rarely inclined to have these parties and dances and whiskey. He wouldn't have any liquor. I grew up in a sober family. You have people, and the first thing they'll do is give you something to drink, but take all that drink, and they can have it all 'cause I don't want it. Like one lady said when she was sick and the doctor or somebody gave her whiskey, "If I'm going to die, at least I can die sober." That's what I say: "Let me die sober." A person can live without it.

I had nine children and I've got eight living. I done everything you can think of doing. You could rent your house for [Princeton University's] Commencement; I could rent my house if I wanted, if I could accommodate the people that were coming. Those times were different than they are now. There's so many hotels, and big people can go to them now and don't need house roomings.

Albert Hinds, 99 years old, washing his car (2001)

And I worked for a family. I've done cooking and laundry work and housecleaning—anything you can think of and put your hands on, I mostly can do it. But it's housework I'm talking about, not those high educational things. With laundry, that was an enormous operation in those days, because it meant you did all the laundry on a washboard, hung 'em up, dried 'em, and ironed 'em. And I'd have to get 'em and I'd have to carry 'em back again. You had to stick those irons on the stove and let 'em get hot, and when they got cool, put 'em back on the stove and get hot, and get another iron.

After the years, I got to a place where women wore uniforms. A regular uniform was simply a blue material with a white collar and a little cuff or something like that. We didn't have uniforms like they do nowadays. They're getting into pants and near everything. Why can't women be women? That's what I want to know.

I'm ninety-six and a half. I've outlived my father who was ninety-four. My people are old—long livers. My father's mother, I understand, was at least a hundred years old when she died. I went down to the South to visit a cousin of my father's when she was 109 years old, and her mind was just as good as could be. I've always tried to do almost what I thought was right. And any mistakes I've made I trust God to forgive me, and everybody else.

Meet the Residents: Speakers' Biographies

BLACK, HATTIE SMITH (1934–), born to William Marshall Smith and Gillie Ann Bartee, is a lifelong resident of Princeton. After graduating high school in 1951, her father encouraged her to apply for a secretarial position at Princeton University. She got the job at age seventeen and began working in the Geology Department, thus making her one of the first black professional employees of the university. Later on, she became the administrative secretary for the African American Studies Program, where she worked until her retirement. In 2001, Black was celebrated for reaching the half-century mark in her career and received the President's Achievement Award for excellence and dedication to her work. She recalls the joys of growing up in Princeton among a close family and the Birch Street community. Her great-grandfather was a slave who lived to be 113 years of age. Celia Riechel interviewed Black in her office in the African American Studies Program at Princeton in November 2000. On December 11, 2001, Kathryn Watterson conducted a follow-up interview.

BROADWAY, ROMUS (1939–) was the eighth of nine children born to John R. Broadway Sr. and Jossie Broadway in Belle Mead, New Jersey, just outside Princeton. He grew up on Birch Avenue in Princeton, washed dishes on the avenue during high school, joined the military, and later became a lab technician and jack-of-all-trades. For many years, he also had a courier service. After starting with a camera won in a craps game, Broadway became a photographer and social historian of the neighborhood. For forty-five years, his photographic collages have chronicled lives and events in Princeton's

African American community. Broadway, the father of four children, still lives on Birch Avenue. Shawn Sindelar interviewed him in October 2000, as did Kathryn Watterson in April 2001 at Broadway's home.

BURRELL, DORIS (1919–2015), who grew up in New Brunswick and attended integrated schools, moved to Princeton when she married her husband, Frederick, in 1941. She was the owner of Burrell's Salon on Leigh Avenue, and her husband ran his own florist business. In 1946, more than two years before the Princeton Plan, she enrolled her oldest daughter, Sondra, at Valley Road School, making her the first black student in school history. Her youngest daughter, Fredericka, enrolled at Valley Road School three years later, after the schools integrated. Lauren Miller interviewed Burrell in her beauty salon in Princeton in October 2000.

CALLOWAY, HARRIETT (1906–2005) was born in Princeton, where her parents and grandparents lived. Her father, a jazz musician, had a small jazz band and traveled to Florida every year. Married in 1927 to Blain Calloway, who worked in service for various university eating clubs on Prospect Avenue, Calloway earned money from babysitting children. Vanessa Redman interviewed Calloway at Eighty-One Clay Street in Princeton in November 1999.

CAMPBELL, CONSUELO B. (1929–2013) was born in Washington, DC, and moved to Princeton when she was two years old with her mother, who found steady work as a housekeeper for one family. Raised in Jim Crow Princeton, Campbell recalls segregated seating at Princeton and Trenton theaters, the whites-only ice rink in Trenton, and the Jim Crow coach trains heading south out of Washington, DC. On southbound trains out of DC, African Americans were forced into the dusty, hot, dirty coach car that was attached to the train engine room. She was married to Floyd Campbell, with whom she had five children. Lindsay Hedrick interviewed Campbell at her home in Princeton on November 11, 1999.

CAMPBELL, FLOYD (1924–2005), born in Memphis, Tennessee, moved to Princeton with his mother in 1927 and attended the Witherspoon School for Children on Quarry Street. Following graduation from Princeton High in 1942, he was rejected from the Marine Corps because of his color, and then drafted into the army. He was soon attached to a marine outfit and won a Bronze Star for piloting the military's amphibious vehicle—the DUKW—in the D-day invasion, providing constant ammunition and cover for the front line while under continuous fire. During the war, he performed for the troops, playing trumpet with a jazz band called the DUKW Cutters. After he was discharged, he and his childhood sweetheart, Consuelo, stayed in Kansas, where he had been stationed and he became a full-time musician. The couple eventually returned to Princeton, where Campbell took a job with the post office. He worked there for thirty years. He and his wife have five children, eight grandchildren, and four great-grandchildren. Catherine Holahan interviewed Campbell in April 2001 at the Campbells' home on Leigh Avenue in Princeton.

CARSON, EULA (1909–2003) was born in North Carolina in 1909. She had one sister and one brother. Her father died when she was nine, and when her mother remarried, they moved to the area where her future husband, Jim Carson, lived. She said she and Jim "started looking at each other" when they were in the sixth grade. When she graduated from high school, she moved to New York with the intention of going to college but found that even getting a housecleaning job was difficult. She joined Jim in Princeton when he was working at the YMCA camp. She also worked at the Nassau Club on Mercer Street. They were married for more than seventy years and had one daughter, Linda. Emily Espenshade interviewed Carson at the her home in Princeton in 1999.

CARSON, JIM (1909–2001) was born in Old Fort, North Carolina. He had two brothers and two sisters, and when he was six, he moved in with his grandmother, who lived nearby. She had been enslaved and was eleven years old when slavery ended. He lived with her until her death at 104, when he was sixteen. He went to a segregated elementary school and to AT&T College in Greensboro for high school. In 1930, he got a job teaching at a one-room school in the mountains. He loved teaching, but in the summer of 1931, he came north and began working at a restaurant in Princeton. His greatest desire was to teach in the South where they needed teachers, but he ended up working as head chef at the Nassau Club on Mercer Street for more than forty years. He was married to Eula Carson for more than seventy years. Emily Espenshade interviewed Carson at his home in Princeton in 1999.

CARTER, JAMES (1928–2000) was born in Trenton, New Jersey, and moved to Princeton in 1941, when he was thirteen years old. A lifelong athlete, Carter pitched in the Negro Baseball League. He describes playing baseball for the Newark Eagles in the Negro League. He recalls a segregated Princeton where blacks could not enter certain establishments. In contrast, he recalls the great fun enjoyed at the famous black-owned Griggs' Restaurant. Carter worked for eighteen years in Princeton University's boiler room. Ethan Leidinger interviewed Carter at his home in Princeton in October 1999.

CARTER, REV. JUDSON M. (1938–2009) was born in Princeton. His father worked in the US Army Depot in Belle Mead, and later as a custodian at Princeton University. His mother worked primarily as a homemaker, but in the summertime, she traveled to Hyannis Port and different areas to work for the Kennedy family. Following the example of diligence and hard work set by his family, Carter often had two jobs as an adolescent. After graduating from Princeton High School, he served a brief stint in the armed forces. After that, he became a cement mixer and later found his calling in religious service as a minister. Rev. Carter has six children and eight grandchildren. Lou Arrindell interviewed Carter in May 2001 at his home in Princeton.

CRAIG, ERIC (1934–) was born in Princeton to Peyton Craig and Harriet Nixon Craig. Craig, a collector of antique tools, worked as a carpenter for Princeton University for more than thirty years. Upon his retirement, the university presented him with a special saw. For more than twenty-eight years, he has served as a member of the Princeton Borough School Board and has been on the Board of Trustees for Princeton at Blairstown. He is married to Minnie Louise Craig and has four children: Tracy, Donald, Glen, and Miriam. Kathryn Watterson interviewed Craig in March 2001 at his home in Princeton.

CRAIG, FRANCES BROADWAY (1943–), an educator, the youngest of nine children, was born in her parents' house on Birch Avenue in Princeton. Her two sisters and six brothers include Romus, Houston, and John. She attended integrated schools at Stony Brook for kindergarten, then Valley Road School for first through eighth grades. She went to college at West Virginia

State College, finished her graduate work at Trenton State College in 1965, and began teaching that same year. She was married the next year and has a son, Julian, and a daughter, Sydney, as well as a granddaughter, Spencer. Craig has been teaching at Community Park for twenty-seven years, and also worked at the John Witherspoon School for three years. She's a current resident in Princeton and was interviewed by Jenny Hildebrand at Community Park School in October 2000.

CRAIG, JAY JEROME (1930–), born in Princeton, was the ninth of twelve children born to Peyton and Harriet Nixon Craig. He attended the segregated Witherspoon School and graduated from Princeton High School in 1944. Early in his career, Jay worked as a grip with a film company, and for twenty-five years, he worked as superintendent of maintenance for the Princeton Jewish Center. Previously married to Francis Broadway Craig, he is the father of a son and three daughters, three grandchildren, and two great-grandchildren. Kathryn Watterson interviewed Craig at his home at 245 Nassau Street in Princeton in March 2001.

CRAIG, LOIS (1927–), the eighth of twelve children, was born in Princeton to Harriet Nixon and Peyton Craig in the house just next door to her current residence on Margerum Court. She married Simeon Moss and has one son, Kim. From 1957–68, Craig worked in the Registrar's Office at Princeton University. Micah Carr interviewed Craig at her home in Princeton in November 1999.

DENNIS, JOHNNIE (1903–2007), born in Old Abbeville County (now called Mount Carmel), South Carolina, came alone to Princeton as a teenager and worked as a maid and housekeeper in various homes all her life. Her sister, Beatrice Dennis, who also did domestic work in the area, died at 102 in 2001. Dennis speaks of being a motherless child who took what she could get for work. Jessica Lautin interviewed Dennis on March 2, 2001, at Merwick Rehabilitation Center in Princeton.

EDWARDS, KATHLEEN MONTGOMERY (1924–2000), known as Kappy, Kathy, Katie, and Mommy Kappy, was born in Marion, South Carolina, to George and Mattie Johnson Montgomery. She came to Princeton with her parents in 1929 and graduated from Princeton High School in 1942. She worked in civil service for fifty-six-and-a-half years and was an administrator at the 305th Medical Group Walson Air Force Clinic at Fort Dix up until her death after a brief illness in October 2000. A member of Trinity Episcopal Church and the Committee for Social Justice, she was active in housing advocacy and civil rights groups in Princeton. During the 1960s, she was the first black female elected to Princeton's Board of Education. She and her husband, Richard E. Edwards, had five children. Micah Carr interviewed Edwards at her home in Princeton in November 1999.

EDWARDS-CARTER, PENELOPE (PENNEY) S. (1947–) was the first of Kathleen M. and Richard E. Edwards' five children. She married Keith J. Carter, a fellow Princeton resident, in 1978, and they have one daughter. In 1979, Edwards-Carter became the first female and first African American to serve as Princeton Borough clerk and the first African American Municipal Clerk in Mercer County. She recalls watching the Birmingham riots on television and race dynamics following the assassination of Dr. Martin Luther King Jr. and speaks of Princeton politics and the entry of African Americans

Community Coordinator Penelope S. Edwards-Carter

into leadership positions. Kathryn Watterson interviewed Edwards-Carter in March 2001 at the Clay Street Learning Center in Princeton.

EPPS, EMMA GREENE (1902–1989) was the granddaughter of a slave, and two other aunts and one uncle were born into slavery. Her maternal grandmother was Massai Indian and her paternal grandfather was part Seminole. As a black student barred from high school in Princeton, she went to Danville High School in Virginia, where she was valedictorian of her class. She enrolled at the Lynchburg Theological Seminary and College but returned to Princeton in 1919 to help her mother, Mrs. Joseph Greene, who had founded the Witherspoon branch of the YWCA with fifteen young black girls. In the late 1930s, Epps, a passionate activist, fought against Princeton University's plan to tear down black homes to build Palmer Square. She worked for more than fifty years with the NAACP, the NJ State Federation of Women's Clubs, and forty-four years with the Friendship Club. This narrative, edited and shaped by Saloni Doshi, was pulled from the transcript of an interview by D. Reese King found in the archives of the Historical Society of Princeton thought to be from the late 1970s.

FLETCHER, LAMONT (1942–) was born in Princeton and raised in the Witherspoon neighborhood. He graduated from Princeton High School and then went to Winston-Salem State University in North Carolina. He went into the service at a hospital in Germany and later finished college in 1969. He holds a degree in elementary education with a minor in social studies and is also certified in English. He was a kindergarten teacher at the Johnson Park School, and at the time of this interview had been teaching for thirty-two years. Jenny Hildebrand interviewed Fletcher in Princeton in October 2000.

FLOYD, FANNIE REEVES (1924–2008), born in Princeton to George Reeves Sr. and Daisy Hampton Reeves, was the youngest of seven children. She attended the Witherspoon Street School and later Princeton High School. She went on to graduate from Virginia State University in 1945 with a degree in English. When she returned to Princeton, she met James Floyd Sr., whom she married in September 1946. The Floyds had two sons, James Jr. and Michael. She was employed as a copy editor by the Educational Testing Service for more than twenty years. Floyd was involved in a multitude of civic, social, charitable, and religious organizations. Some of these included the Princeton YMCA Board of Directors, the Planned Parenthood Board, being a Cub Scout den mother, a Churchwoman United Member, a Community House Surrogate Parent participant, the NAACP Legal Defense and Education Fund, McCarter Theatre Associates Board, Princeton Nursery School, Princeton Community Democratic Organization, and the Witherspoon/Jackson Neighborhood Association. Andrew Ferrar interviewed Floyd in Princeton in the fall of 1999.

FLOYD, JAMES A., SR. (1922–) was born in Trenton and moved to Princeton after college to live with his wife, longtime Princeton resident Fannie Floyd. Throughout his life in Princeton, he was an active civic leader and a member of Witherspoon Presbyterian Church. In the 1960s, he and his wife started a Princeton Family Sponsor Program for minority students at the university. He retired as vice president of the Educational Testing Service (ETS). He was a founding member of PAHR, which later evolved into the Princeton Community Housing Group. His involvement in local politics began with the zoning board, which eventually led him to become Princeton's first African American mayor in 1970. Floyd was interviewed by Ethan Meers in Princeton in October 2000.

GRIGGS, BURNETT (1888–1977), born in Farmville, Virginia, moved to Princeton in 1909 and became a legend there during the first half of the twentieth century. He worked for many years as a waiter, fought in World War I, and in 1919 he opened his own place, Griggs' Imperial Restaurant, on Hulfish, which was popular up until 1962, when it closed. Upon his death on July 28, 1977, to honor his memory, his daughter, Burnetta Griggs Peterson, with her husband, Dr. Chester Peterson, a local dentist, sold Mr. Griggs's property on Route 206 at a very reasonable price so as to enable the building of affordable housing for low- and moderate-income families; it's called Griggs Farm. Griggs's interview was conducted by the Historical Society of Princeton when he was eighty-three years old.

GRIGGS PETERSON, BURNETTA (1931–2013), daughter of Burnett Griggs and Ruth Evans Griggs, was born in Princeton. As a child, she attended the Witherspoon Street School and later graduated from Princeton High School. She went on to pursue a career as a teacher in 1951 after graduating from

Adelphi College. She taught second grade at the Parker School in Trenton and the Nassau Street Elementary and Valley Road Schools in Princeton. She married Chester Peterson in 1956 and moved with him to New Brunswick before returning to Princeton to raise their two daughters. Peterson and her husband constructed the attractive low-income housing units known as Griggs Farm as a perpetual tribute to her father Burnett Griggs. Peterson was interviewed via telephone by Sara Kippur in November 1999.

HILL, JOAN (1942–) was born in Princeton. Her parents, Mr. and Mrs. Douglas Thomas Hill, had both moved to the borough at a young age. Her mother, who loved math, worked at the Campus Club at Princeton University, and later in the library. Hill's father worked for Princeton University, at various state institutions, and, finally, at Greystone Hospital in North Jersey. The third oldest in her family, Hill assumed a leadership role early on in her life. Aside from performing her daily chores, she was responsible for taking her five younger siblings to and from school. She continued to be a leader in high school where she excelled in both sports and academics. After attending Central State University, Marshall County Community College, and Rutgers University, Hill took a position with the Princeton Civil Rights Commission. Later, she became director of the Civil Rights Commission. In addition, she was responsible for starting many programs, including the Witherspoon-Jackson Development Corporation. Lou Arrindell interviewed Hill in October 2000 at the Clay Street Learning Center in Princeton.

HINDS, ALBERT (1902–2006), born in Princeton, was the grandson of slaves and the oldest of Sophia and Arthur Henry Hinds' eight children. He worked a variety of jobs as a young boy, doing everything from polishing shoes to grooming horses to make money. One of a handful of first black students at Princeton High School, he tells of sports events and local tensions, as well as his time away, when he attended Straight College in New Orleans and Talladega College in Talladega, Alabama. He helped to establish and run YMCAs in New Orleans, Atlanta, and New Jersey. He worked for the US Postal Service, the New Jersey State Hospital, and served on Princeton's Zoning Board for twenty years. Hinds was interviewed by Cheryl Hicks in 1995 for the Historical Society of Princeton and by Kathryn Watterson in July 1999, when he was ninety-eight years old.

HINDS, SOPHIE HALL (1875–1974), one of Mr. and Mrs. Robert Hall's eight children, was born on a farm just north of Princeton. Her father, born into slavery, escaped and came north before the Civil War. Hinds worked as a housekeeper most of her life. She was an active member of Mount Pisgah AME Church and the Missionary Society. She and her husband, Arthur H. Hinds, had nine children, and eight—four sons and four daughters—lived to adulthood. Hinds had nine grandchildren, nine great-grandchildren, and several nieces and nephews. In 1971, when Emily C. Stuart interviewed Hinds for the Historical Society of Princeton, he was ninety-six years old.

HOAGLAND, HELEN BALL (1920–2009) was born on John Street, to parents who had moved here from Maryland and Virginia as youngsters. She relays a harrowing racist event at Princeton University that forced her hardworking father to leave his Canon Club job. From Princeton High School, she went to Trenton State College, which in 1937 admitted 2 percent black students. She recalls the racism she experienced there when black students were not permitted to live on campus, so she took rooms in Trenton and elsewhere. She has three children, six grandchildren, and three great-grandchildren. Katherine Jackson interviewed Hoagland in November 1999 in her home on Quarry Street in Princeton.

JOHNSON, ESTELLE (1919–2011) was born in Trenton, New Jersey. After her grandmother died, Johnson moved to Princeton and lived with her mother and father in a house on Birch Avenue and then on Witherspoon Street until 1952. Johnson worked at Nassau Inn as a chambermaid, and her husband worked there as a waiter. She describes the destruction of a strong black community in Princeton once the Princeton Plan of urban renewal was put into action. She tells of the tearing down of black-owned and rented homes, the harsh dispersement of black families, and the failure of Princeton leaders to address urgent housing needs of black families. Dwandalyn Reece King interviewed Johnson for the Historical Society of Princeton in July 1995.

JOHNSON, WILLIAM (1938–), born in Englewood, New Jersey, and raised in Harlem, New York, is a civic activist, teacher, and military veteran. His mother grew up in Englewood and was a nurse at Lincoln Hospital, and his father was a postal worker in New York City. In 1952, the family moved to

Englewood. Johnson graduated from high school in 1956 and attended college in Springfield, Massachusetts, where he majored in physical education and science. After college, he enlisted in the US Marine Corps. He came to Princeton in 1976 to be the principal of the town's middle school. Johnson and his wife, Susie Smith Johnson, have two daughters and reside in Ewing, ten miles from Princeton. Jenny Hildebrand interviewed Johnson in November 2000.

LEWIS, REV. DR. ARTHUR (1931–2013) was born in Princeton to Blanche Taylor Chase and George Peter Lewis. He received a BS in management and an MA in public administration from Rider College, an MA degree in religion from the Lutheran Theological Seminary at Philadelphia, and a DMin from the Lutheran School of Theology at Chicago. After his time in the US Air Force, he pursued a thirty-plus-year career in public service in New Jersey with a special emphasis on employment training and economic empowerment. He worked for the New Jersey Department of Labor, was the director of the Public Service Career Program, the director of the Division of Human Resources, the assistant commissioner for Human Affairs in the New Jersey Department of Community Affairs, and the director of African American Affairs in the governor's office. Lewis was also the pastor of three Lutheran churches as well as a lifetime member of the Alpha Phi Alpha fraternity. Along with his wife, Rose Lewis, he raised two daughters. Ravi Sangisetty interviewed Lewis at the Clay Street Learning Center in Princeton in March 2001.

MACK, JAMES ("JIMMY") (1935–) was born in Virginia and moved to Princeton when he was twenty-one years old, following four years in the navy. In 1962, he opened Jimmy's Barbershop on John Street in 1962 and continued to work there until he retired in 2012. He and his wife, Audrey, live in Princeton. Their two children, Joyce and James Jr., who attended public schools in Princeton, live in Atlanta and Marietta, Georgia. Lauren Miller interviewed Jimmy Mack at his barbershop on John Street in November 2000.

MITNAUL, PAUL (1927–) was born in Greensboro, North Carolina, and moved with his family to Princeton in 1933 when he was six years old. He attended the Witherspoon Street School for Children and Princeton High School. He worked at Nassau Appliance and later set up his own business at 250 Nassau Street. In 1962, he joined the RCA–Astro Space Center in Hightstown, and a year later he moved to RCA Laboratories in Penns Neck, where he remained until his retirement in 1987. When Ethan Meers interviewed Mitnaul in December 2000, he was seventy-three years old.

MOORE, DONALD (1932–) was born in Princeton, where his family has owned several buildings on Spring Street for more than eighty years. Moore, who manages those properties, relays his lifelong struggle to live with dignity despite racism in a segregated Princeton, and despite the racism he experienced during his extensive travels. An army veteran, Moore recalls being refused service and train seating while in military uniform. Moore graduated from Pierce Business School in Philadelphia. His first job was at Paul Fields Linoleum Store. He has lived and worked in various places along the East Coast for the last forty years with his wife, Ruth, a social worker. Molly Spieczny interviewed Moore in November 1999, and Kathryn Watterson interviewed Moore and talked with his wife at their home in Princeton in March 2002.

MOORE, JOSEPH P. (1941–), one of the first African American deans at Princeton University, was born to Evelyn Lamar Moore and Cornelius Arthur Moore. He grew up with ten brothers and sisters on Jackson Street in Princeton and attended the segregated Quarry Street School, the integrated Nassau Street School, and Princeton High School. He graduated from Central State University in Ohio with a major in social work and a minor in philosophy. He worked as a Job Corps leader and later started two special achievement schools within Trenton Central High School. During his tenure as a dean at Princeton, he was elected to two consecutive terms on Princeton's Borough Council, where he served as fire commissioner and police commissioner. Later, he was a member of the Princeton Board of Education and an administrator at the Ford Foundation. Ethan Meers interviewed Moore in October 2000, and Kathryn Watterson did a follow-up interview in March 2001.

MOSS, SIMEON (1920–2007) was the first of four children born to Simeon C. and Mary B. Moss. He attended Princeton Nursery School, the Quarry Street School, and Princeton High School, where he graduated in 1937. Moss earned a bachelor's degree in education from Rutgers University in 1941.

During World War II, he fought in the segregated Ninety-Second Division of the US Army from 1942–46, became a captain, and was awarded a Silver Star and a Purple Heart. Upon his return, he became the first black graduate student admitted to Princeton University, where he studied at the Woodrow Wilson School and received a master's degree in public and international affairs in 1949. Moss was then recalled to the army and served in the Korean War from 1950–52; he retired from the military in 1975 with the rank of colonel. He also was a teacher and superintendent of schools in Newark, New Jersey, worked with the State Department of Labor, later became director of the Newark Youth Career Development Program, and was a lifelong member of the NAACP. In 1946, he married Edith Moss, with whom he had two children. She died in 1997, after 51 years of marriage. He and Lois Craig were married in 1999. Micah Carr interviewed Moss in October 1999 at Moss and Craig's home on John Street in Princeton, and Kathryn Watterson did a follow-up interview with them at their home in May 2001.

PANNELL, HENRY (HANK) (1939–), born to Peter and Francis Tilotson Pannell, grew up on Jackson Street in Princeton and attended Princeton Nursery School, the Witherspoon School for Colored Children, and Princeton High. In 1957, Pannell was the first African American to work at Princeton's Jet Propulsion Lab, and in 1966, he became the first black maintenance mechanic for Palmer Square. In the late 1960s and early 1970s, he was an editor and the printer of the local newsletter, the *Black Word*. He became chief of maintenance for the Housing Authority of the Borough of Princeton in 1972. In the 1990s, he helped to create and build the Clay Street Learning Center; cofounded an organization, the Alliance, to bring together black, Hispanic, and white neighborhood residents; started computer classes for adults and children at the Clay Street Learning Center; collected, repaired, and provided computers for them in their homes, as well as for children at the Harlem YMCA and in Ghana; and was a founder and president of the Jackson-Witherspoon Development Corporation, formed to preserve the integrity of the neighborhood by purchasing and renovating properties to support homeownership at affordable prices. Pannell, a father of four and grandfather of six, lives with his wife, Eileen, on Clay Street. Kathryn

Community Coordinator Henry F. (Hank)
and his wife Eileen Pannell

Watterson interviewed Pannell in June 2000 at the Clay Street Learning
Center in Princeton.

PARAGO, BESSIE (1907–2007) was born in Providence, Rhode Island, married her husband Wilson in 1930, and moved into her home on Leigh Avenue
in Princeton, New Jersey, where she lived the rest of her life. Throughout
most of her life in Princeton, Parago did domestic work in private homes, as
well as in local churches, schools, and the YMCA. She relays her shock upon
moving to a segregated Jim Crow Princeton with segregated restaurants and
theaters. She describes her struggle to have a daughter properly tracked into
academic studies rather than general studies in Princeton's newly integrated

high school. The Paragoes had three daughters, all of whom still live in the Princeton area today. Julie Straus interviewed Parago in November 1999 at her home in Princeton.

PHOX, THOMAS (BUDDY) (1920–2008) was born in Palls, Virginia, where his parents worked on a plantation. They moved to Princeton in 1929, where he went to Quarry Street School and graduated from Princeton High in 1939. He worked as a golf caddy, delivered milk, and then during World War II, he served in the US Army Infantry and received a Bronze Star, a Purple Heart, and commendation for saving troops. He attended Pennsylvania State on a football scholarship and then under the GI Bill attended the New York Technical Institute. He became a film technician and the first African American electrician in the Film Guild/Union. Later, as an assistant director, he became one of the first African American members of the Directors' Guild of America. He and his wife commuted to New York City from Princeton—he to work for ABC, CBS, NBC, and Channel 15, and her to work for Young & Rubicam. They have two children, three grandchildren, and one great-grandchild. Celia Riechel interviewed Phox in December 2000, three days after his eightieth birthday, at the family's home on Ewing Street in Princeton.

REDDING, EVA (1922–1997) was born and raised in Princeton. She was a lifelong civic activist and entrepreneur whose world vision of peace and understanding was exemplified when, as a teenager, she worked with the American Legion and the International Friendship League. During this time she was chairman of the regional March of Dimes, a Princeton Committee Woman, and a member of the Princeton Community Housing Board. Redding was active in Princeton's integration of the Ys in 1948 and was the first African American in the Mercer County American Legion. Her interview was conducted for the Historical Society of Princeton.

RHODES, EMANUEL (1921–) was born in Halifax County, North Carolina, and moved to Princeton with his parents in 1933, during the Depression. His father had quit farming because he was making no money, but the family was able to move in with Rhodes's uncle Heziki in Princeton. During World War II, Rhodes joined the Ninety-Second Division, an all-black unit called the Buffaloes that fought in Italy. Mayling Ganuza interviewed Rhodes on November 1999 at Rhodes's John Street home in Princeton.

RIVERS, HAZEL LEWIS (1910–2007), born in Little Rocky Hill, just north of Princeton, was one of seven children of Mary Evelyn Salter Lewis and David Lewis. Her father was an orphan, so his parentage wasn't known. Lewis attended Princeton High School for four years and went to work as a live-in housekeeper. She married Robert Joseph Rivers Sr. and they had two daughters and two sons. An actress, wife, mother, domestic worker, and civic supporter with strong religious beliefs, Rivers recalls moving to a segregated Princeton as a young bride. She reflects on the realities of growing up with limited financial resources, the pain of segregation, and the joys of family and community. Kathryn Watterson and Rivers's granddaughter, Naomi Dunson, a student at Princeton University, interviewed Rivers in February 2002 in her retirement apartment in West Windsor, near Princeton.

RIVERS, LEONARD (1934–), born to Hazel Lewis Rivers and Robert J. Rivers Sr., is a retired educator who taught and coached for forty years. Starting in the late 1970s, he coached football and baseball at Princeton University. As head baseball coach there, he led the Tiger baseball team to more than a hundred victories. He also worked with professional basketball, serving as director of Community Relations for the New Jersey Nets. David Sackler interviewed Rivers in November 1999 at the Clay Street Learning Center in Princeton. The following year, after he had retired from coaching and teaching history, biology, math, and physical education at Lakewood High School, Kathryn Watterson interviewed him again at the Franklin Township office, where he was working full time as a consultant recruiting new teachers for the superintendent of schools.

RIVERS, DR. ROBERT JOSEPH, JR. (1931–), born to Robert Joseph Rivers and Hazel Lewis Rivers in Princeton, went to the Witherspoon School for Colored Children, and graduated from Princeton High School in 1949. During the time he attended the Witherspoon for Colored Children, he stayed with his mother at the house where she was a live-in cook and housekeeper during the week and got to be at home with his whole family on the weekends. After the V-12 naval officers broke the color barrier at Princeton University during World War II, he was the second student from the neighborhood—after Joseph Moss—to attend Princeton University. He graduated cum laude in biology in 1953, and, in 1957, graduated from Harvard Medical School as a vascular surgeon. He was a lieutenant in the US Navy from 1959 to 1961. From 1964 to 1989, he practiced medicine in Rochester, New York, and was a professor of clinical surgery at the University of Rochester School of Medicine. He served as a member of Princeton University's Board of Trustees and in other advisory positions, with a special focus on opening opportunities for minorities in higher education. He and his wife, Ruth Lewis, are parents to four children. Rivers, a pilot and community activist, retired in 1989. He and his wife live in Cape Cod and Virginia. Kathryn Watterson interviewed Rivers in the Clay Street Learning Center in Princeton in May 2001.

SATTERFIELD, ALICE MAY (1922–2010), born to Annie E. Van Zandt Moore May and William Henry May, was the youngest of seven children. As a young woman, she worked in the kitchen at the Institute for Advanced Studies, where she became friends with Albert Einstein. In the 1960s, she went to work in maintenance for the Princeton Regional School System. She later became their central telephone operator and receptionist and worked there for thirty-one years before she retired in 1987. A lifetime member of Witherspoon Presbyterian Church, Satterfield was interviewed at her Quarry Street home in Princeton in November 2000 by Linda Madeume and again in May 2001 by Kathryn Watterson.

SATTERFIELD, SHIRLEY ANN (1940–), born in Philadelphia to Alice May Satterfield and Claude W. Satterfield, returned to Princeton with her mother when Shirley was a baby. Six generations of her family lived in Princeton, dating back to Satterfield's great-grandparents, Wayman and Martha Boile VanZant. She attended Witherspoon School for Colored Children and the Nassau Street Elementary School. She graduated from Princeton High School, attended Rider College, and graduated from Bennett College for Women. She taught school in Las Vegas, Nevada, Syracuse, New York, and in Summit and East Windsor, New Jersey, before becoming a guidance counselor at Princeton High School. She's on the Board of Trustees for the Historical Society of Princeton and has founded a walking tour of African American Life in Princeton. She is a member and historial of Witherspoon Street Presbyterian Church and several community organizations. Satterfield has two daughters and one granddaughter. Shashank Mathur interviewed Satterfield in October 2000 in her guidance office at Princeton High School.

SINKLER-ROBINSON, JOYCE (1942–), a lifelong Princeton educator, is a fourth-generation college-educated family member. Her strong-willed mother forced the Princeton Board of Education to enroll her in the Valley School, only open to whites at the time. Sinclair-Robinson's interview was conducted by Lauren Miller in March 2001 in Princeton.

SWAIN, JACQUELINE (JACQUI) LENORE (1944–) was born to parents Harold E. Johnston and Rosalee Sullivan in Princeton Hospital. She went to Public School 179 in Rahway, New Jersey, but spent much of her life in Princeton with her grandparents. She graduated from Rider College, where she was a member of a singing group called "The Rosebuds." She became the first black secretary to work at the Woodrow Wilson School at Princeton University. She's been a social activist and worked for many organizations, including the Civil Rights Commission, Joint Commission of Civil Rights, the Paul Robeson Community Center, Housing Authority of the Borough of Princeton, the Community House Board, and the Prospect Association Board, among many others. Kathryn Watterson interviewed Swain in April 2001 in her office as manager of the Teacher Prep Program at Princeton University.

THOMAS, CLYDE (BUSTER) (1934–2004) was born to David and Sylvia Ann Thomas in Princeton, attended the Princeton Nursery School, and, in 1948, graduated in the last segregated class from the Witherspoon School for Colored Children. At Princeton High School, he was a champion track, basketball, and football player. Thomas won twenty-seven consecutive dual track meets and was Princeton High's first thousand-point scorer in basketball. After graduation from PHS in 1952, he attended Pennington Prep and was selected for First Team All-State in football. He won a full scholarship to Pennsylvania State University, where he graduated in 1958 with a major in business administration and labor relations. In his professional life and his volunteer work, Thomas has worked for civil rights and fair hiring practices. He developed the Affirmative Action Plan for the New Jersey Sports Exposition,

Community Coordinator Clyde (Buster) Thomas

which is responsible for the operation of the 177 Meadowlands racetrack, basketball, and hockey arena. He lived in Lawrenceville with his wife of forty years, Bette Thomas, until his death from cancer in 2004. The Thomases have two children and six grandchildren. Kathryn Watterson interviewed Thomas in June 2000 at the Clay Street Learning Center in Princeton.

TROTMAN, MILDRED (1941–), a successful businesswoman, became Princeton's first black and second female mayor. She moved to Princeton from the South in 1962 and spent decades serving on Princeton's Borough Council in addition to excelling in other political roles. Trotman is a graduate of North Carolina State University and the College of New Jersey. She is the president of SAM Management Company. Ethan Meers interviewed Trotman at her office in Princeton in October 2000.

TWYMAN, FLORENCE (1916–2001), born in Princeton, recalls a segregated Princeton where African Americans couldn't get bank loans to build their homes, white construction workers wouldn't work on black homes, and where a visiting black congressman, a black NAACP representative, and traveling black musicians had to rent rooms in black homes because Princeton's public accommodations were closed to them. Twyman recalls the humiliations that came with her first job in Princeton as a white Princeton University professor's domestic worker. Twyman was interviewed by Celia Riechel at her home in Princeton in November 2000.

WAXWOOD, SUSIE (1902–2006), born Susie Ione Brown in Gray, Louisiana, was the fourth of seven children. Her parents, both teachers, sent her to a church school in New Orleans from fifth through twelfth grades. She graduated from Howard University with a BA in English in 1925. She married Howard Waxwood and moved to Princeton in 1935. Her husband was principal of Witherspoon School and a key mover in the implementation of the Princeton Plan to integrate local schools in 1949. Waxwood, executive director of the black branch of the YWCA for eight years following the integration of the black and white branches, was active in the NAACP Legal Defense Fund. She and her husband had one son, Howard Waxwood Jr. At ninety-seven, Waxwood packed up her house on Witherspoon Street to move with her dog, Lucky, to the mountains of North Carolina to live with her granddaughter's family. As this narrative was being edited in September 2002, she was about to celebrate her one hundredth birthday. Kathryn Watterson originally interviewed Waxwood in September 1999 and then talked with her again in 2000 as she was packing for her move.

WRIGHT, BRUCE MCMARION (1917–2005) was born in the Princeton Hospital to Alice Thigpen Wright and Bruce Wright. He graduated from the Quarry Street School for Colored Children, Townsend Harris High School in New York City, and Lincoln University. Following his army service in World War II, he graduated from New York University Law School and began to practice law in New York City. He lived in Harlem, was a published poet, and a good friend of Langston Hughes. He served as judge for New York City's Criminal and Civil Courts, where, because of his disdain for false arrests and inflated charges, newspaper reporters dubbed him

"Turn 'Em Loose Bruce." He was elected to and served on the New York Supreme Court for ten years. The father of five sons, Judge Wright and his wife, Elizabeth Mara Davidson, lived in Old Saybrook, Connecticut. Kathryn Watterson and Hank Pannell interviewed him at his home there on May 25, 2002. At the time, he was recovering from brain surgery and a series of strokes, but he had just come from the gym, where he'd been working out. Later that day, he went to the public library, where he read to the children three afternoons a week. Judge Wright died on March 24, 2005.

YATES, MARILYN (1935–) was born in Princeton to Ralph and Ethel Mitnaul. Along with her brother, she grew up in the John Witherspoon neighborhood where she completed her elementary school education; she graduated from Princeton High School. She is the mother of six children and is retired from her administrative staff position with the English Department at Princeton University, where she worked for more than thirty years. Linda Madeume interviewed Yates at her Clay Street home in Princeton in February 2001, and Kathryn Watterson did a follow-up interview in May 2001.

A celebration at the Henry F. Pannell Learning Center
with many of the participants in the John Witherspoon
Life Stories Oral History Project (May 2001)

Endnotes

INTRODUCTION: "The North's Most Southern Town"

1. Leslie H. Fishel Jr. and Benjamin Quarles, *The Black American: A Documentary History* (New York: William Morrow, 1970), 129.
2. Nubian Committee, *The Gathering II* (September 4, 2009); Iver Peterson, "As Princeton Changes, a Black Community Fears for Future," *New York Times*, September 3, 2001. While there are no official records of free blacks, more than likely, they were among the black and Irish indentured servants freed by their Dutch masters after they had served their terms or escaped from bondage.
3. https://www.geni.com/people/Richard-The-Builder-Stockton /6000000000946493122
4. Constance M. Greiff, "Views of Morven," *Princeton History: The Journal of the Historical Society of Princeton*, no. 10 (1991): 5–6.
5. Jack Washington, *The Long Journey Home: A Bicentennial History of the Black Community of Princeton, New Jersey, 1776–1976* (Trenton, NJ: Africa World Press, 2005), 2.
6. In the 1630s Dutch settlers brought slaves to the New Netherlands—and often set them free after a specified period of service. When the English seized the land in 1664 and established it as the Colony of New Jersey, they wrote into law that Africans were to be held in perpetual bondage by those who had purchased them.
7. Giles R. Wright and Edward Lama Wonkeryor, *New Jersey's Underground Railroad Heritage:"Steal Away, Steal Away . . .": A Guide to the Underground Railroad in New Jersey* (New Jersey Historical Commission, 2002), 4; Clement Alexander Price, *Freedom Not Far Distant: A Documentary*

History of Afro-Americans in New Jersey (Newark, NJ: Historical Society, 1980), 32.

8. Price, *Freedom Not Far Distant*, 30.

9. "Sale of the estate of President Samuel Finley, to be held on August 19, 1766," *Pennsylvania Journal*, Philadelphia, PA, July 31, 1766.

10. Although whites asserted blacks were dim-witted, lazy, and ignorant, advertisements from the time reveal that in truth they were prized as skilled carpenters, boat builders, and millers. Their expertise as "iron forgers, miners, loggers, and woodworkers came from trades practiced in Africa long before the beginning of the Atlantic Slave Trade" (ibid., 40).

11. Robert Ketchum, *The Winter Soldier: The Battles of Trenton and Princeton* (New York: Henry Holt, 1999), 157.

12. Craig Steven Wilder, *Ebony & Ivy: Race, Slavery, and the Troubled History of America's Universities* (New York: Bloomsbury Press, 2013), 139.

13. Jennifer Epstein, "Slaves and Slavery at Princeton," senior thesis, April 8, 2008. Transcribed from a copy in the Office of the President Records, Box 1, Aaron Burr Sr., Seeley G. Mudd Manuscript Library. Courtesy of the Princeton University Archives.

14. Wilder, *Ebony & Ivy*, 17.

15. Ibid., 139.

16. Washington, *The Long Journey Home*, 4.

17. Jeff Looney, "Slavery at Princeton," Seeley G. Mudd Library, FAQ Slavery at Princeton.

18. DC Slave Code, 1860.

19. Shortly after being finalized on July 4, the first printing of the Declaration was ordered for public distribution. Approximately two hundred broadside prints were produced. The first public reading was July 8 in Philadelphia.

20. Wilder, *Ebony & Ivy*, 111.

21. Fishel and Quarles, *The Black American*, 42.

22. Ibid., 40.

23. In some cases, black soldiers were not freed: one man named Prime from Princeton petitioned the state and had to wait more than two years to settle the disagreement between his previous owner and the state.

24. Fishel and Quarles, *The Black American*, 2.

25. Ibid., 127. Also according to Fishel and Quarles, *The Black American*, in pre–Civil War America, "Colored people without masters numbered 59.557 in 1790 and jumped to 488,070 in 1860."

26. Ibid., 128–29.
27. Sean Wilentz, "Princeton and the Controversies over Slavery," *Journal of Presbyterian History (1997–)* 85, no. 2 (Fall/Winter 2007): 110.
28. Ibid., 110.
29. African American History, Princeton Pubic Library, http://www.princeton.lib.jh.us/history.html, 6/20/2003.
30. Washington, *The Long Journey Home*, 27.
31. Fishel and Quarles, *The Black American*, 130.
32. Wilentz, "Princeton and the Controversies over Slavery," 109.
33. James Forten Jr., *An Address Delivered before the Ladies' Anti-Slavery Society of Philadelphia*, April 14, 1836, 10–13. In Fishel and Quarles, "Abolitionism and the Crisis of the Fifties," in *The Black American*, 193.
34. Consuelo Campbell, "Princeton Residents Reflect on Local Civil Rights Movement," Tape 3, MLK Day Celebration, January 14, 1991, Broadcast Center Recordings, Box 3, Princeton University Archives, Department of Rare Books and Special Collections, Princeton University Library.
35. Paul Robeson, *Here I Stand* (Boston: Beacon Press, 1988), 10.
36. Rev. Dr. Martin Luther King Jr., "I Have a Dream," August 28, 1963, Washington, DC.
37. This site is now called the Henry F. Pannell Learning Center in honor of Hank Pannell, who, as chief of maintenance for the Housing Authority of the Borough of Princeton, had supervised and constructed the building with the help of borough employees, friends, and neighbors.
38. Manning Marable and Leith Mullings, eds., *Let Nobody Turn Us Around: Voices of Resistance, Reform, and Renewal* (New York: Rowman & Littlefield, 2000), 351.
39. Nubian Committee, *The Gathering II*, "Education," by PULSE (Pride, Unity, Leadership, Sisterhood, Esteem) of Princeton High School, 3.
40. Fred Jerome, *The Einstein File: J. Edgar Hoover's Secret War against the World's Most Famous Scientist* (New York: St. Martin's Press, 2002), 78.
41. James Baldwin, *Notes of a Native Son* (New York: Beacon Press, 1955), 92–95.
42. Lauren Miller, "Black Businesses in Princeton," research essay for oral history project, Fall 2000.
43. Booker T. Washington Papers, Vol. 6, October 1902, University of Illinois Press, 548.
44. Jerome, *The Einstein File*, 78.

45. Albert E. Hinds Memorial Walking Tour: African-American Life in Princeton, Historical Society of Princeton, www.princtonhistory.org.

46. Kevin Gaines, "Reflections on a Surviving Issue of *The Citizen*," *Princeton History: The Journal of the Historical Society of Princeton*, No. 14, 1997.

47. The *Black Word*, a newspaper created in the late 1960s by an enterprising group of young Witherspoon activists, gave the community a chance to let their opinions be known. Articles in the paper discussed pressing issues of equal rights, fair housing, and politics. Hank Pannell was the printer; Romus Broadway was the photographer.

CHAPTER 1: Our Grandmother Came from Africa as a Little Girl

1. Thomas Jefferson Wertenbaker, *Princeton 1746-1896*, Princeton, N.J. 1946.

2. Jennifer Epstein, "Slaves and Slavery at Princeton," senior thesis, April 8, 2008, 31. Transcribed from a copy in the Office of the President Records, Box 1, Aaron Burr Sr., Seeley G. Mudd Manuscript Library. Courtesy of the Princeton University Archives.

3. Ibid., 32.

4. John Weeren, "Slavery at Princeton," Princeton University, http://princeton.edu.

5. In all of the extensively detailed history and written records of that time up through the mid-1800s, researchers have not found a single entry dealing with slaves or slavery in connection with students, nor did the floor plans of Nassau Hall have any hint of housing for slaves.

6. Isabel Wilkerson, *The Warmth of Other Suns: The Epic Story of America's Great Migration* (New York: Random House, 2010), 37–38.

7. John Hope Franklin, *The Color Line: Legacy for the Twenty-First Century* (Columbia: University of Missouri Press, 1993), 6.

8. Ibid., 39.

9. Dwandalyn Reece King, "Completing the Historical Record: Princeton's First Exhibition on the African-American Community," *Princeton History: The Journal of the Historical Society of Princeton*, no. 14 (1997): 40.

CHAPTER 2: I Grew Up Hugged to the Hearts of My People

1. Robeson, *Here I Stand* (Boston: Beacon Press, 1988), 7.

2. Donald Moore, interview with Kathryn Watterson, Princeton, NJ, March 2002.

3. Hank Pannell, interview with Kathryn Watterson, Princeton, NJ, June 2000.

4. Alice Satterfield, interview with Linda Madeume, Princeton, NJ, November 2000; and with Kathryn Watterson, Princeton, NJ, May 2001·

5. Romus Broadway, interview with Shawn Sindelar, Princeton, NJ, October 2000; and with Kathryn Watterson, Princeton, NJ, April 2001.

6. Shirley Satterfield, interview with Shashank Mathur, Princeton, NJ, November 1999.

7. Irwin Silber, Paul Robeson, "A 20th-Century Joshua," *Sing Out! The Folk Magazine*, vol. 42, no. 4, 44.

8. Fred Jerome and Rodger Taylor, *Einstein on Race and Racism* (New Brunswick: Rutgers University Press, 2005), 5556.

9. Ibid., 124.

10. Rev. Judson M. Carter, interview with Lou Arrindell, Princeton, NJ, May 2001.

11. Ibid.

12. For many years, George Reeves Sr., a steward and chef at a university eating club on Prospect Avenue, spent his summers as camp cook at the Blairstown Summer Camp. Reeves, a highly respected member of the Witherspoon YMCA, persuaded camp administrators to admit African American boys, which they did. University football players and athletes worked as counselors and Witherspoon boys thrived on the experience.

CHAPTER 3: School Integration: A Big Loss for Black Children

1. Constance K. Escher, "She Calls Herself Betsey Stockton," *Princeton History: The Journal of the Historical Society of Princeton*, no. 10 (1991): 74–75.

2. Ibid., 86.

3. Ibid., 88.

4. Article 1, Section 5, New Jersey State Constitution of 1947.

5. Jenny Hildebrand, "The Princeton Plan: Integration and Its Aftermath," paper for "Life Stories: Writing Oral History" course, Princeton University, January 2001.

6. Doris Burrell, interview with Lauren Miller, Princeton, NJ, October 2000.

7. Coordinating Committee Statement, Witherspoon School Reunion, 1848–1948 (October 19, 1996), 2.

8. Frances Broadway Craig, interview with Jenny Hildebrand, Princeton, NJ, October 2000.

9. Lamont Fletcher, interview with Jenny Hildebrand, Princeton, NJ, October 2000.

10. Clyde Thomas, interview with Kathryn Watterson, Clay Street Learning Center, Princeton, NJ, June 2000.

11. Jack Anderson, "The Structure of the Negro Community with Special Reference to Social Classes," senior thesis, April 1950. Courtesy of Princeton University Archives.

12. Shawshank Mather, interview with Shirley Satterfield in her guidance office at Princeton High School, November 1999.

CHAPTER 4: The University: A Place to Labor, Not to Study

1. Dwandalyn Reece King, "Completing the Historical Record: Princeton's First Exhibition of the African American Community," *Princeton History: The Journal of the Historical Society of Princeton*, no. 14 (1997): 40.

2. Thomas Jefferson Wertenbaker, *Princeton, 1746–1896* (Princeton, NJ: Princeton University Press), 3–27.

3. Reference to the Southern aristocracy.

4. Paul Robeson, "A Home in that Rock," in *Here I Stand* (Boston: Beacon Press, 1988), 10.

5. John Weeren, "Slavery at Princeton," Princeton University, http://princeton.edu.

6. Leslie H. Fishel Jr. and Benjamin Quarles, *The Black American: A Documentary History* (New York: William Morrow, 1970), 145.

7. Ibid., 145.

8. Sean Wilentz, "Princeton and the Controversies over Slavery," *Journal of Presbyterian History (1997–)* 85, no. 2 (Fall/Winter 2007): 103.

9. Ibid., 105.

10. Melvin McCray, producer, *Looking Forward: Reflections of Black Princeton Alumni*, video, 2000.

11. King, "Completing the Historical Record," 40.

12. Lou Arrindell, "Civil Rights in Princeton," paper for "Life Stories: Writing Oral History" course, Princeton University, Fall 2000, 7.

13. Hank Pannell, interview by Kathryn Watterson, Princeton, NJ, June 2000.

14. Robert Rivers would go on to become a professor of Clinical Surgery at the University of Rochester Medical School and a Princeton University Trustee. In 2016, Princeton University awarded him a Doctor of Humanities honorary degree. Simeon Moss became superintendent of schools in Newark, New Jersey.

15. Maggie Shi, "First Black Students Face Isolation, Racism," in *Black Experience Princeton Experiencing Blacks: 50 Years of Reflection*, eight-part series, *Daily Princetonian*, vol. 119, no. 28, March 7, 1995.
16. Maggie Shi, "Black Alumni Recall 1960s," in *Black Experience, Daily Princetonian*, vol. 119, no. 30, March 9, 1995, 1.
17. Ibid., 1.
18. Ibid., 12.
19. Lou Arrindell, "Civil Rights in Princeton," 8.
20. Association of Black Princeton Alumni, "Important Dates in Black Princeton University History," abpa@alumni.princeton.edu.
21. Honorary doctorate degree recipient (and 2016 Nobel Prize for Literature recipient) Bob Dylan was sitting nervously on the dais writing, "Day of the Locusts" at the 1970 graduation.

CHAPTER 5: Every Day, You Work to Survive

1. Kathleen Edwards, interview with Micah Carr, Princeton, NJ, November 1999.
2. James Whitehill Funk, "The Pattern of Negro Labor in Princeton," senior thesis, Department of Economics and Social Institutions, Princeton University, January 8, 1948, 15.
3. Ibid., 16.
4. Ibid., 18.
5. Ibid., 18.
6. Leonard Rivers, interview with David Sackler, Princeton, NJ, November 1999; follow-up interview with Kathryn Watterson, Princeton, NJ, October 2001.
7. In New Jersey, 14,185 free blacks were 20 percent of the state's population.
8. Jack Washington, *The Long Journey Home: A Bicentennial History of the Black Community of Princeton, New Jersey, 1776–1976* (Trenton, NJ: Africa World Press, 2005), 12.
9. Ibid., 14.
10. Dwandalyn Reece King, "Completing the Historical Record: Princeton's First Exhibition on the African-American Community," *Princeton History: The Journal of the Historical Society of Princeton*, no. 14 (1997): 40.
11. Lauren Miller, "Black Businesses in Princeton," research essay for oral history project, Fall 2000, 4.

12. *Black Historic Sites in New Jersey* (New Jersey Historical Commission, 1984), 35; Washington, 19, in Wise, Witherspoon-Jackson Community Project Methodology Report, 39.
13. Ibid., 1.
14. Ibid., 5.
15. Doris Burrell, interview with Lauren Miller, Princeton, NJ, October 2000.
16. Hank Pannell, interview with Kathryn Watterson, Princeton, NJ, June 2000.

CHAPTER 6: A Neighborhood under Siege

1. Hundreds of thousands of white veterans were able to get an FHA loan guarantee for their first-time houses, farm, or business. This was not so for black veterans. The Department of Veterans Affairs, which had the power to deny or grant claims under the GI Bill of Rights, was a formidable foe to African Americans in search of the college degrees, trade schools, or business and agricultural training given to whites.
2. Joyce Sinkler-Robinson, interview with Lauren Miller, Princeton, NJ, March 2001.
3. "The Murder Investigation: County Authorities Collecting Evidence at Princeton Today"; "Punishment for the Crime: Death or Thirty Years; Fine or Imprisonment," *Trenton Times*, July 6, 1899, 1.
4. Arthur Evans Wood, "Some Unsolved Problems of a University Town," PhD thesis, University of Pennsylvania, 1920, 15.
5. Ibid., 5.
6. Celia Riechel, "Where the Workers Go When They're Not Working: Living Conditions in 1917," paper for "Life Stories: Writing Oral History" class, Princeton University, Fall 2000, 3.
7. Wood, "Some Unsolved Problems," 19.
8. Ibid., 3; and Celia Riechel, "Where the Workers Go," 7.
9. Jack Washington, *The Long Journey Home: A Bicentennial History of the Black Community of Princeton, New Jersey, 1776–1976* (Trenton, NJ: Africa World Press, 2005), 175.
10. *Princeton Recollector*, July 1975, 11; and Autumn 1978, 14; Wise Preservation Planning LLC, "Witherspoon-Jackson: Historic District Study Methodology Report," www/nj.gov/HP/wj-survey-report.pdf.
11. Ibid.
12. Valerie Smith, "Princeton and the Struggle for Civil Rights," *Journal of Presbyterian History (1997–)* 85, no. 2 (Fall/Winter 2007): 130.

13. Joan Hill, interview with Lou Arrindell, Princeton, NJ, October 2000.

Chapter 7: Fighting for Our Country in Every War

1. Leslie H. Fishel Jr. and Benjamin Quarles, *The Black American: A Documentary History* (New York: William Morrow, 1970), 41.
2. Ibid., 40.
3. Wertenbaker, *Princeton 1746–1896*, 59–60.
4. Ibid., 59–60. The Redcoats kicked out faculty and staff from Nassau Hall; they pillaged the rooms, destroyed furniture and valuables, and kept their cavalry horses in the basement.
5. Booker T. Washington, quoted in Jack Washington, *The Long Journey Home*, 134.
6. Wertenbaker, *Princeton, 1746–1896*, 61.
7. Alfred Hoyt Bill, *The Princeton Campaign, 1776–1777* (Princeton, NJ: Princeton University Press, 1948), 112.
8. Jack Washington, *The Long Journey Home: A Bicentennial History of the Black Community of Princeton, New Jersey, 1776–1976* (Trenton, NJ: Africa World Press, 2005), 134.
9. The reversal of policy to exclude "any stroller, Negro, or vagabond"—either slave or free—from the Continental army came in response to a shortage of manpower and an offer made by the British giving freedom to any slave willing and able to take up arms in His Majesty's service. Enslaved men had signed up in droves with the British. So, when the colonies began to meet their quotas for the Continental army by recruiting Negroes, they enlisted free blacks and slaves with the clear understanding that enslaved men would earn freedom through military service. Others, including two slaves from Princeton, took their masters' places in the fighting in exchange for their freedom. Giles R. Wright, "Prime: Another Resident of Bainbridge House," *Princeton History: The Journal of the Historical Society of Princeton*, no. 10 (1991): 62.
10. Washington, *The Long Journey Home*, 11.
11. Ibid., 10.
12. Fishel and Quarles, *The Black American*, 215.
13. It should be noted that the navy, unlike the army, enlisted Negroes for service at sea from the very beginning of the war. Black crewmen ate and quartered with whites and had opportunities for promotion.
14. Price, *Freedom Not Far Distant*, 93.
15. Fishel and Quarles, *The Black American*, 216–17.

16. Washington, *The Long Journey Home*, 82.
17. The late Terri Nelson, a librarian at the Princeton Public Library, found these records as part of her untiring work to document the contributions African Americans in Princeton made to this city, state, and country.
18. Woodrow Wilson used his executive orders to segregate federal facilities, including bathrooms, and he even ordered screens set up to separate blacks from whites working in the same offices.
19. Washington, *The Long Journey Home*, 143.
20. Jon Blackwell, "1918: They fought racism on two fronts." *The Trentonian*. www.capitalcentury.com/1918.html
21. Washington, *The Long Journey Home*, 143.
22. Ibid., 144.
23. Fishel and Quarles, *The Black American*, 403.
24. Simeon F. Moss, interview with Kurt Piehler, Melanie Cooper, and Sandra Stewart Holyoak, Rutgers Oral History Archives, Rutgers University, May 2, 1997.
25. Catherine Hallahan, interview with Floyd Campbell, Princeton, NJ, April 2001.
26. Fishel and Quarles, *The Black American*, 451.

CHAPTER 8: Racism Poisons Our Whole Nation

1. *The Crisis*, January 1915, 119–20, reprinted in William Loren Katz, *Eyewitness: The Negro in American History* (New York: Pitman, 1967), 389.
2. Ibid., 390.
3. William Keylor, Boston University "Professor's Voices," Commentary, Insight & Analysis, March 4, 2013.
4. Howard L. Green, *Words That Make New Jersey History* (New Brunswick, NJ: Rutgers University Press, 1994), 31.
5. Ibid., 29. "The potential for slave revolt was a constant fear that spilled over, as it did here, into unfounded claims that rebellious slaves had sexual designs on the white women of the community."
6. Canada was a safe settlement area for runaway slaves since the British Empire had abolished slavery in 1833. Giles R. Wright and Edward Lama Wonkeryor, *New Jersey's Underground Railroad Heritage: "Steal Away, Steal Away . . ."; A Guide to the Underground Railroad in New Jersey* (New Jersey Historical Commission, 2002), 1.

7. Ibid., 2, 3. "While much attention has been paid to the role of white abolitionists and Quakers assisting UGRR [Underground Railroad] fugitives, this role appears somewhat overdrawn. In the South . . . the fugitives . . . were mainly assisted by free blacks and fellow slaves. In the North, it was mainly free blacks and fellow slaves acting individually or in concert with vigilance committees, or members of their own churches and self-help organizations, [who provided] shelter, financial help, and general support to runaways."

8. Ibid.

9. William Switala, *The Underground Railroad in New Jersey and New York* (Mechanicsburg, PA: Stackpole Books, 2006).

10. Washington, *The Long Journey Home*, 55.

11. Wise Preservation Planning LLC, "Witherspoon-Jackson: Historic District Study Methodology Report," www/nj.gov/HP?wj-surey-report.pdf, 47.

12. This demonstration and others helped to pressure the state of New Jersey to change their vote against the Fifteenth Amendment and belatedly join in the ratification.

13. Hank Pannell, interview with Kathryn Watterson, Princeton, NJ, June 2000.

14. *Packet*, November 2, 1923, in Washington, *The Long Journey Home*, 159.

15. Washington, *The Long Journey Home*, 160; NAACP, "Thirty Years of Lynching in the United States, 1921." From 1889 to 1918, 702 whites and 2,552 black men and women were lynched in the United States—not including the many "missing persons."

16. Lou Arrindell, "Civil Rights in Princeton," paper for "Life Stories: Writing Oral History" course, Princeton University, Fall 2000, 4.

17. Ibid., 5.

18. Leonard F. Newton, "Princeton Residents Reflect on Local Civil Rights Movement," Tape 3, MLK Day Celebration, January 14, 1991, Broadcast Center Recordings, Box 3, Princeton University Archives, Department of Rare Books and Special Collections, Princeton University Library.

19. James A. Floyd Sr., interview with Ethan Meers, Princeton, NJ, October 2000.

20. Shawn M. Sindelar, "To Serve and Protect: A Look at Relations between the Princeton Borough Police and Princeton's African American Community," paper for "Life Stories: Writing Oral History" course, Princeton University, January 1, 2001.

21. Arrindell, "Civil Rights in Princeton," 5.
22. Lois Craig, interview with Micah Carr, Princeton, NJ, November 1999.

CHAPTER 9: Standing Strong and Moving Through

1. "Fugitive Slave Case," in *Stories of New Jersey: Its Significant Places, People and Activities*, compiled and written by the Federal Writers' Project of the Works Progress Administration for the State of New Jersey (New York: M. Barrows, 1938), 268.
2. Ibid.
3. Constance K. Escher, "She Calls Herself Betsey Stockton," *Princeton History: The Journal of the Historical Society of Princeton*, no. 10 (1991): 71.
4. Ibid., 71.
5. Ibid., 74.
6. One abolitionist gain for slaves in New Jersey was legislation in 1789 that provided that "masters were obliged to teach their slaves how to read and were not to abuse them." Clement Alexander Price, *Freedom Not Far Distant: A Documentary History of Afro-Americans in New Jersey* (Newark, NJ: Historical Society, 1980), 53. Of course, there was no enforcement of this law.
7. Escher, "She Calls Herself Betsey Stockton," 78.
8. Ibid., 83.
9. Excerpted from *African-American Religion: A Historical Interpretation with Representative Documents*, ed. David W. Wills and Albert J. Raboteau (Chicago: University of Chicago Press, 2006).
10. Escher, "She Calls Herself Betsey Stockton," 86.
11. Ibid., 94.
12. Maria Louisa Bustill Robeson's great-grandfather, Cyrus Bustill, a founder of the Free African Society, the first known black self-help organization in America, had been a slave in New Jersey and purchased his own freedom. He baked bread for Washington's troops during the Revolutionary War.
13. Sheila Tully Boyle and Andrew Bunie, *Paul Robeson: The Years of Promise and Achievement* (Boston: University of Massachusetts Press, 2005), 10.
14. Paul Robeson, *Here I Stand* (Boston: Beacon Press), 9.
15. Herbert Aptheker, ed., *A Documentary History of the Negro People in the United States* (New York: Citadel Press, 1951), 2:798.
16. Lloyd L. Brown, *The Young Paul Robeson: "On My Journey Now"* (Boulder, CO: Westview Press, 1997), 24.

17. Ibid., 27; italics in original.
18. Ibid., 28.
19. Paul Robeson, *Here I Stand*, 11–12.
20. Ibid., 12.
21. Irwin Silber, "Paul Robeson: A 20th Century Joshua," *Sing Out! The Folk Magazine*, vol. 42, no. 4, 48.
22. Ibid., 44
23. Ibid., 45.
24. Ibid., 50.
25. Lloyd Brown, *The Young Paul Robeson*, 160.
26. Paul Robeson, "Reflections on Othello and the Nature of Our Times," *American Scholar*, 14 (Autumn 1945): 391, quoted in Sterling Stuckey, "Introduction to the 1988 Edition," *Here I Stand*.

CHAPTER 10: Yesterday, Today, and Tomorrow

1. Donald Gilpin, "Making History: Council Approves Witherspoon-Jackson," *Town Topics*, April 13, 2016, 1.
2. Wise Preservation Planning LLC, "Witherspoon-Jackson: Historic District Study Methodology Report," www/nj.gov/HP/wj-survey-report.pdf, 6.
3. Ibid.
4. 2016-16 ordinance by Princeton, www.princetonnj.gov/ordinances/2016/2016-16.pdf
5. Wise, *Preservation*, 3.
6. Ibid., 5.
7. Gilpin, "Making History," 1.
8. Lloyd L. Brown, *The Young Paul Robeson: "On My Journey Now"* (Boulder, CO: Westview Press, 1997), 26.
9. Ibid., 27.

Bibliography

Achenbach, Joel. "Princeton's 'Ghetto'; Neighborhood of Subtle Riches." *Daily Princetonian*, February 20, 1980.

————. "Longtime Residents Express Concern as Changes Affect 'Ghetto' Community." *Daily Princetonian*, February 20, 1980.

Albert E. Hinds Memorial Walking Tour: African-American Life in Princeton. Historical Society of Princeton, www.princtonhistory.org.

Alexander, Michelle. *The New Jim Crow: Mass Incarceration in a Time of Colorblindness.* New York: New Press, 2012.

Aptheker, Herbert, ed. *A Documentary History of the Negro People in the United States.* Vol. 2. New York: Citadel Press, 1951.

Arrindell, Lou. "Civil Rights in Princeton." Paper for "Life Stories: Writing Oral History" class, Princeton University, Fall 2000.

Baldwin, James. *The Fire Next Time.* New York: Dial Press, 1963.

————. *Notes of a Native Son.* New York: Beacon Press, 1955.

Bill, Alfred Hoyt. *The Princeton Campaign, 1776–1777.* Princeton, NJ: Princeton University Press, 1948.

Blackmon, Douglas A. *Slavery by Another Name: The Re-Enslavement of Black Americans from the Civil War to World War II.* New York: Anchor Books, 2009.

Boyle, Sheila Tully, and Andrew Bunie. *Paul Robeson: The Years of Promise and Achievement.* Boston: University of Massachusetts Press, 2005.

Brown, Lloyd L. *The Young Paul Robeson: "On My Journey Now."* Boulder, CO: Westview Press, 1997.

Bustill-Smith, Anna. "Reminiscences of Colored People of Princeton, New Jersey: 1800–1900," 1913. Courtesy of Princeton Public Library.

"Council Reassures on Urban Renewal: Plan Must Win Majority Approval, Mayor Informs Residents of Area Under Study." *Princeton Herald*, May 9, 1956.

Du Bois, W.E.B. *The Souls of Black Folk.* New York: New American Library, 1969.

Epstein, Jennifer. "Slaves and Slavery at Princeton." Senior thesis, April 8, 2008. Transcribed from copy in Office of the President Records, Box 1, Aaron Burr Sr., Seeley G. Mudd Manuscript Library. Courtesy of the Princeton University Archives.

Escher, Constance K. "She Calls Herself Betsey Stockton." *Princeton History: The Journal of the Historical Society of Princeton,* no. 10 (1991): 71–101.

Finkelman, Paul. *Thirty Years of Lynching in the United States, 1889–1918.* New York: NAACP, 1921.

Fishel, Leslie H., Jr., and Benjamin Quarles. *The Black American: A Documentary History.* New York: William Morrow, 1970.

Forten, Jr. *An Address Delivered before the Ladies' Anti-Slavery Society of Philadelphia,* April 14, 1836. In Fishel and Quarles, "Abolitionism and the Crisis of the Fifties," in *The Black American,* 10–13.

Franklin, John Hope. *The Color Line: Legacy for the Twenty-First Century.* Columbia: University of Missouri Press, 1993.

Franklin, John Hope, and Loren Schweninger. *Runaway Slaves: Rebels on the Plantation.* Oxford: Oxford University Press, 1999.

Funk, James Whitehill. "The Pattern of Negro Labor in Princeton." Senior thesis, Department of Economics and Social Institutions, Princeton University, January 8, 1948.

Gaines, Kevin. "Reflections on a Surviving Issue of *The Citizen.*" *Princeton History: The Journal of the Historical Society of Princeton,* no. 14 (1997).

Gilpin, Donald. "Making History: Council Approves Witherspoon-Jackson." *Town Topics,* April 13, 2016.

Green, Howard L. *Words that Make New Jersey History.* New Brunswick, NJ: Rutgers University Press, 1995.

Greiff, Constance M. "Views of Morven." *Princeton History: The Journal of the Historical Society of Princeton,* no. 10 (1991).

Hageman, John F. "Chapter XXIV: The Witherspoon Street Church." In *The History of Princeton and Its Institutions.* Philadelphia: J. B. Lippincott, 1879.

———. "Chapter XXV: The African Methodist Episcopal Church." In *The History of Princeton and Its Institutions.* Philadelphia: J. B. Lippincott, 1879.

Hersh, Pam. "Witherspoon Presbyterian Celebrates 150 Years of Love." *Princeton Packet,* February 2, 1990.

Hildebrand, Jenny. "The Princeton Plan: Integration and Its Aftermath." Paper for "Life Stories: Writing Oral History" class, Princeton University, January 2001.

Housing Authority. "Urban Renewal Authority: Ultimate Authority in the Carrying Out of the Urban Renewal Project Rests with the Mayor and Borough Council." *Princeton Herald*, May 23, 1956.

"Housing Authority Urges Withholding of Judgment on Urban Redevelopment." *Princeton Herald*, no. 70, June 23, 1956.

Irvin, Dona. *The Unsung Heart of Black America: A Middle-Class Church at Midcentury.* Columbia: University of Missouri Press, 1992.

Jerome, Fred. *The Einstein File: J. Edgar Hoover's Secret War against the World's Most Famous Scientist.* New York: St. Martin's Press, 2002.

Jerome, Fred, and Rodger Taylor. *Einstein on Race and Racism.* New Brunswick, NJ: Rutgers University Press, 2005.

"Keep Housing Out of Politics—Mayor." *Princeton Herald*, June 13, 1956.

Ketchum, Robert. *The Winter Soldier: The Battles of Trenton and Princeton.* New York: Henry Holt, 1999.

King, Dwandalyn Reece. "Completing the Historical Record: Princeton's First Exhibition on the African-American Community." *Princeton History: The Journal of the Historical Society of Princeton*, no. 14 (1997).

Kirk, Donald. "Princeton and the Negro—I: Unbiased Housing Here Fostered by Committee." *Daily Princetonian*, October 23, 1956.

———. "Princeton and the Negro—II: Negroes Buy Houses after Six-Year Effort." *Daily Princetonian*, October 23, 1956.

Knight, Edgar W. "Notes on John Chavis." *North Carolina Historical Review* 7, no. 3 (July 1930).

Kolchin, Peter. *American Slavery, 1619–1877.* New York: Hill and Wang, 1999.

Leitch, Alexander. *A Princeton Companion.* Princeton, NJ: Princeton University Press, 1978.

Looney, Jeff. "Slavery at Princeton." Seeley G. Mudd Library, FAQ Slavery at Princeton.

Marable, Manning, and Leith Mullings, eds. *Let Nobody Turn Us Around: Voices of Resistance, Reform, and Renewal.* New York: Rowman & Littlefield, 2000.

McCray, Melvin. *Looking Forward: Reflections of Black Princeton Alumni.* Video, 2000.

Miller, Lauren. "Black Businesses in Princeton." Paper for "Life Stories: Writing Oral History" class, Fall 2000.

Moss, Simeon F. Interview by Kurt Piehler, Melanie Cooper, and Sandra Stewart Holyoak. Rutgers Oral History Archives, Rutgers University, May 2, 1997.

"The Murder Investigation: County Authorities Collecting Evidence at Princeton Today." Trenton Times, July 6, 1899.

Nubian Committee. *Gathering II*. Booklet. Princeton, NJ, 2009.

The Orange and Black in Black and White: A Century of Princeton through the Eyes of the "Daily Princetonian." Compiled and Written by the 1992 Managing Board and the Staff of the *Daily Princetonian* in Commemoration of Its First Hundred Years of Daily Publication, 1892–1992. Princeton, NJ: *Daily Princetonian*, 1992.

Painter, Nell Irvin. *A History of White People*. New York: W. W. Norton, 2010.

———. *Exodusters: Black Migration to Kansas after Reconstruction*. New York: Alfred A. Knopf, 1977.

———. *Southern History across the Color Line*. Chapel Hill: University of North Carolina Press, 2002.

Peterson, Iver. "As Princeton Changes: A Black Community Fears for Future." *New York Times*, September 3, 2001.

"Planners Vote 'No Blight'; Will Revise Master Plan." *Princeton Packet*, January 4, 1962.

Price, Clement Alexander. *Freedom Not Far Distant: A Documentary History of Afro-Americans in New Jersey*. Newark: New Jersey Historical Society, 1980.

"The Quiet Approach to Integrated Housing." *Daily Princetonian*, October 24, 1956.

Riechel, Celia. "Where the Workers Go When They're Not Working: Living Conditions in 1917." Paper for "Life Stories: Writing Oral History" class, Princeton University, Fall 2000.

Robeson, Paul. "Reflections on Othello and the Nature of Our Times." *American Scholar* 14 (Autumn 1945): 391. In Sterling Stuckey, "Introduction to the 1988 Edition," *Here I Stand*.

Robeson, Paul, Jr. *The Undiscovered Paul Robeson: An Artist's Journey, 1898–1939*. New York: John Wiley & Sons, 2001.

Robeson, Paul, with Lloyd L. Brown. *Here I Stand*. Boston: Beacon Press, 1988.

Schlegel, Sharon. "Emma Epps Is One Tough, Proud Lady." *Trenton Times*, April 23, 1983.

Seitz, Phillip Seitz. *Slavery in Philadelphia: A History of Resistance, Denial and Wealth*. Philadelphia: History for Healing, 2004.

Shi, Maggie. "First Black Students Face Isolation, Racism." In "Black Experience Princeton Experiencing Blacks: 50 Years of Reflection." Eight-part series, Daily Princetonian 119, no. 28 (March 7, 1995).

———. "Black Alumni Recall 1960s." "Black Experience Princeton Experiencing Blacks: 50 Years of Reflection," ." Eight-part series, *Daily Princetonian* 119, no. 30 (March 9, 1995).

Silber, Irwin. "Legendary People's Artist: Paul Robeson, 'A 20th Century Joshua.'" *Sing Out! The Folk Magazine* 42, no. 4 (Spring 1998).

Sindelar, Shawn M. "To Serve and Protect: A Look at Relations between the Princeton Borough Police and Princeton's African American Community." Paper for "Life Stories: Writing Oral History" class, Princeton University, January 1, 2001.

Smith, Valerie. "Princeton and the Struggle for Civil Rights." *Journal of Presbyterian History (1997–)* 85, no. 2 (Fall/Winter 2007).

Starobin, Robert, ed. *Blacks in Bondage: Letters of American Slaves.* New York: Marcus Wiener, 1988.

Stuckey, Sterling. *Slave Culture: Nationalist Theory and the Foundation of Black America.* Oxford: Oxford University Press, 1987.

Switala, William. "The Underground Railroad in New Jersey." In *The Underground Railroad in New Jersey and New York.* Mechanicsburg, PA: Stackpole Books, 2006.

"University Sells Square for $17 Million: Expansion of Central Business District Long Considered." *Princeton Weekly Bulletin* 70, no. 13 (December 1980).

"Urban Renewal Authority." Princeton Herald, May 21, 1956.

Washington, Jack. *The Long Journey Home: A Bicentennial History of the Black Community of Princeton, New Jersey, 1776–1976.* Trenton, NJ: Africa World Press, 2005.

———. *The Quest for Equality: Trenton's Black Community, 1890–1965.* Trenton, NJ: Africa World Press, 1993.

Weeren, John. "Slavery at Princeton." http://libguides.princeton.edu/c.php?g= 84056&p=544524.

Wertenbaker, Thomas Jefferson. *Princeton, 1746–1896.* Princeton, NJ: Princeton University Press, 1946.

Wilder, Craig Steven. *Ebony & Ivy: Race, Slavery, and the Troubled History of America's Universities.* New York: Bloomsbury Press, 2013.

Wilentz, Sean, "Princeton and the Controversies over Slavery." *Journal of Presbyterian History (1997–)* 85, no. 2 (Fall/Winter 2007).

Wilkerson, Isabel. *The Warmth of Other Suns: The Epic Story of America's Great Migration.* New York: Random House, 2010.

Wills, David W., and Albert J. Raboteau, eds. *African-American Religion: A Historical Interpretation with Representative Documents.* Chicago: University of Chicago Press, 2006.

Wintz, Cary, ed. *Harlem Speaks: A Living History of the Harlem Renaissance.* Naperville, IL: Sourcebooks, 2007.

Wise Preservation Planning LLC. "Witherspoon-Jackson Community: Historic District Study, Municipality of Princeton, New Jersey," November 19, 2015, http://www.princetonnj.gov/HP/wj-survey-report.pdf.

Wood, Arthur Evans. "Some Unsolved Problems of a University Town." PhD thesis at the University of Pennsylvania, Philadelphia, 1920.

Wright, Giles R. "Prime: Another Resident of Bainbridge House." *Princeton History: The Journal of the Historical Society of Princeton*, no. 10 (1991): 60–69.

Wright, Giles R., and Edward Lama Wonkeryor. *New Jersey's Underground Railroad Heritage: "Steal Away, Steal Away . . ."; A Guide to the Underground Railroad in New Jersey*. New Jersey Historical Commission, 2002.

Permissions and Notes on Photographs

INTRODUCTION. "The North's Most Southern Town"

(*p. xiv*) First Baptist Church of Princeton (1925); founded as Bright Hope Baptist Church in 1885. Courtesy of the Collection of Harriett Calloway, Historical Society of Princeton

(*p. 3*) Map of the Borough of Princeton, based on a map prepared by William L. Ulyat (1917). Courtesy of the Collections of the Historical Society of Princeton

CHAPTER 1. Our Grandmother Came from Africa as a Little Girl

(*p. 31*) The Thomas Sullivan Grocery Store at 74 Witherspoon Street, on the corner of Jackson Street, now known as Paul Robeson Place (1887). Some of the men are playing musical instruments. In 1896 the store became Dennis Sullivan's Grocery; it was Murray's Meat & Grocery from 1910 until Flory Toto took it over in 1927. Courtesy of the Rose Collection, the Historical Society of Princeton

(*p. 33*) Nancy Greene and Emma Greene (Epps), (1904). Courtesy of the Emma Epps Collection, the Historical Society of Princeton

(*p. 36*) Stereographic portrait of a Princeton man, to be viewed with stereoscope (about 1800). Courtesy of the Collections of the Historical Society of Princeton

(*p. 39*) Women in the Witherspoon neighborhood (about 1800). Courtesy of the Collections of the Historical Society of Princeton

(*p. 45*) Kane Children on their front steps, Jackson Street (1898). Courtesy of the Collections of the Historical Society of Princeton

(*p. 47*) Three Generations of Moore-May-Satterfield women (1944); *top left to right*: Louise Holland (May), Alice May Satterfield, Annie Van Zandt Moore May, and Shirley Satterfield. Courtesy of Alice Satterfield

CHAPTER 2. I Grew Up Hugged to the Hearts of My People

(*p. 52*) YMCA Father-Son Banquet at the First Baptist Church of Princeton (1934). Courtesy of the Collection of Mrs. Martha Barbour, the Historical Society of Princeton

(*p. 55*) Fred and Carrie Hoagland Family (1907); *back left*: Blanche, Sarah (deceased), Father Fred, Carrie, Mother Carrie, Fred Junior; *front*: Ernest Vernon. (Five children not pictured.) Courtesy of the Collections of the Historical Society of Princeton

(*p. 59*) Neighborhood boys with baby sister (about 1840). Courtesy of the Collections of the Historical Society of Princeton

(*p. 61*) Ping Pong at the YMCA (about 1940). Courtesy of the Witherspoon YMCA Collection, the Historical Society of Princeton

(*p. 67*) YMCA basketball team (1950s). Courtesy of the Witherspoon YMCA Collection, the Historical Society of Princeton

(*p. 73*) Eric Craig, three years old, with his dog, Chips (1937). Courtesy of Eric Craig

CHAPTER 3. School Integration: A Big Loss for Black Children

(*p. 76*) Students at the Witherspoon School for Colored Children (1922–29). Gift of Shirley Satterfield, courtesy of the Collections of the Historical Society of Princeton

(*p. 80*) Beloved teachers of the Witherspoon School for Colored Children (about 1940). Courtesy of Henry F. Pannell

(*p. 84*) Young Y basketball team (about 1936). Courtesy of the Witherspoon YMCA Collection, the Historical Society of Princeton

(*p. 91*) Witherspoon neighborhood children (1933). Courtesy of the Collections of the Historical Society of Princeton

(*p. 97*) Howard B. and Susie Waxwood (1980s). Mr. Waxwood was the principal of Witherspoon School for twenty-five years—both before and after the integration of the schools. He attended the Witherspoon School for Colored Children as a child and in 1922 was one of the first black students to graduate from Princeton High School. He earned his BA and MA at Rutgers University and did graduate work at the University of Chicago. Courtesy of Susie Waxwood

CHAPTER 4. The University: A Place to Labor, Not to Study

(*p. 106*) 1944 James Everett Ward '47 and Arthur Jewell Wilson '47 outside Laughlin Hall, 1946. They and two others integrated Princeton in 1942 through the United States Navy's V12 officer training program. Historical Photograph Collection, Campus Life Series (AC112), Box MP215, Image No. 5644. Courtesy of the Seeley G. Mudd Manuscript Library at Princeton University

(*p. 111*) James (Jimmy) Johnson, outside East Pyne Hall, next to Nassau Hall (about 1890). Courtesy of the Seeley G. Mudd Manuscript Library at Princeton University

(*p. 117*) Firestone Library's maintenance and janitorial staff (around 1940). Historical Photograph Collection, Campus Life Series (AC112), Box MP5, Image No. 110. Courtesy of the Seeley G. Mudd Manuscript Library at Princeton University

(*p. 127*) The Hill House on Green Street (1914); Booker T. Washington is fourth from right. Courtesy of the Witherspoon YMCA Collection, the Historical Society of Princeton

(*p. 136*) Robert J. Rivers, graduate, Princeton University, class of 1953. In 1949, Robert J. Rivers was the second student from the Witherspoon neighborhood admitted to Princeton University; the first was Joseph Ralph Moss, class of 1951. Courtesy of Mrs. Hazel Lewis Rivers

CHAPTER 5. Every Day, You Work to Survive

(*p. 138*) Princeton Rug Washing and Carpet Cleaning Works, 23 John Street, Theodore L. Williams, Proprietor (about 1925). This photograph shows John Street before Palmer Square was created. Courtesy of the Collections of the Historical Society of Princeton

(*p. 146*) Phillip Diggs, First African American Police Officer in the Borough of Princeton (1920). Courtesy of the Collections of the Historical Society of Princeton

(*p. 148*) James A. (Connie) Carter of the Negro Baseball League Newark Eagles, (1949–50). Courtesy of James A. Carter

(*p. 152*) Live Chicken Store at Witherspoon and Spring Streets (1919). Courtesy of Collections of the Historical Society of Princeton

(*p. 160*) Jacqui Swain (*top*) and the Rosebuds *left to right*: Joyce Gillette, Sonya Massey, and Jacqueline Beasly) (about 1960). Courtesy of Jacqueline Swain

(*p. 166*) Quarry workers in the Old Quarry on Spruce Street (abourt 1890). Courtesy of the Collections of the Historical Society of Princeton

CHAPTER 6. A Neighborhood under Siege

(*p. 171*) View of Baker's Alley, looking south toward Nassau Street (1925). Courtesy of the Collections of the Historical Society of Princeton

(*p. 178*) Mr. Burnett Griggs' home next to Griggs' Imperial Restaurant, 64 Witherspoon Street (late 1940s). Courtesy of Henry F. Pannell

(*p. 182*) A home at 82 Witherspoon Street, at the corner of Jackson and Witherspoon Streets; it was destroyed by the expansion of the commercial district (late 1940s). Courtesy of Henry F. Pannell

(*p. 187*) Paul Robeson and Christine Moore in front of Sport Moore's furniture and clothing store on Spring Street (about 1930). Courtesy of the Gift of Donald Moore, collections of the Historical Society of Princeton

CHAPTER 7. Fighting for Our Country in Every War

(*p. 194*) The Drum & Bugle Corps, World War I Charles W. Robinson Post 218 of the American Legion (1917). Courtesy of the Gift of Shirley Satterfield, Collections of the Historical Society of Princeton

(*p. 199*) Thomas (Buddy) Phox in Italy (1943). Courtesy of Delores Phox

(*p. 205*) Floyd Campbell (1943). Courtesy of Penelope S. Edwards-Carter

(*p. 211*) James and Martha Phox Barbour (1944). Courtesy of the Collection of Martha Barbour, the Historical Society of Princeton

(*p. 217*) Military Wives' Tea at the YW-YMCA (1944). Courtesy of the Collection of Martha Barbour, the Historical Society of Princeton

Chapter 8. Racism Poisons Our Whole Nation

(*p. 221*) Woodrow Wilson at his desk in the Oval Office (about 1913).

(*p. 228*) The Joe Lewis and Jackie Robinson teams for YMCA membership drive (1948). Courtesy of the Witherspoon YMCA Collection, the Historical Society of Princeton

(*p. 232*) Boys' Boxing Club at the YMCA (about 1920). Courtesy of the Witherspoon YMCA Collection, the Historical Society of Princeton

(*p. 236*) Members of the Friendship Club, who raised scholarship funds, fed the poor and elderly, and supported black education and the NAACP (about 1940). Courtesy of Henry F. Pannell

(*p. 245*) Leonard Rivers, Princeton University's baseball coach from 1976 to 1980. Courtesy of Leonard Rivers

(*p. 249*) The Witherspoon YMCA Phantom Baseball Team, the 1947 City-wide Softball Champions, A-League. Courtesy of the Witherspoon YMCA Collection, the Historical Society of Princeton

Chapter 9. Standing Strong and Moving Through

(*p. 252*) The 1903 Chauffeur and Butler Club Formal. Courtesy of the Collection of Martha Barbour, the Historical Society of Princeton

(*p. 258*) Family with hats, banjo, and accordion (about 1880). Courtesy of the Collections of the Historical Society of Princeton

(*p. 262*) Four women friends (about 1900). Courtesy of the Collections of the Historical Society of Princeton

(*p. 270*) Princeton family at the beach (1925). Courtesy of the Emma Epps Collection, the Historical Society of Princeton

(*p. 273*) Kathleen Montgomery Edwards as a young bride (1947). Courtesy of Penelope S. Edwards-Carter (*p. 276*) Clyde (Buster) Thomas, football captain at Princeton High School (1952). Courtesy of Clyde Thomas

CHAPTER 10. Yesterday, Today, and Tomorrow

(*p. 285*) Black and white friends (about 1930). The boy on the left was in the May's family, the boy on the right, in the Servis family. Courtesy of the Collections of the Historical Society of Princeton

(*p. 297*) YMCA Men's Meeting (about 1947). Courtesy of the Witherspoon YMCA Collection, the Historical Society of Princeton

(*p. 305*) Albert Hinds, 99-years old, washing his car (2001). Courtesy of the photographer, Katrina Robinson

MEET THE RESIDENTS: Speakers' Biographies

(*p. 312*) Community Coordinator Penelope S. Edwards-Carter. Courtesy of Penelope S. Edwards-Carter

(*p. 320*) Community Coordinator Henry F. (Hank) and his wife Eileen Pannell. Courtesy of the photographer, Romus Broadway

(*p. 325*) Community Coordinator Clyde (Buster) Thomas. Courtesy of the photographer, Romus Broadway

(*p. 327*) A celebration at the Henry F. Pannell Learning Center with many of the participants in the Witherspoon Life Stories Oral History Project, May 2001. *First row (from left)*: Jessica Hafkin, Celia Riechel, Lauren Miller, Mia Powell, Katherine Jackson, Jenny Hildebrand, Jessica Lautin, Saloni Doshi. *Second row (from left)*: Hank Pannell, Fannie Floyd, Harriett Calloway, Joan Hill, Kathryn (Kitsi) Watterson, Paul Mitnaul, Trisha Thorme, Romus Broadway. *Third row (from left)*: Rev. Judson Carter, Tom Hartman, Martha Hartman, Wilma Pannell, Shirley Satterfield, Clyde (Buster) Thomas, Marilyn Yates, Jim Floyd Sr., Karim Thomas, Marlo McGriff, Janet Dickerson, Jim Floyd Jr. Courtesy of the photographer, Iming Lin

Acknowledgments

Nearly two decades ago, Hank Pannell introduced me to Mr. Albert Hinds and set this book in motion. I'm grateful to everyone who has helped bring it to life. This starts with Hank Pannell, Penney Edwards-Carter, and Buster Thomas, and with each and every one of the Witherspoon neighbors who shared their stories. The light that shines from you is contagious. And now with this book, the world has a chance to experience the radiance of this beloved community.

I Hear My People Singing couldn't have happened without the heartfelt efforts of my Princeton University students, as well as the enthusiasm of Princeton University administrators whose backing made it possible for us to carry on. Thank you, president emeritus Harold Shapiro; vice-president and secretary Robert Durkee; former vice president for Campus Life, Janet Dickerson; former director of communications, Lauren Robinson Ugorji; former provost Jeremiah Ostriker; former vice provost Joanne Mitchell; former dean of the college Nancy Malkiel; former associate dean of the college Hank Dobin, and Project 55's Mary Miller. Here's a shout-out to Trisha Thorne, director of the Community-Based Learning Initiative, who managed events, microphones, and student stipends; Judith Friedman, former director of Development Communications; former Third World Center director Heddye Ducree, and Community House director Marjorie Young. I would also like to thank Princeton University's current President Christopher Eisgruber for his encouragement.

I'm especially grateful to the former Program in African American Studies—most especially professor and former director, Nell Irvin Painter, and Howard Taylor, Noliwe Rooks, Claudia Tate, Jean Washington, and Hattie Black—for giving me a welcoming academic home for the university's first full course dedicated to the Witherspoon-Jackson neighborhood. I also thank the Princeton Writing Program; Albert Raboteau, Henry W. Putnam Professor of Religion,

Emeritus, as well as Shirley Satterfield, educator and Witherspoon resident, for their contributions to our class sessions.

I also express my immense gratitude to Brother Cornel West for writing the foreword to this book and endorsing it from the beginning.

I deeply appreciate Princeton archivists Ben Primer and Daniel Linke of the See-ley G. Mudd Manuscript Library; Firestone librarian Emily Belcher, African American Studies selector; Gail Stern, Maureen Smyth, and, more recently, Izzy Kasdin of the Historical Society of Princeton; the late Terri Nelson, of the Princeton Public Library, for her research on Princeton's Civil War veterans; Romus Broadway for his photographs; Dana Hughes, director of the Clay Street Learning Center; Emily Espenshade, a member of the Witherspoon Street Presbyterian Church, for her interviews of Jim and Eula Carson; Dwandayln Reece King, who conducted earlier interviews for the Historical Society of Princeton, and Victoria Billups-Sanderson for providing research about a murder-for-land in Princeton in 1899.

I also want to acknowledge the New Jersey Historical Society, the Bonner Foundation, and the Historical Society of Princeton, for grants and awards to back the project. I've gained new appreciation of documentary history through this work, and I was inspired by Jack Washington's *The Long Journey Home: A Bicentennial History of the Black Community of Princeton, New Jersey, 1776–1976;* Fred Jerome and Roger Taylor's *Einstein on Race and Racism;* and Phillip Seitz's *Slavery in Philadelphia: A History of Resistance, Denial and Wealth.* My special appreciation to Wilbert H. (Bert) Ahern, Horace T. Morse-Alumni Distinguished Professor emeritus at the University of Minnesota, Morris, who was a great champion of this book. I also value the anonymous historians, "Readers 1 and 2," whose astute suggestions contributed greatly to its outcome.

The majority of these interviews were meticulously transcribed by Jane Shipley, and the process was enhanced by early layouts from designers Donna Ching and Jonathan Foster of ChingFoster. I thank Christina Sun for her design advice; Katie Sanders, whose editorial prowess was pivotal to bringing these testimonies to the page; Kristin Cashioli, whose research and editing sharpened the text; Tara McGowan, who shaped narratives for the initial project and pitched in again on the final manuscript, and Mindy Erhart and Shelagh Davis, who did early administrative work. I'm especially grateful to Lee Gruzen, who spent hours discussing, editing and fact-checking this manuscript. I also thank Lou Ann Merkle, and Elizabeth Naismith Picciani for their photographic and editorial assistance.

Many others have nurtured me as we've made this journey: Emily Mann, Lawrence Thomasson, Zachary Watterson, Alice Watterson, Susan Danoff, Shannon

Oberg, David Solomon, Margie Boynes-Brown, Eileen Pannell, Pamela Groves, Jane Shapiro, Sharon Dougherty, Sarah Watterson, Jane Nakashima, Gerry Groves, Charlene Kwon, Sarah Green, Judy Wicks, Ronald Sitts, Marie Stoner, Gail Walker, Joyce Turner, Michael Robertson, Ben Lewis, Dawn Ryan, Donna Musial-Manners, Pamela Hersh, Niyonu Spann, Hugh O'Neal, Dominic Cartwright, and Brother Robert Carter.

Deepest gratitude goes to my agent, Ellen Levine, of the Ellen Levine Literary Agency, Trident Media Group, who has been of constant support through a very long process. I also thank Brigitta van Rheinberg and the terrific team at Princeton University Press, including Eric Crahan, Debbie Tegarden, Cathy Slovensky, Hannah Zuckerman, Mary Bearden, Pamela Schnitter, and Demitri Karetnikov, for their diligent work in creating a beautiful book, and Colleen Boyle, Theresa Liu, and Debra Liese for promoting it.

Author's Note

We are donating documents and photographs used in preparation of this book to the Historical Society of Princeton and to the Paul Robeson Collection for African-American Family History at the Princeton Public Library. At the public library, these archival materials will be housed in the Robeson Collection in the Special Collections Room, along with the library's excellent genealogical materials for those interested in researching their African American roots.

The Historical Society of Princeton, which donated a great deal of time to preparing photographs for this book, will also have copies of research materials gathered by students and community available to the public.

Half of the profits from royalties for this book will be donated to the Jean Riley Scholarship Fund for the Princeton Nursery School, 78 Leigh Avenue, Princeton, NJ 08540. Jean Riley grew up in the Witherspoon neighborhood and put her heart into the nursery school for fifty years, beginning in 1955. She was head teacher until 1973 and served as director from 1974 until her retirement in 2005.